# TO THINE OWN
# SELF BE TRUE

# Lewis M. Andrews, Ph.D.

# TO THINE OWN SELF BE TRUE

## The Relationship Between Spiritual Values and Emotional Health

DOUBLEDAY

*New York   London   Toronto   Sydney   Auckland*

PUBLISHED BY DOUBLEDAY
a division of Bantam Doubleday Dell Publishing Group, Inc.
666 Fifth Avenue, New York, New York 10103

DOUBLEDAY and the portrayal of an anchor with a dolphin
are trademarks of Doubleday,
a division of Bantam Doubleday Dell Publishing Group, Inc.

ISBN 0-385-23737-5
SEPTEMBER 1989
10 9 8 7 6 5 4 3

*in memory of my cousin*
*Harry Sebolt*

# ACKNOWLEDGMENTS

It would be impossible to acknowledge everyone who has contributed to a book that has been almost a decade in the making and has seen at least eighteen completed drafts. I have included many of the formal interviews I conducted during that time in the References section at the end, though very special thanks are again due Dr. Allen Bergin, Dr. Thomas Hora, Joel Kanter, and, as will shortly become evident, Dr. Jon Davidson.

My grateful appreciation, of course, to my editor and friend Loretta Barrett, whose two thoughtful critiques were invaluable, and to my agent, Roberta Pryor, whose diligence and good humor are priceless assets. My thanks also to Mary McCarthy for her editorial assistance.

I am indebted as well to Dean Harry Adams and Dean Abraham Malherbe of the Yale Divinity School for granting me a research fellowship that gave me access to some of the best library facilities in the world, to my friend Barrows Peale and to my sister Mary for their thoughtful support, to Gene Young who gave me helpful ideas for organizing earlier drafts of the book, to my mother Katherine Andrews who patiently proofread the last three drafts of the manuscript, and to my copy editor, Anne Lesser.

On a more personal level, I owe much to Dr. Marvin Karlins, who taught me most of what I know about professional writing in particular and a good deal about life in general, to Roy Fairfield who knows more about values than all the psychology books I read in college and graduate school put together, and to Tony Collins and his wife Belinda for being better friends than I sometimes deserved.

My thanks also to the makers of the Compaq Plus, which has served me faithfully through many drafts.

# CONTENTS

# INTRODUCTION

Having spoken widely and often on the connection between spiritual values and emotional health over the past few years, I've become increasingly aware of three rather striking developments.

The first is the extent to which people from all walks of life have become fascinated by this subject. One might naturally expect an audience among the clergy and mental health workers; but there is also a strong interest from the general public, particularly from business executives, teachers, artists, government administrators, students, doctors in family practice, lawyers, and from the so-called "average citizen." Even when I give a workshop that is designed for some specific professional group, such as ministers or nurses, there is always a large percentage of interested laypeople who "just happened to hear about it" and decide to attend.

The second striking fact is that the quality of the questions raised by people who are interested in the connection between values and health is remarkably consistent, no matter what the audience. Reading a transcript of the question and answer period following one of my own lectures or workshops, you could not easily tell whether I had just addressed a convention of psychologists or some housewives at a local church prayer breakfast, whether I had spoken to a group of pastoral counselors or some recovering drug addicts. It is almost as if the country as a whole were undergoing a profound intellectual evolution, with certain pressing issues cutting across the traditional boundaries of work, education, and class background.

Finally, there is a striking consensus, even among professional therapists, that something fundamental is missing from modern conceptions of mental health—an ethical or spiritual dimension which is essential to overcoming such difficult emotional problems as depression, guilt, feelings of worthlessness, indecision, boredom, fear, frustration, loneliness, and anxiety. Whenever I attack the ineffectiveness of conventional psychotherapy, in fact, it is usually the therapists themselves who are nodding most firmly in agreement.

There was a time when I dreaded the prospect of confronting the mental health professionals in my audiences, fearing that many would storm out in protest against my call for a synthesis of psychology and spirituality. And while I do occasionally offend a few of my colleagues, I'm much more likely to have a psychologist or doctor privately thank me for putting into words what he's "been thinking to myself for years."

Why this new openness to the spiritual dimension of emotional healing?

Part of the answers is purely demographic. With the baby-boomers now headed into their late thirties and forties, the average age of the population is getting older; and there is a natural shift away from the superficial simplicities of "pop" psychology toward a deeper and more profound wisdom. The growing interest in spiritual healing is part of a much broader cultural emphasis on traditional values, an emphasis reflected in the classroom by the call for a return to basics in education and in business by the public's demand for higher ethical standards.

Another reason for the openness to spiritual healing is the bankruptcy of conventional psychiatry. After more than a half century of putting psychotherapists with their "value-free" theories of human behavior on a cultural pedestal, the public is finally catching on to the fact that no major school of psychotherapy has accomplished very much in the way of improving the nation's mental health. Indeed, many helping professionals appear hard pressed to solve their own emotional problems, let alone anyone else's.[1]

In contrast to the failing light of conventional psychotherapy is the remarkable success of many grass-roots spiritual movements, particularly Alcoholics Anonymous, a self-help organization founded in the 1930s by a group of recovering drinkers. As we shall see in later chapters, the basic tenants of A.A.—a belief in a "higher power" and the practice of certain ethical values—have proved so successful in the treatment of alcoholism that many nonalcoholics around the country have begun to employ these same methods to treat their own emotional problems. Depressives Anonymous, Kleptomaniacs Anonymous, Fundamentalists Anonymous, Parents Anonymous, Emotions Anonymous . . . these are just a few of the latest variations on Alcoholics Anonymous, all based on a spiritual approach to healing.

At the same time that people are becoming more interested in the connection between spiritual values and emotional health, even the most curious who approach this subject are sometimes limited by certain prejudices. For some, the biggest problem is the memory of a very strict or punitive religious upbringing. They have difficulty distinguishing the word "religious" from the word "spiritual" and need to be reminded that the phrase "spiritual values" refers to the elevating ethical beliefs at the heart of all great religious traditions—what Aldous Huxley called "the highest common denominator"—not some narrow interpretation of scripture or arbitrary dogma.

And if some are handicapped by a repressive religious upbringing, others are blinded by a misguided conception of intellectual sophistication—by the false assumption that being spiritual is somehow the opposite of being scientific or logical. They have been conditioned to scoff at any mention of the "G-word"—God—and have never been told that the greatest scientific minds from Newton to Einstein were themselves deeply spiritual people.

As we shall see in the second chapter, the still fashionable idea that spiritual beliefs are somehow intellectually naïve—an expression of childlike fantasy or a throwback to the Spanish Inquistion—is itself a naïve belief and one which stands on very weak intellectual ground. It was Einstein himself who observed that the person lacking "a lively feeling for values . . . more closely resembles a well-trained dog than a harmoniously developed person."[2]

Even those who believe themselves open to a spiritual understanding of their emotional problems may fall prey to a very powerful distraction. Rather than address the unethical conduct which is at the root of most psycholgical discomfort, they instead attempt to mask their symptoms in the quest for an intense "cosmic," "holy," or "transpersonal" experience, a spiritual "high."

Every generation has this fascination with what I call "special effects" spirituality. For my contemporaries it was the psychedelics, particularly LSD, mescaline, and marijuana: "beholding God in a pill," as it were. The focus today may appear to be different—channeling, psychic phenomena, out-of-body experiences, and healing with crystals— but the motive is too often the same, to evade a serious look at the relationship between one's values and one's health.

This is not to attack the validity of psychic research and related studies or the importance of pursuing them, but to focus our attention on the real source of our emotional distress. It was the great psychologist William James, a pioneer in the attempt to bridge psychology and spirituality, who observed that the "hell we make for ourselves in this world" is the hell we create "by habitually fashioning our characters in the wrong way."[3]

Deliberately reforming our characters, "assuming the virtue"[4] as Shakespeare put it, is the essense of effective self-help. This begins with an awareness of the kind of ethical violation which usually causes the emotional problem we suffer from—to see that depressed feelings, for example, stem from resentful attitudes or that chronic frustration with others comes most often from our attempts to manipulate them. My book has been organized to clarify the connections between the most common negative emotions—anxiety, guilt, fear, loneliness, etc.—and the particular unethical behaviors which typically cause them.

Once we know the value violations underlying our emotional difficulties, there are specific steps we can take to improve the quality of our behavior . . . and, therefore, our happiness. I have outlined the broad historical evolution of this "ethical therapy" in the second chapter and provided a more detailed discussion of the exact ethical treatment for each of our psychological complaints within the chapters that follow.

When people begin to approach their psychological problems from a deeper, more spiritual point of view, some remarkable things can happen. Negative feelings that had lasted for years begin to dissipate; and social difficulties with friends, colleagues, and family that had always troubled us are resolved in fascinating and unexpected ways. There is a newfound confidence and enthusiasm for living.

But perhaps the most remarkable development of all is the recognition that this spiritual therapy is not really a new discovery, revealed by some outside authority, as much as it is a reminder of the basic truths we have always known in our own hearts. In healing ourselves, we learn that the greatest wisdom of all lies not in listening to others but in being true to our deepest selves.

LEWIS M. ANDREWS
*Redding Ridge, Connecticut*
*March 1989*

# Chapter 1

---

# THE REVOLUTION
# IN THERAPY

They are blind who have no clear standard.

PLATO[1]

(Ask) not what kind of disease the person has,
ask what kind of person has the disease.

SIR WILLIAM OSLER (1849–1919)[2]

Modern psychology is on the verge of a transformation which may
prove as important a turning point in the history of psychotherapy as
relativity was to physics or DNA to biology. After nearly a century of
doggedly refusing to acknowledge any possible connection between effective therapy and traditional ethical values, increasing numbers of
practicing psychiatrists are choosing to describe their own patients'
emotional problems in ethical, moral, and even spiritual terms.

And like those revolutions in physics and biology, the implications
of this new "ethical" approach for the quality of everyday living extend
well beyond the boundaries of professional theorizing. In the chapters

to come we will see how ethical therapy is leading to dramatic advances in the treatment not only of major emotional problems such as depression, guilt, and fear, but of many related physical complaints as well.

As to my own interest in the therapeutic importance of values, I suppose I have never been quite comfortable with the tendency of modern academic psychologists to equate the purity of their science with the complete rejection of ethical tradition. One of my most vivid memories from my undergraduate years at Princeton was listening to a professor argue that a "good" psychologist had to be absolutely "value-free" in his approach, for any discussion of ethical discipline or moral responsibility would be admitting a degree of freedom which negated any hope of scientifically predicting human behavior. There was also the thinly veiled warning that legitimizing a subject so often associated with traditional religion would make psychology vulnerable to subversion by the worst kind of theological dogma and superstition.

Even then it seemed to me that my professor's fears were a bit exaggerated. Although treating patients as people capable of making independent ethical choices might conflict with some psychologists' dream of reducing man to a completely predictable biochemical machine, there was still plenty of room for valuable scientific research. One could measure, for example, whether habitually honest people are happier or more successful than their dishonest counterparts. Or how different ethical values are related to the incidence of various emotional disorders.

Of course, if there had been any hard evidence to support a "value-free" approach to psychotherapy, I probably would have given my professor's prescription more serious consideration. In point of fact, though, neither psychoanalysis nor behavior modification—the two most prominent psychiatric schools of that time—had ever really proven themselves very effective in alleviating patients' emotional problems. Indeed, what research had been done up until that point suggested that the long-term effect of conventional psychotherapies could just as easily be negative as positive,[3] even on patients who themselves were therapists.[4]

(Today, psychoanalysis and behavior modification are still the leading schools of therapeutic thought, but the inability of either to distinguish itself in a meaningful way[5] is a problem that continues to haunt the profession.[6] As recently as January of 1985, Dr. Saul Levine, a Professor of Psychiatry at the University of Toronto, had to admit that "in spite of years of accumulated knowledge, well-controlled, reliable and valid studies (of psychiatric success) are still hard to come by."[7]

The threat of incorporating ethical choice into psychiatric treatment, I began to sense, was not that it would interfere with the possibility for useful scientific research, but that the human dignity and mystery implied by this approach would prevent the professional psychologist from feeling as superior as he might like to his patients and to the "less sophisticated" layman in general. I also began to wonder if psychology's persistent allergy to any subject even faintly connected to traditional religion or philosophy might not be exactly the kind of dogmatic and negative thinking a "good" psychiatrist ought to be trying to cure.

How exactly I made the journey from this vague undergraduate dissatisfaction with the "value-free" bias of academic psychotherapy to finally embracing the traditional values of *honesty, tolerance,* and *intuitive self-reliance* as a primary form of treatment is a long story, combining more personal and professional experience than could easily be condensed. Yet, to the extent such evolutions can really be summarized, two incidents have always seemed particularly important.

The first happened over fifteen years ago while I was still in graduate school at Stanford. Through a series of circumstances I had gone into therapy with an unusually talented and iconoclastic Palo Alto psychologist named Jon Davidson. I don't remember what problem I had presented on this particular day, only that I was trying to make a case for telling some kind of white lie.

"Do you really want to do this to yourself?," Jon interrupted provocatively.

"Do what?," I replied blankly.

"Lie," he answered. "Don't you realize that by trying to manipulate somebody else you're only going to hurt yourself."

"Oh, well . . . maybe if you believe in some kind of afterlife justice. . . ."

"No, no!," Jon continued in his animated way. "I'm talking about right *now,* what you're going to feel *today!*"

After some further discussion, I finally realized what Jon was getting at. Lying, if I took the trouble to be aware of it, was really a terrible psychological state. My vision dimmed, my pulse quickened anxiously, and there was a noticeable loss of contact with the outside world, all this in addition to any long-term physical effects of such stress.

Indeed, the more I experimented with disciplining my deceitful impulses in the days and months that followed—forsaking the temptation to manipulate other people's feelings and stating my real intentions without the usual rationalizations—the more confident and peaceful I began to feel. The improvement in my social life was particularly noticeable. After months of living a rather lonely and isolated campus life, I suddenly found myself with a new girlfriend and full weekend schedules of skiing and tennis.

The second pivotal incident in the development of my thought occurred roughly ten years ago while I was driving back to California from a trip East. It lasted no longer than a second, though it can fairly be said that the emotional turmoil leading up to it, including guilt over a girlfriend's recent abortion and the mishandling of some writing projects, had gone on for some time.

The time was about an hour after dark when I noticed what seemed to be a flash in an otherwise clear sky. At first I thought I had seen lightning, but quickly realized that the flash was an incredible internal transformation. Suddenly, after years of doubting and uncertainty, I had accepted the existence of an inner self—a *soul* if I dared use that most unpsychiatric of words—whose knowledge and wisdom extended well beyond my biological conception of brainpower.

I already knew that reports of such inner realizations were quite common in people rebounding from emotional stress—Gallup polls suggest that as many as 70 percent of all Americans can expect a similar experience at least once during their lives.[8] But I was quite unprepared for the lasting authority of the event or for the unavoidable intellectual implication that many of the intuitions I had so often dismissed as irrelevant fantasies or wishful thinking—my hunches, instincts, and "gut" feelings—might actually represent a higher form of wisdom.

The more I dared to test this proposition, however, the more truth there seemed to be to it. Following an intuitive impulse to organize some seemingly trivial part of my life, for example, or to investigate some oddly intriguing subject I'd happened to hear about, would prove just days or weeks later to have an unexpected utility. I would also find, when hiring someone for a job, that the briefest personal impression was a far better predictor of his or her performance than any recommendation or résumé. Even the impulse to call a distant relative or contact an old friend I hadn't seen in years would turn out to demonstrate exceptionally good timing.

Indeed, my experience with trusting my intuition was so successful that I found myself in a strange quandary. In the months and years following my discussions with Jon Davidson, I had become convinced that certain ethical restraints, particularly honesty and the willingness to curb judgmental tendencies, were absolutely essential to personal happiness; yet now it was becoming clear that being more spontaneous also had something to do with it. How could somebody believe in both discipline and spontaneous intuition at the same time?

Fortunately, it soon became apparent that these seeming opposite approaches to life were quite compatible and, indeed, had the surprising effect of reinforcing each other. This is to say that the more I learned to trust my intuitive wisdom, the less I felt I had to judge and manipulate other people. Similarly, it was my willingness to be more open and tolerant with others that seemed to strengthen and clarify my intuitive perceptions. The juxtaposition of ethical discipline and intuitive self-reliance proved not to be a psychological paradox after all, but two aspects of the same therapeutic process.

In the decade since that remarkable drive back to California, I have had many opportunities to share these conclusions with scores of professional friends and colleagues, and each year the response becomes so increasingly sympathetic that what at first seemed like a solitary undergraduate's futile rebellion against a "value-free" psychiatric establishment now appears as but one expression of a much broader movement. The continued inability of conventional therapies to produce anything approximating a cure, coupled with a broader cultural interest in traditional values, has created a situation where even the most stubbornly avowed *psychoanalyst* or *behavior modifier* will admit, in the relaxed atmosphere of late night conversation, that no patient has ever really been healed who has not adopted a more spiritual point of view.

Indeed, I don't think it is a coincidence that as of this writing the board of directors of the American Psychiatric Association is facing widespread resistance from its own rank-and-file members to its attempt to publish an official manual of recommended treatments for emotional disorders. It is one thing to require would-be psychiatrists to study "value-free" theories in order to get a license to practice, quite another to force them to continue using these theories on innocent patients with real problems.

Of course, the most important question of all is not how I personally stumbled upon the therapeutic wisdom of traditional values, or why I believe so many working professionals will be openly supportive of the ethical techniques described in this book, but how someone currently suffering the throes of depression, guilt, or some other emotional problem can begin to apply this emerging therapy to his or her particular situation. Conventional psychology's long neglect of this topic has so debased our everyday language that even the person who senses the need to be more honest, tolerant, or intuitive can easily get lost in semantic confusion over the meaning of such words. The seemingly paradoxical nature of traditional values—the simultaneous belief in ethical discipline coupled with a faith in the wisdom of spontaneous expression—only appears to compound the problem.

Fortunately, the therapeutic use of traditional values proves surprisingly straightforward once we understand a few basic concepts. In this respect, the motivated layman, whose only concern is his own happiness and the well-being of loved ones, has a distinct advantage over many academic psychologists who have made a career out of defending psychoanalysis, behavior modification, or some other "value-free" point of view.

Approached with an open mind and a bit of courage, ethical therapy can provide lasting relief from a wide variety of emotional problems. The only prerequisite is some historical sense of how ethical therapy, whose effectiveness has been obvious for the better part of the last two thousand years, could have become so thoroughly obscured to modern eyes—and a willingness to question the sorry assumptions that still cloud conventional psychiatric wisdom.

# Chapter 2

---

# WHAT IS
# ETHICAL THERAPY?

. . . the study of history is the best remedy for a sick
mind.

LIVY[1]

. . . it is important to recognize that a movement is
occurring. . . . . it is a widespread cultural phenomenon, a kind of return to the study of values including
spiritual values, but is happening with new sophistication and a more systematic and empirical analysis.

DR. ALLEN BERGIN[2]

Beneath the thin veneer of official psychology with its stubborn insis-
tence on an objective, "value-free" approach to the cure of emotional
problems, a quiet but profound revolution is taking place.

Prominent professors still teach psychology as if mental disorders
were strictly a function of impersonal social forces; academic researchers continue to describe depression or feelings of worthlessness or lone-

liness as if those who suffered from such problems had no control over their fate; and the well-known heads of famous institutes speak as always about the determining influence of early childhood experience. But among the thousands of psychologists, psychiatrists, and social workers who actually practice therapy day-to-day, something dramatically unexpected is happening: many are promoting ethical discipline *as an explicit form of psychotherapy.*

Consider the resident psychiatrist at a Midwestern hospital who encourages patients to end each day by meditating briefly on how honestly they have behaved during the past twenty-four hours. Or the New York City drug counselor who encourages a recovering cocaine addict to make a list of all the people he has harmed, for the purpose of making amends. Or the private therapist in suburban Connecticut who listens patiently to his client's complaints of being unable to make a career decision, then says "Okay, those are the logical arguments. What do you feel like doing in your *soul?*"

Statistically this growing reliance on traditional ethical and spiritual values reveals itself in collective attitudes which would have been considered unthinkable less than a decade ago. A recent national survey of 425 practicing psychologists, marriage and family counselors, psychiatrists, and social workers,[3] is revealing. Queried on what they believed to be the essential requirements for mental health, 96 percent stressed the importance of patients becoming more "open, genuine, and honest." 100 percent agreed on the importance of "assuming responsibility for one's actions," 99 percent on "increasing one's capacity for self-control," 93 percent on "being able to forgive parents or others who have inflicted disturbance in oneself," and a remarkable 96 percent on "acquiring an awareness of inner potential and the capacity to grow."

Dr. Allen Bergin, now of Brigham Young University, recalls a telling event.[4]

"During my graduate education," he remembers, "I had the fortunate experience of working with several leaders in psychology. . . . These were good experiences with great men for whom I continue to have deep respect and warmth; but I found our view on values to be quite different. . . . I felt constrained from full expression of my values by . . . the prevailing, sometimes coercive, ideologies."

Frustrated by these attitudes, Bergin finally made a case for his own, more ethically explicit approach in a 1980 issue of the *Journal of Consulting and Clinical Psychology*. The response since that time from what Bergin himself called the "hidden society" of values-oriented psychologists, psychiatrists, and social workers has been well over a thousand congratulatory letters and speaking invitations, a near record for replies to this type of academic publication.

How is it possible that such large numbers of therapists have come, seemingly independent of one another, to be sympathetic to a point of view so radically at odds with the ideological basis of their own academic training? And what does this emerging ethical therapy mean for the treatment of specific emotional problems?

First, we should understand that the idea of advocating ethical discipline as a therapeutic treatment, while provocative, is really the oldest and most enduring form of therapy, dating all the way back to the first philosophers of ancient Greece. Indeed, the very concept of psychotherapy was born of Plato's attempt to remedy the emotional problems surrounding the economic and military decline of his native Athens with an explicit and practical code of moral values.

How Plato came to see ethical discipline as the key to emotional rejuvenation is part history, part conjecture. We know that he was profoundly influenced by the example of his own teacher, Socrates, an amateur philosopher whose own personal integrity created such a radiant presence that his very glance could stop traffic in the marketplace.[5]

We also know that Plato fled Athens at age twenty-eight, probably to escape a political tyranny which had condemned even Socrates, and spent a good part of the next twelve years trading throughout the Mediterranean, researching and writing as he traveled. Some historians believe he was influenced by the mystery religions of Judea, others detect the Vedic influence of distant India, while still others would say that the concepts Plato chose to express in the form of his famous *Dialogues* between Socrates and other Athenian Greeks were, in fact, the literal transcription of conversations he had overheard as a young student.

Whatever the blend of his sources, by the time Plato finally returned to settle in Athens at age forty, he was already laying down a concept of ethical therapy that would prove the basis of effective mental health care for centuries to come.

He didn't use the word *psychotherapy*, of course; the word hadn't even been invented yet. But there is hardly a page in Plato that is not concerned with *justice*, a word he uses to mean the systematic application of ethical discipline to amplify the natural healing power of the intuitive mind, what he called man's *rational soul*. By becoming more honest in one's business and family affairs—balancing a tolerance for the opinions of others with reverence for the dictates of one's own heart—he believed it was possible to "treat"[6] even the severest afflictions.

So powerful was Plato's ethical therapy that he was emulated, not only by lesser contemporaries[7], but by virtually every great doctor and practical philosopher who has followed over the centuries. The Greek physician Galen, St. Augustine, the influential twelfth-century Jewish doctor and philosopher Moses Maimonides, the Persian seer Jalal-uddin Rumi, Sir Francis Bacon, Benjamin Franklin—all readily acknowledged their debt to Plato. From the universities at ancient Alexandria to the academy of Renaissance Salerno to the "cradle of the modern clinic" in eighteenth-century Leiden, the very history of medicine up until the advent of immunization and anesthesia is in large part the progress of Plato's original therapy.

Of course, every generation has made its own contributions. Just as Freud produced Neo-Freudians and behaviorism has produced Neo-behaviorists, so the history of Plato's ethical treatment is really the history of Neo-Platonism. From Galen came the idea of relating particular psychological problems to particular lapses in ethical conduct, from Augustine a fuller understanding of willpower, and from Maimonides a broader appreciation of psychosomatic problems. Rumi added a poet's insight on the nature of intuition, while Bacon demonstrated that any person, even a politician or lawyer, could benefit from what he called "the wisdom of the ancients." Benjamin Franklin[8] added the use of his famous pocket diary, showing for the first time that the therapeutic power of ethical self-discipline—what he called "the science of virtue"[9] —could be empirically measured.

The emerging ethical approach of today's working therapist, then, is much less a break with established authority than a rediscovery of history's most enduring and successful therapeutic tradition. Not only has the idea of ethical therapy been around since ancient Greece, but its basic themes of increased honesty, restrained judgment, and intuitive self-reliance were well established principles by the beginning of the nineteenth century.

We need only to go back to Franklin's day when Benjamin Rush, the famous physician and Revolutionary War hero, was lecturing Pennsylvania medical students on "moral treatment" of the mentally ill. Although Rush's use of the word *moral* referred more to the idea of providing patients with humane living conditions than to any particular technique, it nevertheless reflected the popular perception of mental disturbance as a psychological phenomenon—and one that could be treated with a basic reverence for human values.

By the mid-nineteenth century, in fact, Americans had established more than thirty hospitals for the "moral" treatment of emotional problems. Worcester State Hospital in Massachusetts, the best known of these facilities, achieved annual patient recovery rates as high as 71 percent,[10] astonishing even by today's supposedly advanced standards. Europe, too, was taken with moral treatment, thanks in no small part to the efforts of a reform-minded writer named Charles Dickens, who traveled widely to promote it, and of the nearly forgotten Dr. Ernst von Feuchtersleben, who taught a popular course in psychiatry at the Viennese University Medical School.

Of course, if the nineteenth century was a high point in popular enthusiasm for ethical therapy, it was also the time most of us have learned to associate with the beginnings of modern scientific psychiatry. It was in the latter part of this century when the distinguished Boston medical professor William James founded Harvard's psychology department, when Sigmund Freud began publishing his first observations of the unconscious mind, and when advanced psychological laboratories were being established in both Germany and the United States.

How, the question naturally arises, could the modern ideal of "value-free" psychiatry emerge from such an unlikely environment?

The short answer is, "it didn't."

Certainly James, who authored such essays as "The Moral Philosopher and the Moral Life" was very much an advocate of ethical therapy, as were a great percentage of his colleagues. The vision which inspired the early pioneers of modern social science—Herbert Spencer,

James Mark Baldwin, Leonard Hobbhouse, Sir James Frazer, and Samuel Alexander—was not, as we have been taught, the prospect of debunking traditional values, but of *clarifying* their power, establishing in Spencer's own words the "rules of right conduct on a scientific basis."[11]

Many believed traditional values so crucial to human happiness that they openly speculated on the possibility of certain character traits actually selecting themselves out over generations, turning Charles Darwin's "survival of the fittest" into something more like the "survival of the nicest." A steady upward development of ethical values was considered such an inevitable part of human evolution that many scientists thought people would try to be more honest and tolerant just to prove their evolutionary superiority.

Even Sigmund Freud's original views were much closer to the legacy of classical psychiatry than most of us have been led to think.[12] Openly acknowledging his debt to Plato's *Dialogues,* Freud's emphasis in his word *psychoanalyse* was definitely on the *psyche,* a term he used with full knowledge of its ancient Greek meaning, "the soul."

"My psychical treatment," he wrote in an article called "Treatment of the Soul,"[13] signifies "treatment originating in the soul, treatment—of psychic or bodily disorders—by measures which influence above all and immediately the soul of man."

Furthermore it was never Freud's intention that therapy should become a protracted and murky process, replacing the need for ethical self-discipline with years of dispassionate and complicated analysis. To the end of his life he lobbied for a profession of "lay" analysts, neither physicians nor priests, who would hopefully develop psychoanalysis to the point where it could educate large numbers of people to become more self-reliant without their ever having to visit a doctor's office.

The real beginning of "value-free" psychiatry as we know it today came not at the end of the nineteenth century but some twenty years later and seems to have had more to do with American medicine modifying psychoanalysis to suit its own professional purposes than with any kind of scientific insight. Physicians began insisting, for example, that only medical school graduates who had trained at an approved site were competent enough to call themselves "psychoanalysts"; and a concerted effort was made to politically enforce these restrictions—a bill which finally passed the New York State legislature in 1926.

But the most drastic alteration in this professional perversion of psychoanalysis was in the therapy itself. Medical organizations in America and other countries outside central Europe produced gross mis-translations of Freud's original German texts, with English language versions actually deleting his many and often impassioned references to ethical and spiritual concepts.

Perhaps the most serious of all was the attempt to turn Freud's original argument in favor of a judicious balance between self-expression and moral constraint (in *Civilization and Its Discontents*) into a blanket condemnation of all ethical discipline as a form of repression. Slowly but surely medical psychoanalysis came to equate mental health, not with Freud's ideal of responsible independence, but with the endless weekly probing of morbid fantasy; and the therapy which had been invented to cultivate man's ethical dependence on his own internal authority was well on its way to serving the vested interest of a now thriving medical establishment.

Sadly, this "value-free" thrust in medical psychiatry was accompanied by a nearly parallel development in departments of academic psychology. After years of promising research in the area of ethical discipline—including an impressive study by Columbia University's Teachers College on the psychological consequences of truth telling[14] —the subject of traditional values suddenly became, in the words of one terse observer, "as dead as last week's newspaper."[15]

How did this happen?

Official psychology's own explanation points to the influence of a young researcher named John Watson who, from 1908 to 1920, attempted to show that the behavior of animals and even humans could be systematically altered through the careful administration of external rewards and punishments. It was the success of Watson's experiments which supposedly persuaded increasing numbers of psychologists to reject the importance of inner values and concentrate instead on the manipulation of overt behavior, the approach we today call *behaviorism*.[16]

But to really understand the success of behaviorism, we must look not to the period of Watson's experiments, but to the mid-1920s, when large infusions of cash from the Laura Spelman Rockefeller Memorial and similar foundations began to have a subtle effect on the orientation of psychological research. For until that time, most psychologists did not really take Watson very seriously. It was only when researchers discovered that there was considerable support available to those who shared the philanthropic ideal of using science to engineer social change that behaviorism began to flourish.

While it would be unfair to suggest that the psychologists of those days deliberately altered their theories for the sake of professional advancement, the behaviorists' emphasis on external measurement and control clearly made any proposal for the funding of new research and training facilities very attractive to many philanthropic organizations. For example, Beardsley Ruml, an ardent behaviorist sympathizer who became director of the Laura Spelman Rockefeller Memorial Foundation in 1922, made generous grants available to like-minded protégés at Yale, Minnesota, Berkeley, Chicago, and other newly founded research institutes.[17]

Such radical departures by both organized medicine and academic psychology from the ethical spirit of classical psychiatry did meet with considerable resistance at first. Freud himself continually disparaged the American version of psychoanalysis, insisting that it "signif[ied] neither a friendly attitude toward [the] essence [of psychoanalysis] nor any extension and deepening of its understanding."[18] And as for the academic psychologists' increasing flirtation with behaviorism, the distinguished Columbia University professor F. J. Woodbridge saw full well that his colleagues were trading truth for power and professional advancement. This "emphasis on behavior," he warned a 1925 conference of colleagues in New Hampshire, is "an important shift in scientific emphasis, a shift from understanding to control . . . from the search for truth . . . to management, direction, [and] greater effectiveness."[19]

Yet the fact that medical psychoanalysis and academic psychology were separated by different concepts and terminology gave many the illusion that psychiatric science was progressing with a genuinely open mind. Less clearly visible was the fact that for all their superficial disagreements, *both* the psychoanalytic and behaviorist schools of therapy succeeded in making taboo subjects of history's two most tested and durable therapeutic principles: ethical discipline and intuitive self-reliance.

From the 1930s on, virtually all psychiatric textbooks, whether psychoanalytic or behaviorist, ignored the ethical foundations of their own science, and courses in the history of psychology were given no more than a token priority by graduate school departments. The word *ethics* came to have a such narrow meaning in professional circles—therapists might discuss the ethics of professional conduct, but never the use of ethics *as* therapy[20]—that almost none of the federal money that became available for social science research after World War II was ever used to study traditional values as an explicit form of psychotherapy.

Even many religious counselors who might have been expected to lend traditional therapy a sympathetic hand were themselves seduced by these new objective theories. Forty years ago, a prophetic teacher at the University of Chicago[21] complained that new ministers were too eagerly mimicking the psychiatrist's blind rejection of traditional values, sending troubled parishioners back into the world with more problems than when they first asked for help. Unfortunately, it wasn't too long after this futile plea that divinity schools began teaching their own courses in "value-free" psychiatry.[22]

Only such a widespread and prolonged bias against traditional values could explain how so many of today's professionals who pride themselves on a fearless probing of the human condition could at once congratulate a client for following a recommended treatment schedule, yet refuse to concede that this same client may have had something to do with creating his pain in the first place.[23]

When the patient gets better, the case report will always say "the patient has been very industrious," but never the converse—that the patient has been lazy or unmotivated. Then the report simply says that the patient has been "passive," as if some uncontrollable biological or physical problem has taken over.

A similar contradiction exists between the high standard of personal responsibility a psychiatrist will often apply to his own private life versus his professional assumption that everyone else he encounters is really just a biological machine with no real power of choice or independence of mind. A therapist might spend his entire weekend coping with such important obligations as caring for the children, fixing up the house, and staying up late on Sunday night to be sure the month's bills are paid on time, but then walk into his office on Monday morning and presume that the patient sitting across from him is the inevitable product of hapless childhood experience, whose only hope for real change lies with some mood-altering drug or conditioning technique.

But of all the contradictions of "value-free" psychiatry, perhaps the most striking is that the same therapist who insists on the importance of a scientific approach to understanding human emotions will refuse to acknowledge the documented conclusion of such research—namely, that a code of personal values is critical to long-term happiness. Despite all the elaborate scientific surveys which have demonstrated that the essentials of a happy life—good relationships, positive attitudes, and job satisfaction—are conditioned upon a belief in firm ethical standards,[24] the conventional psychiatrist continues to equate being a "scientific psychiatrist" with being "value-neutral." Such narrow thinking is reminiscent of the failed military commander who insisted on building an elaborate intelligence network, only to ignore those reports that contradicted what he wanted to believe in the beginning.

Of course, there have always been perceptive therapists who dared to protest the myth of an effective "value-free" therapy. George Mora, the respected Yale psychiatrist and medical historian, argued forcefully in the early 1960s, for example, that the character of the therapist was much "more important than his adherence to a particular school of thought."[25] And Dr. O. Hobart Mowrer, an early pioneer in the development of behaviorism who eventually became disillusioned with this "value-free" approach, actually held what he called weekly "integrity" group meetings for training young therapists at his home near the University of Illinois.[26]

Another reformed behaviorist, the late Brandeis University psychologist Abraham Maslow, was even more outspoken. "Plato's words still hold," he once told an interviewer. The man who lives by "ultimate value[s] . . . stands in the sunlight and sees the real world."[27] Maslow came to believe that the happiest individuals "are ordinarily concerned with the basic issues and eternal questions of the type that we have learned to call philosophical or ethical."[28]

Even Dr. Carl Jung, who today we associate with mysticism and

Eastern religions, was in fact a lifelong champion for a return to traditional values in contemporary psychology. Tracing the therapeutic idea of an ethical-intuitive balance all the way back to the ancient Greeks, Jung frequently warned that to privately "cherish secrets and to restrain emotions are psychic misdemeanors for which nature finally visits us with sickness."[29]

What makes for the modern revolution is that the ethical conviction which has always surfaced among a few dissenting luminaries has finally spread well into the ranks of working professionals. Different psychiatrists may use different terms to describe their emerging beliefs, but the growing emphasis on tolerance, honesty, and intuitive self-reliance is unmistakable.

Some of these new ethical therapists, like Jon Davidson, can be found in the relative seclusion of private practice, while others, like Joel Kanter, a thirty-six-year-old therapist at the Washington (D.C.) School of Psychiatry and nearby Mt. Vernon Mental Health Center, continue to work within the institutional structure of establishment psychology, all the while patiently lobbying for a more enlightened approach. Helping troubled patients and their families to take a more disciplined and responsible approach to their problems, Kanter is typical of a growing institutional "underground" that daily walks the fine line between acceptable "value-free" procedures and a more experienced sense of what really works.

In the pages to come we will hear from many other working professionals, including Milwaukee-based therapist Victoria Brundage, a former classical scholar who now specializes in treating the families of physicians and other helping professionals, and Frances Vaughan, a California psychologist and consultant who has become an internationally recognized authority on the subject of intuitive thinking.

But what is particularly fascinating is to see how pressure from the rank-and-file of psychology's working therapists, combined with the continued public embarrassment over official psychiatry's inability to produce anything even remotely approximating a reliable cure, has even begun to force a serious reconsideration of ethical therapy within the highest levels of the professional establishment.

Behaviorist thinkers are finally conceding that internal values do indeed color a person's emotional state. The University of Pennsylvania

Medical School's Dr. Aaron Beck, with the help of colleagues, has developed a new technique he calls *Cognitive* Behavior Therapy, which encourages patients to reexamine their most negative kinds of thoughts and beliefs.[30]

The typical application would be the depressed patient who habitually thinks to himself "you can't trust anyone" or "I'm just no good—I never amount to anything." In the past, behavioral therapists might well have ignored such private statements, concentrating strictly on how to recondition the client's overt behavior: late sleeping habits, poor working hours, and other external symptoms. But in Cognitive Behavior Therapy, there is a direct attempt to make the depressed person aware of how psychologically defeating such internal dialogues can be.

In the very first sessions he is encouraged to begin monitoring the self-statements he makes during the course of his daily activities, always reminding himself that there is a more optimistic way of looking at things. He is even told to schedule work breaks, snacks, movies, and other pleasurable activities as a reward for thinking more constructively.

Words like *ethics* and *intuition* do not yet have any formal role in this kind of therapy, but it is intriguing to note just how much of such "cognitive restructuring" has to do with teaching people to suspend their most hostile thoughts and deceitful impulses, at the same time becoming more receptive to hunches and gut feelings. In an earlier time such training would clearly have fallen within the province of what Plato himself called "moral science."

For their own part, many psychoanalytic researchers have also made a significant, if equally well-camouflaged, move in the direction of traditional values. Interpersonal Psychotherapy, a product of fifteen years' research by Yale University's Dr. Gerald Klerman, Eve Chevron, and other members of the New Haven-Boston Collaborative Depression Research Project, typifies a growing trend away from the lengthy analysis of residual childhood memories toward a shorter-term therapy with major emphasis on developing certain disciplines. Patients who enter Interpersonal Psychotherapy are encouraged to focus their efforts almost exclusively on the improvement of current social relationships and altering the self-defeating way they habitually react to problematic situations.[31]

The net effect of emphasizing the client's need to take responsibility for distorted thinking and a lack of assertiveness is a rather thorough and forceful reevaluation of his or her basic values. "Ours is a therapy," confides Chevron,[32] "where in fact I assume there is a value system. . . . We start with the therapeutic assumption that unless you're having good or fulfilling relations with other people, it's awfully hard to be happy."

Interestingly, this subtle shift toward values in two major areas of conventional clinical psychiatry has been accompanied by parallel developments in psychosomatic medicine, business management, education, and many other fields of psychology.

Take the work of Dr. James Pennebaker, a graduate of the University of Texas who now teaches and conducts research at Southern Methodist University. Fascinated by the apparent relationship between psychological attitudes and the onset of various physical ailments, Dr. Pennebaker began some years ago to measure the medical impact of specific character traits. Not only has his research suggested a direct connection between personal honesty and increased immunity to the stressful consequences of major traumatic events, but between habitual openness and improved health in general.[33]

Dr. Carl Thoresen, a professor of counseling education at Stanford University, is interested in the relationship between character and health, specifically the impact of habitual judging on the incidence of heart disease. Studying coronary patients with a history of resentful and hostile behavior, Thoresen has found evidence to suggest that those who deliberately cultivate a more tolerant disposition are significantly less likely to suffer a second heart attack than those who continue to indulge their old negative attitudes.[34]

In the field of management, there is the intriguing work of Daniel Isenberg, a Harvard Business School professor who has spent many years studying the qualities which differentiate a dynamic executive from his less successful contemporaries. Contrary to the popular stereotype of the high achiever as an arrogant autocrat, impatiently judging colleagues and insensitive to the needs of subordinates, Isenberg has found the most successful senior managers are quite extraordinary in their ability to refrain from overt criticism of others, often humorously conceding when they themselves are wrong. They also take a greater than normal interest in the emotional comfort of their fellow workers and have a tendency to transform everyday resentments over unexpected problems into constructive questions about how to improve their company's operations.

Successful managers also have one other surprising quality, according to Isenberg—they tend to rely quite heavily on their "gut feelings." It may seem inconsistent with everything we've come to expect from movies and television, Isenberg readily admits, but "[my] observation is that intuition plays a very central role in the thinking process used by senior managers."[35]

Even in the field of educational psychology, the experimental playground for all manner of psychoanalytic and behaviorist theories, there is now growing concern that the same "value-free" ideas which have so inhibited the effectiveness of conventional psychotherapy may also be standing in the way of needed educational reforms. One past president of the American Psychological Association, D. T. Campbell, has suggested that the profession's "background assumption that . . . moral traditions are wrong"[36] may be harming the mental health of an entire generation of Americans. ". . . in propagating such a background perspective in the teaching of perhaps 90 percent of college undergraduates [and increasing proportions of high school and elementary school pupils]," Campbell warns his colleagues, "[we] may [actually] be contributing to the undermining of . . . extremely valuable social-evolutionary inhibitory systems which we do not yet fully understand."

Outside the relatively conservative boundaries of academic psychology, the rebound from "value-free" therapy is even more explicit. Perhaps the most obvious example is in the area of treating alcohol, drug, and other addictive behaviors where conventional psychoanalysis and behaviorism are rapidly conceding defeat to the so-called "anonymous" programs, which emphasize recovery through the cultivation of ethical values and inner guidance.

Inspired by the original Alcoholics Anonymous, there is now a Narcotics Anonymous, a Gamblers Anonymous, an Overeaters Anonymous, and most recently a Cocaine Anonymous. Total participation is difficult to estimate, though A.A. conservatively estimates its membership alone at "well over one million."[37] When combined with sister organizations dedicated to helping relatives of addicts, such as Adult Children of Alcoholics and Al-Anon, the ethically oriented anonymous self-help programs currently constitute the single largest treatment program in American life.

Another area where values are clearly making a strong comeback is family therapy. If any institution has suffered the most from the conventional ideology of ethical neutrality, it is family life; and it is in the offices of therapists who attempt to deal with fractured family relationships where the basic importance of honesty and tolerance has become most obvious.

Family therapists have pioneered the move away from conventional psychiatry, explains Harold Goolishian of the Galveston Family Institute, because "they have to deal with what really works." Therapists who work one-on-one with just individual patients have the luxury of not having to be right—"they can be more accepting of deviance."[38] Therapists who work with the whole family, on the other hand, can see immediately the results of their work with one person on the other family members.

Finally, we can see a resurgence of traditional values in the so-called "personal growth" market: lectures, seminars, and workshops dedicated to helping large numbers of already healthy people feel even better. Dr. M. Scott Peck, author of the highly acclaimed *Road Less Traveled,* and Hasidic scholar and therapist Dr. Edward Hoffman, are both increasingly in demand as guest speakers at civic meetings and university classes across the country. "I meet many people who share [this interest in values]," notes Hoffman,[39] "and we all feel we are doing something important."

Dr. Thomas Hora, a European-born psychoanalyst with a private practice in New York City and suburban Bedford Village, has attracted a considerable following in recent years with his attempts to breathe life into the "dry bones" of behaviorism and psychoanalysis. Hora has called for a new school of *metapsychiatry* (literally, "beyond psychiatry") that would include long neglected ethical and spiritual concepts.

To date, Dr. Hora's own New York Institute of Metapsychiatry claims an active membership of over 700 and publishes professional books and newsletters around the world. A 1985 summer conclave of "metapsychiatrists" in Oosterbeek, Holland, attracted participants from all over the Netherlands and Belgium, even as far away as Frankfurt, West Germany, and finally had to be conducted in three languages.

What do all these developments mean for someone who is currently suffering with some seemingly intractable emotional problem?

They mean first of all that very few psychological maladies—not depression, guilt, boredom, indecision, feelings of worthlessness, fear, frustration, loneliness, or even prolonged anxiety or addiction—are natural states, nor need be endured. As we shall see in the chapters to come, each of these negative states has its roots in a particular judgmental or manipulative habit; and it is through understanding the proper connection and by taking some simple remedial steps to correct our conduct that many of our emotional troubles can finally be alleviated.

Of course breaking any unethical habit is probably the last thing any unhappy person wants to try. For trusting in the discipline of our habitual judgments or manipulations often feels like we are being asked to give up conscious control of our lives at precisely the most difficult moment—when we are in the throes of emotional pain.

The more pain we feel, the more convinced we have become that the universe is completely hostile to our welfare and that no promise of eventual psychological relief is worth the risk of being more forthright and trusting. Our unethical habits and manipulations, no matter how self-destructive, at least offer a semblance of order amidst the seeming threat of complete chaos.

Fortunately the operative word is *experiment*. We don't need to be firmly convinced of ethical therapy in order to begin using it in a tentative way. Gradually restraining our most self-destructive habits, we take what steps we feel comfortable with until the benefits become so obvious that our hesitation to venture further vanishes of its own accord.

The only real requirement for progress is a willingness to look beyond the conventional view of emotional health as a commercial object—something we buy in the form of pills, gimmicks, or pat insights—and begin to define it as every great healer since Plato has defined it: as a personal responsibility, our *ethical* responsibility.

# Chapter 3

---  ⤐

# *BEYOND DEPRESSION*

The melancholic acts differently:
they show fear and depression, discontent with life
and hatred of all people.

GALEN[1]

And since he is ignorant of what *principally* concerns
him, tho' it has been told him a thousand Times
from Parents, Press, and Pulpit, the Vicious Man,
however learned, cannot be a *Man of Science*, but is a
Fool, a Dunce, and a Blockhead.

BENJAMIN FRANKLIN[2]

Occasional exhaustion is a normal and even healthy fact of life. Every day we are subject to thousands of pressures, from job-related stress to family squabbles to changes in body chemistry, and we all have periods of adjustment when we feel "sluggish," "unusually tired," "sad," "discouraged," "burned out," or "disillusioned."

There is also a small segment of the population which falls victim to extreme mood fluctuations, alternating between episodes of wild restlessness and grandiose thinking, on the one hand, and the blackest feelings of despair on the other. An estimated two million Americans, or just under one percent of the country, suffer from this "manic-depression" syndrome, apparently because of an inherited genetic defect on chromosomes 'X' and '11.' (Fortunately most cases of this genetic disorder can be treated with medically supervised doses of lithium.)[3]

But if you are among the estimated 25 percent of all Americans who feel continually depressed over a long period of time[4] (what professional therapists call *clinical depression*)—if you are one of the fifty-million plus adults who take powerful mood-elevating drugs on a regular basis[5] or if your depressed state is accompanied by thoughts of suicide, loss of appetite, or lack of sexual interest—then you may be afflicted by something much deadlier than the ordinary pressures of everyday life or even a genetic defect: you may be the victim of your own resentful judgments.

Is a good portion of your daily life spent fantasizing revenge or indulging hostile thoughts toward a family member, former loved one, boss, colleague, teacher, even a political cause or organization?

Perhaps you can identify with Anne R., a housewife who became increasingly despondent for no apparent reason. Her life was comfortable enough, her family healthy, and she had the freedom to work or not as she chose. Yet day by day things seemed to grow blacker, and as they did she began to nag.

Anne did not like growing into a nag—she knew she could be unpleasant to live with—but the temptation to sling an occasional resentful arrow often seemed the only relief to her ever-deepening despair. If Anne's husband came home early, for example, she'd complain shrilly that the house was too dirty and wonder out loud why he didn't clean the ashtrays or put his newspapers away. If he worked late, she whined with secret pleasure about his neglecting her. She made it hard for him to pin down weekend and vacation plans, then criticized his poor planning when it was finally too late to make reservations.

Or perhaps you are more like Chris, a busy consultant who became habitually abrupt and short-tempered as the pressures of his work seemed to blend into one bleak drone. Impatient at home, he resented having to cope with the problems of an insecure wife and two rebellious youngsters. At work he was obsessed by the failings of colleagues and employees. Finally driven into therapy, Chris readily admitted to being "a bit much on the critical side," but what was the alternative? His life had become such a "turn-off" he couldn't conceive of handling people without saying what he "really thought."

What both Anne and Chris have yet to realize is that their hostile impulses are not the *result* of their depressed states but the *cause*. Anne may feel justified in complaining of her family's neglect because she's so miserable; but it is also her *complaining* of neglect that deepens her misery. Similarly, Chris may believe that his depressed state gives him the right to vent a certain amount of resentful venom; but it is this very venting which undermines his effectiveness both as a father and businessman.

How is it possible that an impulse like resentment, which seems to carry with it such a strong emotional charge, can end up being such a depressing drag on our lives?

The answer, as Plato himself hinted long ago, is that what we mistake for a cathartic impulse is really the egotistic giddiness that comes from the triumph of objective thinking over our intuitive mind, not unlike the seductive narcotic effect of certain poisons. The ancient therapist was so convinced of hostility's illusory allure that he refused to ever discipline a servant when he was in a bad mood. Indeed, he once delegated the responsibility to a visiting friend, because he himself was feeling the deceptive "passion."[6]

One of Plato's most famous successors, the Greek physician Galen (129-200 A.D.), was even more explicit on the subject, perhaps because he had witnessed such a radical disparity between his own father, a good-tempered and benevolent architect, and his irascible mother, who was so quarrelsome that she would bite her serving maids in fits of spite. The interesting thing about "this enormous difference between my parents," Galen observed was "that [father] was never depressed over any affliction, while my mother became annoyed over the merest bagatelle."[7]

Later, as Galen advanced in his career—first as physician to the gladiators in his native city of Pergamum and later as medical advisor to many Roman nobles, including the emperor Marcus Aurelius—the self-defeating resentment of envious colleagues only furthered his interest in the persistent juxtaposition of animated hostility and melancholic despair. Summarizing his thoughts in a psychological treatise *On the Passions and Errors of the Soul*, he finally agreed with Plato that depression was the result of a fatal blindness on the part of those who suffered from it, an inability to recognize that venting resentful impulses in the name of self-expression was really a form of spiritual suicide.

Today's ethical therapist knows only too well the danger of confusing a resentful impulse with genuine desire. "As long as we blame someone for anything," observes Dr. Thomas Hora, "we are angry and resentful, and . . . we usually hurt ourselves. . . . To carry a grudge is a very crippling mental condition."[8]

Of course, this is not the easiest psychological message to convey in today's world: the idea that expressing our resentments could ever make us feel bad contradicts a powerful social myth. We pick up the latest novel about life among the mighty and read that only those who "take care of the competition" ever get to the top. Or go to the local theatre and Clint Eastwood grimly demonstrates how self-righteous homicide can "make our day." The notion that it is perfectly reasonable, healthy—even *moral*—to make our enemies "pay" is epitomized by that popular phrase so often attributed to the late Senator Robert Kennedy: "Don't get mad—get even."

Yet even the research of conventional psychologists is beginning to confirm the eternal diagnosis of depression. In one recent study, for example, where eighty men and women were asked to reflect on their most recent verbal expressions of hostility, more than two thirds confided feeling depressed for some time afterward. About half used words like *unhappiness, gloom, anxiety,* and *nervousness* to describe their state.[9] Carol Tavris, author of *Anger, the Misunderstood Emotion,* claims several studies show that venting resentment can so diminish people's self-esteem that they "feel depressed for several days [and . . . ] a gloomy pall envelops them."[10]

But the most intriguing indictment of resentment comes from a just completed study by the National Institute of Mental Health, which attempted to compare the relative effectiveness of psychotherapy versus psychoactive drugs, such as *imipramine*, for the treatment of depression.[11]

Called the Treatment of Depression Collaborative Research Program or TDCRP for short, the Institute's project involved more than six years of planning and execution, 239 patients, twenty-eight therapists, a medical center and five universities, a budget of ten million dollars, as well as some unusually rigorous controls. To insure an accurate comparison of talk-therapy to drug-therapy, for example, all those who administered the antidepressants were given strict dosage guidelines. The talk-therapists were divided into two groups, one representing psychoanalysis and the other behavior modification, and each was given at least eighteen months' additional training in his or her assigned technique.

It was "one of the largest and most rigorous and really probably the best study [of depression] conducted yet,"[12] observed Robert Hales, an associate professor of psychiatry at the Uniformed Services University of the Health Sciences in Bethesda, Maryland.

Now, TDCRP was not designed specifically to measure the relationship between resentful judgments and depression. If anything the study was motivated by the desire of conventional psychology to bolster its sagging image at a time when public opinion was becoming increasingly skeptical that either psychoanalysis or behavior modification could really accomplish anything.

What makes the study so relevant is that the two therapies chosen to represent psychoanalysis and behavior modification in this showdown with drug-therapy were Interpersonal Psychotherapy and Cognitive Behavior Therapy—the two variations of conventional psychiatry which come closest to expounding ethical values and which make the discipline of resentment a fundamental part of therapy. These two therapies were chosen, explains Morris Parloff, a former Institute director who helped frame the study, "because they are brief and very definable. . . ."[13] Irene Elkin, Washington coordinator of the project, adds that both Interpersonal Psychotherapy and Cognitive Behavior Therapy are simple and systematic enough to be taught to therapists from official manuals.

Whatever the reason for their being chosen, the outcome of the study was most enlightening. The talk-therapies proved at least as effective against depression as the antidepressant drug. In fact, both Interpersonal Psychotherapy and Cognitive Behavior Therapy completely eliminated the most serious symptoms of depression in 50 to 60 percent of the normal cases assigned to them. Where resentful behavior is dramatically reduced, it seems, scientific measures of depression decline rapidly.

Modern scientific research not only confirms the impact of resentment on depression but also suggests severe physical symptoms if left unchecked.

Many readers may remember a well-publicized mid-1970s study[14] by two San Francisco cardiologists, Dr. Meyer Friedman and Dr. Ray Rosenman, which showed that the single greatest reason for heart attacks was not overeating, not even smoking or cholesterol, but a psychological attitude they called *Type A* behavior. Back then, *Type A* was thought to embrace a wide range of stressful behaviors including excessive planning, a sense of time pressure, general competitiveness, as well as resentful thoughts and hostile behavior.

Interest in *Type A* behavior has continued over the decade, but a considerable body of research by Dr. Friedman and others has narrowed the possible spectrum of contributing psychosomatic factors to just one. Dr. Robert Case of the St. Luke's-Roosevelt Hospital Center, who is senior author of one of the most respected studies of *Type A* behavior to date, has observed in the *New England Journal of Medicine* that "hostility and unexpressed anger correlat[e] well with the extent of coronary disease," noting that the other factors have "no relationship" to mortality risk.[15] A possible reason for resentment's uniquely dangerous effect is its potential influence over critical cardiovascular variables, such as blood pressure and the endogenous production of cholesterol and free fatty acids in the bloodstream.

Dr. Carl Thoresen, a collaborator with Dr. Friedman in Stanford University's Recurrent Coronary Prevention Project, agrees about the dangers of resentment. "Hostility," he observes,[16] "particularly those facets of hostility that might be termed 'retributional'—the view that one should get back at others, that others should be punished for their perceived wrongdoings—is linked to the increased risk of fatal or nonfatal infarction." Thoresen's conclusion is based on a five-year clinical study of nearly a thousand men and women who had suffered at least one myocardial infarction and were willing to undergo extensive psychological and physiological monitoring over the period.

Dr. Thomas Hora is so convinced that resentment "can break through within us in the form of a physical disease"[17] that he advises his depressed patients to immediately begin "cleansing themselves" of all malicious thoughts. "Never, never," he advises, "allow [yourselves] to entertain malicious thoughts under any circumstances, no matter what the provocation."[18] We have to "understand," he adds, "that by forgiving people, we are not doing them a favor. We are hurting ourselves by carrying a grudge, and that is no way to live."[19]

Fortunately, the kind of "cleansing" Dr. Hora talks about has always been possible for anyone with a sufficient awareness of the problem to want to do something about it.

Galen himself recorded the typical case of a traveler from Crete whose resentful habits included rebuking tardy slaves with the sharpest edge of his sword. The man was so desperate for relief from his chronic depressions that he was willing to have demons flogged out of him; but Galen suggested he first try a little spiritual discipline instead. The man agreed to consciously break his vengeful impulses, refusing as best he could to translate hostile thoughts into hurtful comments or punitive actions for a period of one year. In much less than that time, Galen was happy to report, the patient "became much better."[20]

Harvard professor William James, perhaps the most famous nineteenth-century American exponent of ethical therapy, cited the case of a writer named Horace Fletcher who with just a little conscious effort at curbing his resentful habits had actually reached the point where, without the slightest feeling of annoyance or impatience, he could watch a train move out of the station without getting angry at the tardy porter carrying his baggage who had caused him to miss it.

This actually happened to Fletcher, who said that when the porter from the hotel finally came panting into the station just minutes later, looking "as if he feared a scolding . . . I said to him: 'It doesn't matter at all, you couldn't help it, so we will try again tomorrow. Here is your fee, I am sorry you had all this trouble earning it.' The look of surprise that came over his face was so filled with pleasure that I was paid on the spot for the delay in my departure. Next day he would not accept a cent for the service, and he and I are friends for life."[21]

Coming up to more modern times, it is striking how dramatically people can alter the expression of hostile thoughts once they begin to understand the self-destructive consequences of their habitual resentments.

One of my favorite stories concerns a young thirty-ish man I know who some four years ago was suffering from what he himself called "anxiety attacks and a generally depressed outlook," which had come to a head after being unceremoniously dumped by a girlfriend.

Uncertain as to the cause of these negative feelings and somewhat methodical by nature, he proceeded to sample one kind of therapist after another, rigorously laying out all the circumstances of his childhood, relating his most traumatic memories, and eventually terminating therapy whenever the psychiatrist appeared to contradict himself in the slightest or make a silly suggestion. In the space of a little over two years he had tried—and convicted—everything from traditional analysis and behavior modification to drug therapy, various self-help groups, and the entire clinical staff of the Yale Medical School.

Naturally his condition grew worse, for not only was he suffering the depressing hostilities that had brought him into therapy, but his new-found resentments against the therapists who failed him were further compounding the problem.

Fortunately, he had become so desperately miserable that he was willing to try anything; and when a friend of mine made the suggestion that the resentment itself might be part of the problem, there began a turnaround over the next few months that even casual acquaintances could not help but notice. The more he was able to check the expression of resentful impulses—sometimes by trying to laugh at how quickly his dark side could emerge, more often by simply biting his tongue—the more he was able to enjoy himself again, even to the point of being able to socialize with some of the people who at one time had so easily aroused his anger.

Now all this isn't to suggest that disciplining the expression of resentment is a snap. For even when we understand that our resentment is an attack, first and foremost, on ourselves, there are still times after someone has hurt our feelings or after we think we have been taken advantage of, when our self-esteem demands a response. No matter how much we may suffer as a result of our own hostility, no matter how much psychological and even physical damage we may incur, we cannot help but want to act out our hostilities. It's almost as if some voice in the back of our head is saying, "if you just take this, you're nothing but a doormat!" Nursing the prospect of a subtle strike—cutting an old foe at a cocktail party or passing some malicious gossip—generates a gleeful rush we often have trouble refusing.

What we don't realize in most of these situations is that giving in to resentment, far from helping us stand up for ourselves, only makes us an accomplice in our further humiliation. Resentment *is* the process of being stepped on, not just psychologically, but in the literal sense of allowing someone else to push us around.

This is a critical point, so let me give you an example of what I mean.

Many years ago when I first entered therapy with psychologist Jon Davidson, he told me a revealing story about another client, a teenage boy who had enormous hostility toward an insensitive and intellectually aloof father. Each semester the father would lecture the boy on the importance of getting good grades in certain subjects, to which the boy would respond by promptly flunking them.

"Don't you realize how completely you've let your father control your life?," Jon finally said to the teenager.

"What do you mean? I never do well in any of the subjects he wants."

"That's the point," Jon explained. "I can predict exactly what grade you're going to get in each subject by how your dad feels about it. If he really wants you to do well, you're definitely going to flunk. If it's not so important to him, you'll probably land a 'D.' And if he doesn't care at all you might even pass. It doesn't matter that you're doing exactly the opposite of what he wants. If you were really free, you wouldn't be so predictable."

The point to be made is that the opposite of being a doormat isn't resentment; resentment is just trading our own foot for somebody else's. The really free person is the one who can quickly step outside the emotional cycles that generate resentment. This is probably what Einstein meant when he said, "Arrows of hate have been shot at me many times, but they never touched me because they came from a world with which I have nothing in common."[22]

How do we achieve this elevated capacity?

One way is by starting to voice our feelings at the first sign of anger, before they have any chance to simmer. When some aggravating situation does catch us by surprise, we should regard the first awareness of hostile plotting in the back of our minds as a signal to calmly but firmly voice our displeasure. To someone who has just cut us off in the movie line, the simple statement, "Excuse me, I don't think this is your place," can preclude a whole half hour of seething resentment—just as immediately calling the dry cleaner who has destroyed one of our favorite shirts eliminates the need to carry that ennervating image throughout what could be an otherwise pleasant afternoon.

This practice of defusing our anger may not appear in many conventional psychology texts, but it is one of the most common survival techniques used by therapists themselves who have to cope with malingering and demanding patients. Instead of endlessly catering to the noisy clinger or hypochondriac, the smart psychiatrists learn to express their frustrations up front, thus avoiding a cumulation of resentment that could actually interfere with their ability as therapists.

The trick is not to be intimidated by any inhibitions we have about appearing too sensitive or vulnerable. People may not always acknowledge the legitimacy of our complaint, but everyone secretly respects a genuine feeling; and this becomes obvious the more we try it.

It is also important not to go to the other extreme and, like Galen's irascible mother, use this opportunity for expressing our legitimate anger as a pretext for punishing others with loud, protracted, or whining complaints. The point of expressing our displeasure is not to "get even," but to communicate our feeling with sufficient clarity that the desire to take revenge is no longer an issue.

Of course, making our displeasure clear is not the same thing as changing someone else's character; and there will inevitably be some people who, while reluctantly bowing to our momentary objection, only present us with another aggravating confrontation some days later. The employee who persistently offends customers, the boy or girlfriend who always says something hurtful when we least need to hear it, the neighbor who's become an incredible mooch—the only alternative in these kinds of situations is to step completely outside of the relationship in such a way as to avoid the recurrence of resentful feelings. In other words, end them. There are very few personal or professional relationships that are worth the price of depression.

Where this gets difficult, of course, is when the aggravating relationship involves a family member or a very old friend. Now we are in what is called a *double bind:* depressed if we continue the relationship yet really not capable or desirous of ending it.

Here there are two levels of response, depending on the ultimate severity of the problem. The first is based on the assumption that in most families or intimate business situations where persistent hostility arises, the resentment is mutual. Furthermore, both parties tend to inadvertently escalate the problem by their misguided attempts to solve it.

"What you have with this kind of resentment," explains Galveston family therapist Harold Goolishian,[23] is a "philosophical battle" where both parties are "trying to rein the other's hostility by getting the other to change his point of view or interpretation of events." Unfortunately, it is the unsolicited attempt by another person to change our point of view which is most likely to make us angry.

The solution in many cases is simply to look for a point of agreement with the other person and hope that our attempt to find common ground will be reciprocated. Goolishian cites the example of the time he was returning from a lecture engagement in a foreign country and being driven to the airport by a colleague. Arriving at the terminal early, the colleague asked his daughter, who had accompanied them, to get some silverware from a nearby café so all three could have some lunch. When the daughter returned with a glass of water, the man became angry.

"I told you to get some silverware!," said the colleague.

"No you didn't," protested the daughter, who was becoming angry herself.

A familiar pattern of mutual resentment was emerging until the man remembered something he had heard in Goolishian's lecture.

"You know, I've had a lot on my mind lately," he said apologetically. "Maybe I did say 'water.' " At which point the daughter softened and said, "It's so noisy in here that maybe I didn't hear you right."

Fortunately, a good percentage of resentful relationships can be resolved through this kind of practical "philosophical" compromise.

Yet sometimes the only answer is to remove ourselves as much as possible from the situation, at the same time leaving the door open to possible reconciliation at some future date. This is what many ethically oriented therapists describe as "detaching with love."

If this sounds like a tricky process with all kinds of qualifications and pitfalls peculiar to the person involved, it is exactly that. Yet I am always amazed by the degree to which any good faith effort to reconcile one's need for peace of mind with concern for preserving what is potentially positive in a relationship invariably leads us up from depression.

A case in point concerns David,[24] a man whose story I learned about at the very beginning of my research for this book.

The problem began when David was thirteen. That was when his mother died, and for the next three years he felt lonely and overworked as he struggled to help his father maintain the farm while every day walking two and a half miles to school. His father was very strict and appeared to have little understanding or caring that David's lot was so hard.

"The onset of depression came when I was sixteen," David remembered. "What had happened to me I did not know. I only knew, from the first, that my mental powers and the ability to do my school work that had always been so easy were impaired. I 'stood alone and the darkness hemmed me in and there was no one to deliver me.' Various doctors, the best general practitioners in the state, ascribed my illness to this and that physical cause. There were several minor operations. A change of climate was recommended for a supposedly virulent form of malaria and I lived in the West for six years."

"The predominating feeling through all of this was that I was insane. I wanted to be put away in an institution where nobody could see me. I started college but gave it up after a year. After that I lived at home but on account of my illness did nothing but occasional jobs. . . ."

Having "suffered many things of many physicians," David finally stumbled onto a psychiatrist of sufficient depth to see his problem as the inevitable consequence of his attempts to get even with his father. The doctor urged David to risk braking his vengeance, to let his resentful thoughts pass without translating them into action and to remember in the process how very sick the father must have been to inspire such hatred. "[He] was only safeguarding [me] as he thought necessary," David practiced telling himself, ". . . he did not know, nor had he the opportunity to know, what he was doing to my emotional life."

David's willingness to *deliberately* forgive his father by physically maintaining distance while refusing to vent his resentment was the pivotal change which finally lead to his remission. His depression gradually lifted, enough so that he could return to college after a ten-year absence, eventually graduating class valedictorian. He moved on to a career in education, counseling children with emotional problems on how to defuse their own depressing resentments with the same loving detachment he had learned to use himself.

Of course it can be argued that a depressed person is not in the best position to diagnose the best treatment for his or her resentments. What arouses hostility on one day may have no effect on the next; and the line between whether we should undercut a growing grudge with an immediate expression of anger or attempt to be compromising or decide we have no choice but to begin to detach with love is not always clear.

Fortunately, if there is one important consistency in the management of resentful depression, it is that any sincere attempt to overcome hostile behavior, no matter how tentative or uncertain, will prove worthwhile. Indeed, the mere *realization* of a relationship between resentment and despair appears to alleviate depressed feelings.

During their five-year study of different methods for reducing hostility in surviving cardiac patients, Dr. Carl Thoresen and his colleagues at Stanford University were astonished to discover that one of the most powerful techniques a patient could use was simply his attitude. The people most likely to continue suffering the effects of their resentful behavior, they found, were the ones who resisted thinking about ethical principles or those people who believed they could go on acting punitively toward others without paying a physical and emotional price. On the other hand, those who recognized a relationship between hostility and physical-emotional collapse seemed to automatically increase their chances of recovery.

Thoresen himself finally had to conclude that the most successful technique a therapist could possess is not a battery of statistics or obscure analytical insights but an "armamentarium of human aphorisms and quotations"[25] that reinforces the time-honored principle of tolerance. Far more effective than the scalpel or the drug, he now concedes, is "an arresting presentation of effectively chosen words, ideas, and images."

Luckily the more progress we make against resentment, however halting and "merely" philosophical it may seem, the more the very temptation to be hostile begins to disappear. "I just don't get that upset any more," says a woman counselor I know who, after years of being weighed down by quietly cumulating grudges, finally learned to make a priority of taming her resentments. "Nobody lives in my head rent free," she adds.

As Galen himself promised almost two centuries ago, ". . . you will yourself some day realize that you are less easily roused to anger than formerly, so that neither great nor small matters excite you."[26]

# Chapter 4

---

# BEYOND GUILT

Of all the infirmities we have,
the most savage is to despise our being.

MONTAIGNE[1]

Sin used to be . . . defined as whatever one does
that puts him in danger of going to Hell. . . . and it
is small wonder that it has fallen into disrepute as the
scientific outlook and method have steadily gained in
acceptance and manifest power. But there is a very
tangible and very present Hell-on-this-earth which
science has not yet helped us understand very well;
and so I invite your attention to the neglected but
very real possibility that it is *this* Hell—the Hell of
neurosis and psychosis—to which sin and unexpiated
guilt lead us. . . .

DR. O. H. MOWRER[2]

A certain amount of guilt, like a certain amount of resentment, is
perfectly natural. Society functions to a large degree by conditioning us

to take pause when certain rules are violated, and it is inevitable that we are going to trigger this little regulating mechanism from time to time.

Some of us even use guilt as a motivator, "putting the screws" to ourselves to get something done when we are either tired or have little interest in the immediate job at hand. As a short-term technique, this is a perfectly acceptable way to get ourselves going, provided we use it sparingly and with some awareness that temporary failure or falling behind is no reason for relentless self-criticism.

But *chronic* guilt—feeling perpetually inadequate and blameworthy, constantly deferring to the wishes of others, holding ourselves accountable for every negative situation we encounter—is something else again. This kind of guilt can so divert us from the business and pleasure of everyday living that even the pain of a serious bodily injury can pale by comparison.[3] Some people become so physically and emotionally drained by such guilt that they may actually require hospitalization.[4]

That guilt should have the same depressing effect as resentment is no coincidence, for both are judgments. The fact that self-blaming hostility is directed inward toward ourselves, rather than outward at others, does not alter the psychological fact that *any* judgmental impulse has a tendency to ennervate our life force. Hence the philosopher Spinoza's famous maxim: "One who despises himself is nearest to a proud man."[5] From a therapeutic point of view, observes Dr. Hora, "to be proud or to be ashamed is the same, [just as to] be vain or embarrassed is the same."[6]

Dr. Aaron Beck, Professor of Psychiatry at the University of Pennsylvania School of Medicine and a pioneer in the development of the new Cognitive Behavior Therapy, has actually graded guilty feelings from *mild* ("I've let everybody down . . . if I had tried harder, I could have made the grade.") to *moderate* ("I'm a weakling . . . I don't do anything right . . . I'm no good.") to *severe* ("I'm a terrible person . . . I don't deserve to live . . . I'm despicable . . . I loathe myself.").[7] Each step up this scale, he finds, triggers a parallel deflation of mood.

Increased guilt, like increased resentment, almost always insures that we will become more deeply dejected, with severely guilty people also suffering such depression-related symptoms as insomnia, indigestion, and even shortness of breath. Guilty people are also more susceptible to degenerative diseases. Combined studies at Harvard, the University of Michigan, and Dartmouth suggest that the physiological effects of prolonged self-blame are cumulative, with rapid physical deterioration becoming obvious around age forty-five.[8]

Interestingly, the approach of both traditional psychoanalysis and behavior modification to guilt is to treat it pretty much as an inconvenient flaw in the human makeup. Ever since the late 1940s, when delegates to the International Conference for Medical Psychotherapy in London decided that the nature of guilt was a metaphysical question, best left to theologians and philosophers[9], the majority of therapists have tended to view guilt as an irrational feeling, something that is best countered by convincing the client that he or she has "nothing to feel guilty about."

Psychoanalysts may use phrases like "overcoming a tyrannical superego," while behavior modifiers talk about "deconditioning inappropriate thoughts," but both kinds of therapists aim for the patient to "accept himself" just as he is and pride themselves on being appropriately "nonjudgmental," "nonpunitive," "nondirective," and "ethically neutral."

Unfortunately the one major difference between resentment and guilt is that responsibility for our misdeeds is not something we can eliminate simply by understanding the full self-destructive impact of guilty thoughts, gradually cutting back on our guilt-inspired behavior, or simply deciding to "forgive ourselves." Conventional psychotherapists may like to view guilt as an irrational product of a bad childhood experience or a negative social environment, but anyone who feels severely guilty is usually blaming him or herself for something quite specific. In other words, he knows he has something to feel guilty *about*.

Even in situations where the pattern of guilty thinking appears to imitate insensitive parental criticism, the repetition of self-critical phrases and attitudes is not automatic or arbitrary. A child may have been raised with inappropriate labels like "stupid," "undependable," "jerk," or "no good," but by the time he begins to direct such language against himself it is usually in response to some situation where he has, in fact, fulfilled some or all of these prophesies.

Our dialogue may have been written by others—our guilt may be exaggerated, we may even legitimately claim to be inclined to delinquent behavior by a lack of early discipline—but virtually all our current guilty thinking can be traced to some event or series of events where we have, in fact, knowingly hurt or deprived a fellow human being. It may have been something as relatively innocuous as fudging on taxes or something much more serious, such as cheating on our spouse or reckless driving that perhaps led to an automobile accident— we may even have committed the crime against *ourselves*, as in the case of promiscuity, drug addiction, or wasting an educational opportunity —yet disabling guilt is usually almost always traceable to very particular failings or transgressions.

Indeed, the result of trying to blindly "accept ourselves" is frequently to increase our sense of inadequacy, for deep down we are unable to make what we are told is the intelligent choice. This feeds the impulse to self-criticism even further and leaves us more deeply dejected than when we first walked into the therapist's office.[10]

One-time behaviorist O. Hobart Mowrer, a past president of the American Psychological Association and until his recent death in 1982 a distinguished leader in the revival of ethical therapy, liked to cite the example of a thirty-eight-year-old depressed man who had sought treatment for a variety of marital problems. Finally deciding to get everything off his chest, he took it upon himself to confess to his wife that he'd had a series of affairs, including one with an older woman who had recently died of cancer.

At first there was a sigh of relief, partly because his wife had reacted so well; but within weeks he felt "the weight of the world on his small shoulders again."[11] As much as he tried to just "accept himself" for what he had done, it simply wasn't possible. He finally had to turn around and commit himself to a hospital.

"Just so long as a person lives under the shadow of real, unacknowledged, and unexpiated guilt," Mowrer explained, "he *cannot* [if he has any character at all] 'accept himself'; and all *our* efforts to reassure and accept him will avail nothing. He will continue to hate himself and to suffer the inevitable consequences of self-hatred."[12]

Fortunately, most guilty patients have the good sense to avoid such "self-acceptance," once they've had a taste of it. I learned this myself many years ago during a semester's counseling internship at Stanford University, when I had the experience of treating an under-graduate from nearby San José College. Each week he would come into my office to talk about his guilt over situations having to do with his family and girlfriend, while I in my naive mimicry of the standard academic line would try to convince him to "just relax and enjoy life."

While he continued to return for the benefit of my supposed wisdom, our communication became increasingly strained to the point where we finally had to agree that he should try something else. Only now do I understand why with each visit, he would become increas-ingly withdrawn and stubborn; for to the extent he was able to take my advice I was probably only aggravating his guilty condition.

How most people do seem to cope with their guilt is by stoically enduring their self-blame and depression in the hope that a time will come when the weight of their suffering will finally cancel out the gravity of accumulated misdeeds. This improvised self-therapy is what accounts for the large numbers of those who quietly suffer the tortures of self-blame without ever asking for help or who, when they do confide the painful drone of inner condemnation, seem incapable of change. What appears to the outside world as masochistic self-abuse is really the hope that a sufficient amount of suffering will some day clear the guilty slate.

We might even be tempted to call this trade-off approach a "com-mon sense" therapy if it were not marred by two critical psychological flaws.

The first is that no amount of self-blaming depression can quell the real intuitive message of our guilt, which is not that we must *suffer* for our past misdeeds, but that we must take steps to *rectify* the damage we've created, insofar as this is reasonably possible. A man who has abandoned his family can punish himself with all the self-abusive be-havior he wants, but this does nothing to feed his struggling wife and children, just as no amount of private regret can ever repay the credi-tors of a bankrupt man. We may not recognize this consciously, but the intuitive pangs of conscience, reflecting our deeper wisdom, are never really satisfied by inappropriate gestures, no matter how painful or costly.

Mowrer himself observed that "lacking formal recognition of the need for atonement following sin," people endure endless "stigma, disgrace, and suffering"[13]—even psychiatric hospitalization—all to no real avail. The promised grace of silent suffering is a tragic illusion which only condemns us to useless sacrifice.

And if this "common sense" trade-off therapy ignores the real correctional imperative of our guilt, it also ignores the secret pleasure we occasionally derive from substituting self-blame for rectification. For all the depression we inevitably suffer, our guilt does have a strangely addicting quality, an appeal based on the degree to which it flatters our ego's manipulative powers.

How can we feel guilty, after all, unless we have done "something big" to feel guilty about? The woman who feels so terribly upset about breaking up some poor man's marriage is also saying to herself, "It's *because* of me. *I* did that!" However guilty a child may feel about behaving so badly at school that his parents have to spend hours with school counselors—no matter how much a husband regrets that his "willful stupidity" has caused everything to go wrong at home—both secretly revel in their abilities to bring about such major family catastrophes.

Tennessee psychologist Richard Driscoll[14] has even seen cases where egotistic self-criticism evolves into a kind of arrogant morality. Deploring one's sins, Driscoll finds, is really a way of insisting that we are beyond reproach, that our standards are never relaxed, that we in fact are *morally superior*. Therapist Thomas Hora puts the problem most succinctly: "We have come to see that guilt is a devious way of boasting."[15]

As ethical therapists have warned for centuries, the combination of our misguided willingness to trade suffering for guilt, coupled with the subtle egotistical compensations of martyrdom, can trap even the most well-intentioned person in a brutal cycle of self-abuse. Moses Maimonides, the twelfth-century beacon of Plato's light, had the misfortune of watching hundreds of Hebrews in the southern Mediterranean communities of Egypt and Morocco become absurdly self-effacing in response to their political misfortunes, even to the point of becoming suicidal martyrs. Those who "err concerning [virtue]," he warned future generations, "becom[e] accustomed to them."[16]

Today we see the powerful grip of egotistically "trading-off" in the familiar stories of wives who quietly endure abusive marriages, of men who seem to enjoy humiliating intimidation, and in all people who repeatedly play the role of patsy without apparent complaint. Mowrer himself believed that the perpetual popularity of electroshock therapy is due primarily to patients' misconceived notions of expiation.

Perhaps you can identify with Tim, a man who by outside appearance would appear the model of consideration. He's the one who can always be counted on to look after the dog when the neighbors take a weekend trip, the first one people think of to borrow money from. Tim is also self-effacing at work, though it hasn't gotten him very far. He's always the last to get a perk because his bosses know "good ol' Tim" won't really mind.

Inside, of course, Tim feels both hurt and unappreciated. He's quite aware that people take advantage of him and that he's seen as a wimp by what passes for friends and colleagues.

Tim's problem is that he doesn't feel justified in doing much about it. With a long history of having willfully sabotaged genuine opportunities for friendship and advancement, he feels he's getting pretty much what he deserves. He also derives a secret pleasure from knowing that learning to adjust to his failures has made him a "better person."

Then there is the example of Jenny, a forty-five-year-old divorcée struggling month to month to raise her three children in a competitive, affluent Connecticut suburb.

Jenny has no lost love for her ex-husband, whom she often remembers with a bitter curl of her lip; but the gnawing sense that she might have been able to save the marriage had she done something differently has led her to be permissive with the children, even to the point of tolerating a noisy household, abusive language, sloppy manners, and incessant demands for money.

The only trouble with Jenny's willingness to suffer for her mistakes is that it hasn't done anything to alleviate her guilt. Gloomy and irritable, she can feel depressed for hours at a time, sometimes wanting nothing more than to lie on her living room couch and sleep her way through the day.

Indeed, complaints from the oldest son's math teacher are beginning to make Jenny think that her willingness to indulge her children's lack of discipline may be backfiring, creating a rebellious delinquent and giving her yet another reason to feel guilty.

Fortunately, such vicious cycles of placating guilt with proud but futile suffering do not have to persist forever. Just as in the last chapter we saw how a better awareness of the relationship between resentment and depression tends to diminish the appeal of hostile thinking, so it is with guilt: the more we begin to understand the fallacy of substituting pain for rectification, the less we are willing to tolerate this very costly ego trip.

The critical step is our willingness to go to the heart of our guilt and consider taking whatever steps we reasonably can to begin making amends for the real damage we've created over the years. In the end, observes therapist Joel Kanter, it is only by restoring a sense of balance that we can be aware of our experience without continuing to judge ourselves for past mistakes. "You really do need to make up for what you do," he says.[17]

Consider the case of Fred,[18] a married salesman whose adult life had been a roller coaster of self-criticism. For weeks Fred had been feeling guilty over his recent affair with a neighborhood housewife.

"What have I done, what have I done! . . . I can't leave my wife and kids, but Ruth [the new woman] says she'll kill herself . . . ! How can I ever make this up to my family!" Such thoughts played over and over in Fred's mind, depressing him at work and creating still another reason to feel guilty. Finally not knowing what else to do, Fred sought professional help from what turned out to be an unusually enlightened therapist.

For the first session Fred seemed eager to mimic the confessional analysis he'd seen in the movies and on television. By the end of the hour he had revealed practically everything he ever remembered doing wrong, from the details of his most recent affairs all the way back to trivial childhood pranks. He talked about working harder (to punish himself) and about how he would resolve never to do it again.

But when Fred returned to his therapist's office, something important still felt unresolved. He'd confessed all his sins, made all the appropriate promises, yet the gnawing guilt was still there.

"I've heard all about how bad you are," the therapist finally said. "Now what are you going to *do* about it?"

"Do about it?"

"Your wife, Ruth, those other things you mentioned. They're not going to go away unless you do something about them."

And that's when Fred's real therapy began. Systematically working through his mental list of guilts, he started thinking of what active steps he could take to correct his history of self-centered behavior—paying more attention to his wife, helping out the children he had neglected, and so on. Within weeks Fred began to feel a sense of lightness and relief he hadn't known in years.

Of course, it is one thing to hear about other people making amends for their guilt, quite another to apply this principle to our own lives. To whom do we make our amends? What do we say or do? What do we really have to feel guilty about, especially when deeds are long done and over?

The "to whom" part is easy. Like Fred, if we've really harmed somebody we already know it. Nobody has to tell us if we've betrayed a trust or cheated a friend or committed a crime or played sadistic emotional games with a loved one. Any relationship we feel vaguely guilty about for a long period of time probably requires our attention.

The tricky part is deciding what it is exactly that we are going to do about it.

Suppose, for example, a man cheats his boss on the company expense account, writing off his frequent visits to the racetrack as business dinners. He might confess to misspending the money and pay it back directly; or he might personally absorb the legitimate expenses of his next business trip until the amount has been paid back. Either way, the amend he has to make is pretty obvious; at least, it can be pinned to an exact dollar figure.

But let's go back to the example of Fred's case and say we're again talking about a man who has had an affair with his neighbor's wife. How does Fred make up this one? Confessing the truth to the husband next door might be the most direct thing to do, but it could also cause more problems than it solves.

Suppose further that the affair had happened years ago when the other couple was going through some crisis; but now they are happily married. Or further still, suppose that young children might be affected by the emotional fallout of such a potentially disrupting revelation.

Should Fred confess his guilt to everyone involved or perhaps think instead of doing some anonymous good deed for the benefit of the offended husband?

There is no objective answer to such a problem, and two equally intelligent people could devise radically different amends.

But there is a right answer for *that* man, an answer that becomes apparent with his *willingness*, first to recognize the need for actively making amends, then to think about different alternatives (perhaps consulting a local priest, therapist, rabbi, or close friend in the process) and finally to follow through on whatever *feels* like the right amends, no matter how unusual or offbeat.

"It's not so much what you *do*," explains Joel Kanter, "as what you *don't* do." The important thing is that we don't try to rationalize our guilt by trying to hold ourselves blameless or suffering in silence. "It is in consciously baring our guilt that the proper acts of atonement will take place."[19]

Now this is admittedly a daring answer, particularly in the context of our "value-free" culture. To admit the possibility that guilt *itself* can guide us is to admit that our intuitive hunches are far more important and perceptive than any behavioral formula conventional psychology would have us adopt.

It might be useful, then, to reflect on one of the truly fascinating anthropological discoveries of the twentieth century, which occurred in 1935 when anthropologist Kilton Stewart discovered an unusual tribe[20] deep in the rain forests of Malaysia. At first these natives, called the Senoi, appeared no different from any other primitive group. Living in thatch and bamboo huts on large piles above the ground, they sustained themselves with simple farming, hunting, and fishing. In the area of social relations, however, they had developed a psychology "so astonishing," in Stewart's words, "that they might have come from another planet."

What the Senoi did, it turns out, was to treat their guilt seriously. Anytime a Senoi tribesman sensed he had needlessly harmed others, he would begin thinking about the best way to make amends. The answer didn't have to make sense, it just had to "feel" right.

Interestingly many of the answers came during sleep; and Senoi children were encouraged first to finish all their dreams—if necessary to

recall where a dream left off when falling asleep on the following evening—and then to carry out what amends they had imagined in real
life. The result was that the Senoi experienced no mental illness, no
suicide or truancy, in fact nothing even approaching what we would
call depressed behavior. Stewart found this tribe to be the most serene
and democratic group he had ever encountered, with a social system
the equivalent of modern man's achievements in communications and
physics.

If there is a modern variation of this intuitive Senoi technique, it
would be represented by the case of a woman I know of who'd been
depressed for years over an abortion she'd had in her early twenties. In
the back of her mind the woman had nurtured the fantasy of making
amends to her unborn child, an idea she had repeatedly dismissed as
"too far out" until an open-minded therapist she finally consulted encouraged her not to be so judgmental of her intuition. Soon hitting on
the idea of a belated funeral service, she found a sympathetic minister
and gave the child the decent burial she felt she owed it. Almost
immediately the guilt and depression she'd lived with for so long began
to lift, and the woman could finally resume a normal life.

Another fascinating amend involved a thirty-four-year-old hospitalized schizophrenic, who took it upon himself to confess the real
cause of his illness in the form of an academic paper for the benefit of
his doctors, which he titled "A New Theory of Schizophrenia." Defining his illness as a conscious and "unethical defense mechanism"
against having to confront guilty deeds from the past, he went on to
suggest that most of what had passed for treatment was really a form of
"perjury" in which he pretended to go along with his therapists' pet
theories in order to avoid discussing "the primary deed."

"What is a schizophrenic?," he went on to diagnose himself. "In
brief, he is a terrified, conscience-stricken crook, who has repressed his
interest in people. . . . He is of no mean Thespian ability. And his
favorite Commandment is . . . 'Thou shalt not get caught.' "[21]

The only way out of this psychological box, the author concluded,
is for the patient himself to begin taking responsibility for the guilt he
has so desperately tried to cover up. In what was surely more than mere
coincidence, it was shortly after writing the paper when the man's own

symptoms remitted to the point where he was finally released from the hospital.

No matter what intuitive solution we come up with, the process of making amends is always easier than we imagine, if for no other reason than the very willingness to go ahead with it tends to commute our obligation. Just as the voluntary confession of a legal crime tends to reduce the sentence the judge might impose, so the voluntary assumption of a deserved guilt always balances the psychological scales in our favor.

It is also important to remember that the part of us which revels in the self-importance of guilt likes to equate the idea of amends with exaggerated notions of self-punishment, imagining that only some grandiose gestures could ever compensate for the magnitude of our destructive past. In fact, the closer we get to making restitution the more we find that the horrible sacrifice we have been anticipating is really a statement of regret.[22]

One of my own experiences with amends involved a telephone call about five years ago to a woman I had previously lived with. This was a loving person whom I had not treated very well during our time together, for I had allowed my fears of intimacy to mask themselves as emotional indifference and my work problems to become an attack on her blooming career, all the while pretending complete ignorance of what I was really doing. Indeed, by the time I had prepared myself to make the call I was half expecting her to hang up on me.

In fact the call proved a pleasant exchange during which I expressed my regret for my lack of maturity and she, in turn, was surprisingly forgiving. Perhaps she herself had done some things for which she felt guilty, perhaps my misdeeds were not as damaging as I had imagined—whatever the reason, I have always found my own attempts at amends to be far less onerous than I had imagined, though always a source of relief.

Finally, when we think of making restitution to people we have harmed, we should not forget any amend which we feel we may owe to ourselves. If we think we've slept with too many people we didn't care about or that we've wasted a valuable educational opportunity or that our drug habit has cost us the promotion we always wanted, there is always the option to recommit ourselves to the goals and values we know are in our best long-term interest.

Dr. Joel Moscowitz of Columbia University has noted a frequent example of this in what he calls "secondary virginity" among formerly promiscuous women. "After a period of promiscuity that they find disillusioning, they become scrupulously chaste, saving further sex for marriage or at least for an emotionally close and stable relationship."[23]

Such willingness to make amends to ourselves serves a double purpose. Not only does it complete the removal of self-blaming judgments and the depression that comes with them, but it also reminds us that the purpose of guilt is not to make us suffer. Suffering is what happens when we ignore our guilt through arbitrary "self-acceptance" or offering pain in place of restitution.

In his famous psychological interpretation of *Old Testament* scriptures, the great ethical therapist Maimonides observed that God punished the Pharoah for his harsh treatment of the Jews, not by death or sickness, not even by the destruction of his kingdom—but by making him incapable of repentance.[24]

# Chapter 5

⤙

# BEYOND BOREDOM

Concern yourself not with the thieflike ego and its business.

JALAL-UDDIN RUMI[1]

He that findeth his life shall lose it. . . .

MATTHEW[2]

If the depression caused by resentment and unexpiated guilt is the most severe emotional problem, boredom is probably the most widespread.

Now by boredom, I'm not talking about the temporary glaze of the housewife standing in the supermarket checkout line or the commuter sitting lifeless in a cramped and humid subway car. When the external conditions that cause these brief imprisonments come to an end, the mind automatically snaps back to life.

What I am talking about is the boredom that lasts—that sense of numbed emptiness which saps meaning from every corner of our lives.

It is the state which has been variously described as *ennui*, tedium, vexation, disquiet, wearisomeness, or perhaps most eloquently by Flaubert as "leprosy of the soul."[3]

"How weary, flat, stale, and unprofitable seem to me all the uses of the world," said Shakespeare's Hamlet. Unfortunately, too many of us know exactly what he meant. When the well-known psychology writer Sam Keen did a small piece on boredom for a 1977 issue of *Psychology Today* magazine, he was flooded with letters and phone calls from all over the country. At least eight magazines asked to reprint the article.[4]

The problem even affects a large percentage of college students, if a recent report by University of Arkansas researchers Donna Darden and Alan Marks is any indication. In a statewide study to learn why young adults attending school were so dissatisfied with courses designed to be "socially relevant," they found that these classes tended to ignore what the students themselves considered the most pressing social issues in their lives, chief among these being the subject of boredom.[5]

Where do our bored states come from?

Again, conventional psychology offers divergent explanations that betray an underlying similarity. To the behavior therapist, for example, the problem is one of poor planning. We need to schedule more exciting events in our lives, this theory goes, such as seeing more movies with friends or having weekend adventure away from home. If we do this with enough consistency, we will gradually condition ourselves to be less bored.

For the more analytically oriented therapist, the answer lies in our unconscious resistance to pleasure—probably due to some early childhood prohibition against erotic stimulation. Here the implication is that we must work through our puritanical qualms, learning to enjoy good food, good sex, and any other gratification which is not physically harmful to ourselves or to others.

Yet the common denominator of both these approaches is their view of boredom as a lack of external sensation. For one therapist the villain may be bad conditioning, for another it is childhood repression; but both see the answer in terms of material satisfaction. If only we just allowed ourselves more sources of external stimulation, then our dreariness would automatically come to an end.

Now the ethical therapist has a great deal of trouble with this conventional view of boredom. In the first place, we know from practical experience there are many people who, from the outside, appear to lead simple and uneventful lives, yet who nonetheless are completely absorbed in their work and family—just as there are many jet-setters who flit nervously from one glittering event to the next without ever escaping their sense of discontentment.

This common sense observation is confirmed by any number of studies[6] which show that the intensity of bored feelings has little direct relationship to the frequency of outside activities, such as the amount of time spent socializing or number of leisure-time hobbies. Quite the opposite, those who would describe themselves as "busy," "active," or "on the go," often prove to be far less satisfied with their lives than people who report a quieter, more easygoing routine.

If boredom were really a problem of external stimulation, notes British historian and sociologist Sean Healy (who has written one of the few well-researched studies of the subject), we would expect conservative or puritanical societies to suffer the most from it. But there is "no evidence that this is true," he finds.[7]

" 'Bored' just is not the word that springs to mind," Healy writes, "when one thinks of the extraordinarily moralistic . . . zealots of the seventeenth century in England, of the followers of John Knox, of the Anabaptist communities of the preceding century, or of the Pilgrim Fathers setting out for the New World and surviving the wilderness. One would more readily think of the latter days of the Roman Empire, a time of relaxed authority and weakened moral imperatives as an epoch of boredom."[8]

We come closer to understanding the true dynamics of boredom by looking at the opposite. Plato himself devoted an entire dialogue[9] to the subject of love, by which he meant not merely romantic love or the affection of a mother for her child, but all the ways in which we come to care passionately for some thing or cause or idea. What all of man's consuming interests have in common, Plato concluded, is the flowing out of energy, like a "spirit" radiating outward from the heart to the world at large.

Abraham Maslow, an early pioneer in the modern revival of ethical therapy, came to much the same conclusion from his unusual studies of men and women who seemed to be leading happy, interesting, and fulfilling lives. (Unlike many of his colleagues, who derived their ideas of mental health exclusively from the study of emotionally disturbed people, Maslow believed much could be learned about healthy behavior by studying people who were, in fact, quite healthy.) One of Maslow's most consistent findings was that the ability to appreciate one's life "with awe, pleasure, wonder, and even ecstasy"—the capacity for "newness," as he called it—went hand-in-hand with a kind of outflowing spiritedness. That is, subjects who rarely complained of boredom were the same subjects who were "relatively spontaneous in behavior and far more than that in their inner life, thoughts, and impulses. . . ."[10]

Boredom, then, is not a deprivation of *external* stimulation but a lack of something from within, a diminished spirit, as it were. Maslow himself interviewed many people who had achieved all the outward appearances of a dynamic life—the high-paying job, material gadgets, and a busy social calendar—and found that those who were motivated more by the desire for external stimulation than by spontaneous curiosity always seemed less satisfied. It wasn't that they were depressed enough to want to crawl under the covers, but neither did they care very much for what they were doing or did they want to stay with it as long.

Why is this kind of boredom so widespread? Certainly not for any lack of natural enthusiasm. We can all remember how as youngsters we could find something of interest in the most mundane setting, spending hours rummaging through an old attic or garage.

The problem as we grow older is that our natural enthusiasm is so easily depleted by the judgments and lies we use to prop up our self-image to others. The hostility we direct against someone who has challenged our authority or "had the nerve" to make us late, the kind of guilt trip which secretly makes us feel like a superior person, the way we twist facts to make ourselves seem more important or to cover up some embarrassing misdeed—all drain our spontaneous energies.

This is the psychological meaning behind the age-old religious injunction against "committing idolatry." To the extent we compromise our integrity to make an attractive image of ourselves, we lose contact with our natural enthusiasm. We become contrived, artificial . . . bored. The old story about the self-centered schemer who is never contented with any of his ill-gotten triumphs is a perennial metaphor for the psychological law that every manipulative effort we make to boost our position in the world only diminishes our natural capacity to appreciate what has been achieved.

Since most of the unethical ways we prop up our self-image are discussed under the headings of other emotional complaints, I'll leave the problem of how to remedy them to separate chapters. But there are two egotistical attitudes which contribute uniquely to boredom and deserve our attention here.

The first of these subtle bores is *arrogance*—that is, thinking, talking, and acting as if our opinions were somehow superior to those of the people around us. While we already know from experience that we can be quickly bored by the arrogant opinions of others, we need to be reminded of the fact that we can be equally vexed by *our own* haughtiness. As Dr. Thomas Hora observes, patients who complain the most about boredom are frequently those with the most condescending and aloof attitudes.[11]

"Isn't it interesting," he says,[12] "that we start out criticizing other people in order to make ourselves feel better. And the more we do this, the worse we are going to feel, because if we criticize others, we [build up] . . . a burdensome load of thoughts which we don't want anyone to know. Consequently, the more we try to feel better the worse we feel. This is the way one cripples oneself socially. It becomes more and more difficult to communicate with one's fellow men and participate in the social process."

Psychiatrist M. Scott Peck, author of *The Road Less Traveled* and popular lecturer on traditional values, describes the case of Betsy,[13] a lovely and intelligent twenty-two-year-old woman who suffered from a severe case of anxious boredom.

On the surface, Betsy seemed to have everything. "My husband is good to me," she had to admit. "We love each other very much." Yet Betsy suffered from feelings of boredom so intense that not even the tranquillizers a general practitioner had once prescribed could stop the growing sense of panic.

At first Betsy blamed her husband for her state. His manners were "uncouth," she said. His interests were too narrow and he watched too much TV. But as therapy progressed, it became clear that Betsy's real problem was an arrogant attitude which isolated her from a more stimulating life. Years before she had quit college because she felt superior to the other students who were "into drugs and sex a lot." She also didn't approve of people who "question the church" and "some of my parents' values." By consistently seeing herself as superior to others, Betsy had cut herself off from the possibility of any genuine excitement.

The second egotistical bore is *defensiveness*, constantly mobilizing our resources to boost our vanity or justify to others what we feel is the stigma attached to some past failing or gap in our lives.

"Defenses limit and kill off our everyday experiences," explains Dr. Robert Firestone,[14] a Los Angeles psychologist who has spent more than twenty-five years thinking and writing about what he calls the "habitual patterns that deaden" patients.[15] "They numb us as feeling persons and rob us of our dignity."

Beverly Hills management consultant Theodora Wells believes that a good deal of what is commonly called *burnout* or *job alienation* is really the dispiriting boredom of defensive behavior. Putting the best light on a bitter divorce when dating a new boy or girlfriend, trying to explain some lack of experience to a new client, giving an envious neighbor the reasons why we need a "fancy new car," even the common practice of jokingly defending our late arrival to work—"many of these recurring situations seem trivial," she says, but "its *repetitiousness* is not. The situations continue to occur; you continue to feel more defensive,"[16] with the result that life seems less and less interesting.

In my own work as a volunteer counselor with chemically dependent adults, I find that those with the greatest need to explain themselves are usually the same ones who give "boredom" as their main reason for getting high. It is almost as if the energy required to rationalize has so completely drained them of any spontaneous feeling that they no longer believe natural excitement is even a possibility. Indeed, for the defensive addict being "straight"—i.e., drug free—is usually synonymous with being dull.

The only reason the boring effect of our defensiveness is not more obvious is that our immediate experience is often one of relief. To the extent our self-justification has silenced some outside criticism, we feel the cosmetic power of our words has saved us from attack. We may even find ourselves apologizing *in advance* for a shortcoming we merely anticipate someone else to be thinking, as if by raising the issue on our own terms, we can become inoculated against someone else's critical opinion. It is not until some time later that we begin to feel estranged and cut off from whatever situation we happen to be in, a sensation we mistakenly attribute to people or circumstances completely unrelated to our defenses.

That both arrogance and defensiveness should have the same droning effect should be no surprise, if we think of it, for both are very judgmental attitudes. One may seem to be motivated by overconfidence, the other by nervous fear, but both are obsessed with sustaining the image of how we think we "should" appear. In this sense, the parallel between arrogance and defensiveness is very similar to that between resentment and guilt, the major difference being that in the latter polarity of judgments tend to be stronger and, therefore, to have a more depressing impact.

Indeed, it is not at all unusual to see extremes of arrogance and defensiveness in the same person, particularly in cases where the lack of esteem being defended is sufficiently hidden to allow an aggressive defense, the arrogance being primarily an attempt to keep potential critics off balance. The irony in such people is that while others may view them as aloof and even snobbish, they themselves feel enormously inadequate.

The relationship between arrogance and defensiveness parallels the resentment-guilt polarity in another important way. Just as the discipline of resentful depression is largely a matter of reining in the expression of hostility until the thoughts themselves begin to ebb, so the discipline of arrogant boredom is largely a matter of learning to keep one's mouth shut. We may not have much voluntary control over conceited thoughts in the short run, but we always have the ability to bite our tongues.

The classic example of how effectively this works is to be found in Benjamin Franklin's early test of the ethical therapy.[17]

The time was 1730. Franklin was still a struggling young Philadelphia printer and had reluctantly accepted the invitation of a rather dry minister to attend a series of sermons on morals. He was so put off by the first lecture that he refused to go again; but the subject continued to fascinate Franklin.

Some days later, he decided—in what was probably the New World's very first psychology experiment—to make a list of desirable character traits, practice them daily, and see what effect they might have on his life. "I made," he wrote, "a little book, in which I allotted a page for each of the virtues. . . . I determined to give a week's strict attention to each . . . marking every evening the faults of the day."

The experiment was an inspired one, a Quaker friend commented, except that one virtue was notably lacking. "[He] kindly informed me," Franklin admitted, "that I was generally thought proud; that my pride showed itself frequently in conversation; that I was not content with being in the right when discussing any point, but was overbearing and rather insolent."

In the end Franklin was persuaded to give a week to humility and, deliberately censoring his most arrogant thoughts, made it "a rule to forebear all direct contradiction to the sentiments of others," even "the use of [expressions] that imported a fix'd opinion, such as *certainly*, *undoubtedly*, and so on."

Astonishingly, the very virtue that Franklin had almost overlooked turned out to have the most electrifying impact on his career. "And to this habit [of enforced humility] I think it principally owing," he wrote in his *Autobiography*, "that I had early so much weight with my fellow citizens . . . and so much influence in public councils when I became a member. . . ."

As to the psychological benefits, Franklin never speaks directly to the issue of boredom, but it is clear from the accounts of his later years that it was his disciplined effort to tolerate petty political infighting, antiquated social rituals, and conservative court customs which enabled him to turn the potential tedium of his many diplomatic assignments into a series of fascinating adventures. "[I] never arrived at the perfection I had been so ambitious of obtaining . . . yet I was by the endeavor a better and happier man. . . ."

Franklin was also careful to emphasize that it was not arrogant thinking itself which needs to be controlled. "In reality . . . there is perhaps no one of our natural passions so hard to subdue as *pride*; disguise it, struggle with it, beat it down, stifle it, mortify it as much as one pleases, it is still alive and will every now and then peep out and show itself."

Our task is much more modest and attainable: to begin policing that critical gap between thought and speech. We may not be able to stop ourselves from thinking that Uncle Bill is a jerk or that our colleague lacks some common sense or that the blonde down the hall is really a bimbo, but we don't have to say it out loud.

"There is a difference between repressing a thought and suppressing a thought," explains Dr. Hora in more modern psychological language. "When we are trying to hide a thought from ourselves, it is called repression. When we are trying to hide it from others, it is called suppression." The latter can be an effective technique for overcoming the negative effect of our judgmental tendencies if we "have compassion for ourselves and we say, 'Well, I may have these feelings and I may have these thoughts, but I don't have to be involved with them because there is something higher and better for me to pay attention to.' "[18] As Franklin himself came to discover, what we "at first put on with some violence to natural inclination," becomes "at length so easy and . . . habitual [that] a dogmatical expression" will never escape us.

Interestingly, Harvard Business School professor Daniel Isenberg finds that most dynamic executives are people who have consciously or unconsciously achieved this kind of discipline. "In fact," says Isenberg, "if you knew what was going on in your boss's mind when he or she was talking to you, you would be shocked. They sometimes think a few nasty things about the people they work with . . . 'crazy,' 'stupid,' 'baloney,' 'bullshit,' and so on."[19]

Their dynamic power, notes Isenberg, comes from the fact that they do not blindly vent their arrogant thoughts and appear quite flexible about reevaluating them, thinking to themselves minutes or even seconds later "maybe that wasn't so dumb after all."

The well-known California psychiatrist Gerald Jampolsky tells the instructive, as well as amusing, story[20] of how, after appearing on a national television show, he was confronted by a bearded and somewhat untidy fan who had hitchhiked all the way from Virginia just to meet him.

Tired and still busy after a long day, the doctor's thoughts were understandably judgmental. "He must be quite disturbed to come across the country to meet me because he saw me on television," the therapist now admits saying privately to himself. But instead of giving voice to that judgment, he suggested they meet the next day to "meditate" on the meaning of the young man's journey. ←

This deliberate softening of his impulsive judgment not only saved his visitor's feelings, but proved just the tonic the psychiatrist himself needed to relieve the numbness of his oppressive schedule. "This man came across the country as a gift to you," the psychiatrist began to think when he met the man the next day, "to tell you he saw . . . something you have difficulty seeing in yourself." Suddenly grateful, the therapist realized that the "awful odor" he thought he'd smelled the day before had totally disappeared.

Now if the discipline of arrogance is simply a matter of keeping our mouths shut, the discipline of defensiveness gets a little trickier. Like guilty behavior, it is not something we can simply stop, if for no other reason than many of the situations which inspire the impulse to rationalize *do* require some kind of response.

Take the example of the typical job interview. You're sitting and discussing your résumé when the potential employer pauses and says something like, "I see here that you don't have much experience with accounting." You may not want to defend against the implied criticism, but neither can you politely just ignore it.

Another common, if less dramatic, situation might involve a community affairs meeting, such as a tenants' group. No sooner do you walk through the door when someone who's never been particularly friendly yells out, "Hey, there you are! Haven't seen you for a while!" Now, on the one hand, you don't want to get into an elaborate public defense of what you've been doing for the group on your own time; yet to let the remark pass would be like admitting you have been sloughing off.

The basic solution in these and, indeed, all defensive situations is to paraphrase the implied criticism in the most accurate nonjudgmental terms. To the job interviewer, for example, it would be perfectly correct to say, "Yes, I'm not very good with figures. That's why I always have a good number cruncher on my team." Similarly, we might reply to the unfriendly tenant with a simple, "Yes, I guess we've missed each other."[21]

These are not particularly difficult responses to invent, once we get the hang of it; but they are usually not on the tip of the tongue, particularly when we feel tense or defensive. The result is that we go blank and blurt some kind of rationalization that always leaves a telltale daze.

This is why it is helpful to develop the habit of buying time to think, to use the initial panic of our defensive feelings as a signal to take what we might call a *therapeutic pause*.

There are many ways to do this, explains Theodora Wells. We can say we "need a minute to think about that" or we can also make a long thought noise, such as "hmmm," to keep our place in the conversation. We also have the choice of responding to the least disturbing part of the question or even admitting that we're not sure what we think and want a chance to "get back" with the answer at a later time.[22]

Which therapeutic pause works best for a given person will naturally depend on the situation. The trick, as Wells tells her own clients, is to try more than one. "When you have a larger repertoire of available quick responses, you are more likely to dispose of these gnats. Then you won't be draining the energy you use in vague defensiveness. You can redirect it to more interesting activities."[23]

Of course, there is one universal technique which helps remove arrogance, defensiveness, and all other unethical barriers to our natural enthusiasm; and that is to place ourselves in a situation where we begin to experience more of our spontaneous impulses without any of the social distractions which normally prompt us to defend our self-image. A weekend in the country, time alone on a vacation, quiet walks or jogs in the park—these are the kinds of situations which naturally rekindle a sense of excitement and zest for living.

Such brief respites from the pressure to control social perceptions do not prevent a recurrence of our judgmental and manipulative habits once we come back to the everyday world, but the invigorations of regular solitude do temper our manipulative tendencies over the long run.

Fortunately these therapeutic escapes do not necessitate a big move or reclusive gesture. Every month, popular magazines feature articles on biofeedback, yogo, relaxation exercises, dance therapy, or some other meditative technique that can be performed in the middle of a busy life. To the extent that any of these methods help us to relax our judgmental and manipulative tendencies—and to the extent we use them with *this* in mind—the relief from boredom will be real and immediate.

There is, finally, the ultimate option of going all the way to the source of our enthusiasm. To seek through silent petition for some kind of direct access to our natural instincts, to have our spontaneous caring restored without having to fight our way through every "idolatrous" habit—in other words, to pray for help.

This is a radical technique, of course, though not for the literal difficulty of execution. The physical act of getting down on our hands and knees is by far the easiest of therapies.

The problem is what prayer says about the real nature of our enthusiasm. It is one thing to talk about the existence of a spontaneous energy which we can reach through the discipline of our manipulative habits. We may have some trouble conceptualizing what this energy is or where it comes from; but at least we can intellectualize it as a kind of biological wisdom, perhaps something contained in our genes or an energy field hidden in the curvature of space, and we're willing to give it a try.

But to talk about the kind of energy that can be liberated through prayer is to begin to identify our essence with something spiritual—a soul, in other words—and it is this potential for a deeper conception of self which ironically makes the most miserable person stubbornly unwilling to avail himself of the most effective option for dissipating his boredom. In fact, the more we try to persuade him, the more stubborn he becomes.

So I won't try to persuade.

Indeed, it must even be admitted that over the long history of ethical therapy, there are some sharp divisions on this issue of prayer. To the religious heirs of Plato's therapy—St. Augustine, Maimonides and many of today's practicing therapists—prayer is the first and most indispensable tool in the battle against boredom.

Yet there is also a tradition passing from Galen down through Francis Bacon and Franklin which either ignores or downplays the relevance of prayer, perhaps with some awareness that it touches on issues so sensitive that it may alienate the very people who could most benefit from the ethical therapy. Plato himself was uncharacteristically vague on the topic of petitioning God, perhaps for the same reason.

However, for those to whom prayer does not seem to be an outrageous intellectual compromise in the quest for a full and exciting life, two things need to be said:

First, you're not as far out in space as conventional psychology would have you think. Hard-nosed psychoanalysts and behavior modifiers may still lump spiritual practices with witchcraft and superstition, but the vast majority of private therapists who work on the front lines of everyday emotional problem-solving—68 percent, according to the most recent survey[24]—believe that a spiritual relationship to the universe is essential to achieving a healthy, enthusiastic outlook. (A surprising 44 percent would say the same about having "a religious affiliation in which one actively participates."[25])

Secondly, the issue of *how* to pray our way beyond boredom, while certainly colored by private denominational considerations, is surprisingly consistent among all theologically oriented therapists. The way to get spiritual inspiration is simply to ask for it: *"Thy will, not mine, be done."*

This is not particularly difficult for any religiously oriented person, since the popular prayers of every major religion are constructed precisely to this purpose. The only thing that needs to be done in most cases is to listen more carefully to the words we first heard as children and say them with some awareness. "[The] third clause of the Lord's Prayer," author Aldous Huxley once observed, "is repeated daily by millions, who have not the slightest intention of letting any will be done, except their own."[26]

To those who choose to pray for a more inspired life, yet shy away from any formal religious affiliation, the best prayer is the one which reminds us that in order to receive the gift of enthusiasm, we must have the courage to lay aside some of our egotistical notions of self-interest. In my own case, I have come to rely on this excerpt from Fenelon, Archbishop of Cambrai, which I have recited every morning for almost a decade:

"Lord, I know not what to ask of thee. Thou only knowest what I need. Thou lovest me better than I know how to love myself. Father, give to thy child that which he himself knows not how to ask. Smite or heal, depress me or raise me up: I adore all thy purposes without knowing them. I am silent; I offer myself up in a sacrifice; I yield myself to thee; I would have no other desire than to accomplish thy will. Teach me to pray. Pray thyself in me."[27]

I face a lot of problems day-to-day, for my ego is hardly in check, but boredom is not one of them.

# Chapter 6

---

# BEYOND
# INDECISION

Continued observations of this basic dynamic nature
of happiness, especially in clinical psychological practice, leads almost inevitably to the conclusion that
deeper and more fundamental than sexuality, deeper
than the craving for social power, deeper even than
the desire for possessions, there is a still more general-
ized and more universal craving in the human makeup. *It is the craving for knowledge of the right direction—or orientation.*

WM. H. SHELDON, M.D.
(1899–1963)[1]

Thinking only increases my need for therapy.

ANONYMOUS[2]

The option to make choices, to select one course of action from a host
of competing alternatives, has been called the noblest of human abilities.

Lower animals are pretty much the prisoners of automatic reflex, reacting mechanically to almost every situation. Only we humans map our strategies, sift through details, ponder changing conditions, weigh relative benefits—in short, demand to be a creative partner in our own fate, not just an unwitting victim.

But for millions of Americans this remarkable ability to make daily choices is not the divine blessing of poetic lore, but a perpetual burden, a process of appraisal and reappraisal that never delivers on the promise of a firm conviction. For many of us the limited simplicity of the animal's life appears paradise compared with the chronic pain of endless vacillation.

Perhaps you can identify with Willard, an executive in a Seattle marketing firm and the father of three children. With business picking up and his youngest son finally packing off for college, Willard should be busier than ever; yet today he is sitting at his desk, deep in thought, unable to take calls or read reports with a clear mind. Willard is paralyzed with indecision, not about office problems, but whether to buy some new sails for his boat. Ever since he and his wife agreed to spend their vacation cruising the Puget Sound, Willard has been unable to decide if he should stick with the equipment he has or replace it with a new brand. Nor can he understand why so many of these seemingly trivial decisions so often evolve into long, disruptive quandaries. Willard can be running along just fine for a day or two, only to find himself bogged down by the most insignificant problem.

Or maybe you are like Trish, an artist who thinks every decision she makes is a momentous event. When offered a commission to paint a mural in the style she thought she had outgrown, Trish determined in typically grim fashion to "work out" her conflict between going for the money or taking the chance on waiting out a better opportunity. This meant dozens of phone calls to friends and relatives, dramatic sessions with her psychiatrist, and tortuous discussions with her boyfriend. The professional counseling alone cost Trish almost as much as the profit she would make from the commission.

And then there is Luke. For five years in a row now, he has attempted to change his life by entering graduate school. Every spring he applies to new programs in law, sociology, and film; and every fall he agonizes over the old question of what he is going to "do with his life."

Deadlines come and go but Luke never makes a decision; and September always ends with Luke declining all his acceptances, resolving of course to apply to some "better" programs next spring.

These are composite examples, designed to illustrate the wide varieties of contemporary vacillation, for the patterns and complexity of habitual indecision are virtually limitless. Yet no matter what the problem or circumstances, there is one thing all chronically indecisive people have in common: a stubborn tendency to substitute objective judgment for intuitive self-reliance.

Not that we can be blamed for such behavior in the context of extremely ambivalent social pressures. Americans may give lip service to the Harry Truman image of "listening to your insides" or John Wayne's "straight-talkin' " self-reliance; but when it comes to making really serious personal, financial, or professional decisions, it is the computer, not the cowboy, which is the dominant metaphor.

Most of us went to schools that emphasized objective judgment to such an extreme that we are really afraid to be any other way; and while deep down we all love the movies where the hero risks it all on one big hunch, the fact that this kind of risk-taking *is* a movie virtue only reinforces our apprehension of its unreality.

Yet the attempt to be so logical about our decision-making has one fatal flaw. As Plato himself first warned, a logical argument is only as good as the assumptions on which it rests—and, since these are always subject to arbitrary and unexpected revision, any attempt to be rigorously logical about our lives always leaves us on uncertain ground.

Indecisive people already suspect this. We've made enough big mistakes to know we really can't control our life objectively, no matter how thoroughly rational we try to be. We've also had enough uncanny experiences such as vividly predictive dreams, seemingly impossible coincidences, or perhaps even the kind of spiritual encounter I described in chapter 1, to suspect that there are levels of knowing far superior to the limits of conscious deduction.

Our problem is in conceptualizing a trustworthy alternative to logic. Because we've learned to equate intuition with irresponsibility or blind impulse, we feel we have no choice but to continue pursuing our rational approach.

Novelist Saul Bellow described the predicament quite well in his

Nobel address[3] when he said that "almost everyone is aware of [logic's limitations]" but are "reluctant to talk about this because there is nothing we can prove, because our language is inadequate, and because few [other] people are willing to risk talking about it."

This is why Willard repeatedly works over his catalogs, waiting for the one compelling reason that will finally justify choosing one set of sails over another, and why Trish keeps pumping her friends to tell her what she "should" be painting. And no matter how many ways Luke analyzes his graduate school options, he always hopes that some rational answer will finally point him in the right direction.

Plato anticipated very clearly the dilemma of the modern indecisive person when he warned about the dangers of teaching logic to eager students without giving them the kind of insights that would enable them to rely with more confidence on the intuitive wisdom of their "rational souls." Failing to provide the right guidance, he argued, would be to trap them in the intellectual equivalent of trying to wrap water in a package. Things "never stay the same . . . [they would] get lost and disturbed and tipsy, just like a drunk."[4]

What are these ancient insights which give us the courage to cultivate a more intuitive sense of direction?

The first is a simple but very important modification of terms— the realization that giving up our dependence on objective judgments is not the same thing as refusing to think logically. Being intuitive does not preclude the possibility that some instances of logical deduction can be just as instinctive as any gut feeling or hunch.

Certainly we've all had the experience of daydreaming some argument in the back of our minds, all quite spontaneously and without any of the pressures we normally associate with coming to the "right" decision. This is the kind of experience scientists refer to when they talk about their work as "play" or use phrases like "brainstorming" and "connecting."

The pioneering ethical psychologist William James once pointed out that even the most profound philosophical thinking can be an intuitive act—indeed must be, since in the end "absolute existence is absolute mystery."[5] To the outside observer, deep thinking may appear methodically compulsive, but it is much more the product of a person's faith in himself and his emotional inclinations than the result of any objective discipline. Hence James' descriptive phrase: "the sentiment of rationality."

The difference between our dependence on logic and depending on intuition is not a conflict between thought and feeling, but between control and surrender, between the attempt to enforce a solution on our problems and the willingness to just let it emerge. When we take the latter approach, our logical thinking is not only just as intuitive as any hunch or "gut" feeling, but the rational and emotional parts of us begin to converge in a very intellectually powerful way. We become more effective at seeing through conflicts and contradictions, at creating new ideas, and at dressing up our final decisions in terms that other people can readily understand. Einstein himself believed it was *only* through intuition that man could ever solve nature's deepest mysteries.[6]

One of my favorite historical anecdotes concerns the fifteenth-century Chinese statesman and sage Wang Yang-ming,[7] who grew up in a period particularly notable for its lopsided worship of abstract logic and intellectualization. This was a time when powerful governmental positions were filled, not on the basis of ability or success, but on academic rank—a time when ambitious men advanced by dint of bureaucratic theorizing and the capacity to pass examinations. Not coincidently it was also a time of social chaos, with agriculture floundering at the hands of centralized planning, whole regions rebelling against inept governors, and bandit gangs ravaging the provinces.

Yang-ming was clearly a product of his time. He practiced archery (an intellectual discipline as well as a sport in ancient China), memorized intellectual treatises of all sorts, and studied at monasteries throughout China. He even missed his own wedding in order to talk with a scholarly monk he'd happened to meet on the way to the ceremony. Like so many modern intellectuals, Yang-ming believed himself always on the verge of some "thorough understanding"[8] of his problems, if only he could just get the formula down.

Unfortunately Yang-ming could not exaggerate the logical obsession of his age without also suffering the extremes of its consequences as well. Repeatedly dedicating himself to a thorough "investigation of things" that could never be thoroughly investigated, he frequently fell ill from his exhausting efforts, at one point vomiting so much blood that he had to take a leave of absence from his post in the Ministry of Justice.

It was about this time when a remarkable series of events conspired to help Yang-ming realize that a more intuitive approach to living was not the intellectual laziness he always assumed but something quite the opposite. He was thirty-six at the time and had just intervened to save some innocent officials from an unjust imprisonment at the hands of a corrupt bureaucrat named Liu Chin. This so angered Liu Chin that Yang-ming was flogged, jailed, and finally banished to live among the primitive Miao aborigines. Fleeing hired assassins—at one point feigning a drowning suicide in order to throw them off his track—Yang-ming and a few devoted friends finally found refuge in a snake-infested cave.

It was there, living in such fear of Liu Chin's agents that he actually made a coffin for himself, when Yang-ming had to accept the fact that his mad obsession with logically weighing "events and things"[9] really hadn't gotten him very far. In spite of all his efforts to do the sensible thing—his sincere questioning and educated theorizing—in the end he knew no more about the meaning of life or how to conduct himself in a "sagely" manner than when he was a young student. Only a fool could have so mishandled the case of the imprisoned officials that he would be reduced to waiting out a term of exile in some barren province, tending horses and doing coolie labor just to survive.

At first Yang-ming felt hopelessly adrift and, with nothing left to do, sat meditating morbidly in front of his handmade coffin. But then some of his servants became ill and he began attending to their needs, gathering wood and water to cook their meals, even singing songs and telling stories to help pass the time.

It was in the midst of this simple life, having forsaken the pressures of his constant intellectualizing, that Yang-ming began to get a sense of what it was like to live more instinctively. At one moment giving in to some creative, sentimental, or compassionate impulse, then shifting back naturally to a logical train of thought, he gradually discovered how much more easily—and effectively—his intuition enabled him to function. Always having to know the "right" answer, he finally concluded, was "not a small sickness,"[10] when compared to the deeper wisdom of what he called the spontaneous "mind-and-heart."

Completing his term of exile and assuming a probationary position as Kiangsi magistrate, Yang-ming came to see that this willingness to flow intuitively back and forth between logic and feeling was as wise a strategy in the complex world of power politics as it had been among the Miao aborigines. He could arrive at the most important decisions with a previously undreamt clarity, a skill that eventually promoted him to governor of the entire province. "I have finally understood that my human nature is quite adequate for the task of achieving sagehood," he would become famous for saying. "My mistake in the past was seeking principle in events and things [external to my nature]."

The first step toward more intuitive decision-making, then, is not to give up logic but to include one's own heart in the process, to refrain from seeking strictly objective answers to our problems or from imposing solutions that seem perfectly intelligent on the surface but, deep down, feel contrived, artificial, and uninspired. "Out of both [the mind and heart] we came," reflects therapist Jon Davidson, "of both we are constituted, and to both shall we grow within the plane of existence that we define as Life."[11]

Interestingly such advice parallels that given by many executive-search consultants, so-called "headhunters," to clients struggling with new opportunities and career changes. "What the candidate [for a job switch] needs most," says Jonathan E. McBride, president of the Washington-based consulting firm which bears his name, "is a close examination of what makes sense rationally—in the head—and what feels right—in the heart—before proceeding. If an appropriate synthesis of head and heart is achieved, the match has a great chance of success."[12]

McBride should know. It was back in the mid-1960s, just after he had completed his military tour of duty, when a good friend from IBM tried to make a case for McBride joining the company.

"What he said made superb sense and captured my head," recalls McBride, "but something was missing—the 'want' factor. My heart wasn't in selling data-processing machinery to companies. I wanted direct contact with people concerned with their own well-being."

"I followed my heart to Merrill Lynch. I could take the criteria for quality training, industry standing, and breadth of exposure from IBM and apply it to Merrill Lynch. For almost a decade I was more effective at Merrill Lynch than I would have been at IBM because it not only made sense, but I wanted to be there, too."

McBride's story leads us to the second way we develop the courage of our instincts, and that is to appreciate just what a large part intuition plays in the lives of so many supposedly hard-nosed decision-makers. The textbook image of effective decision-maker as some kind of cold, rational automaton may be a popular stereotype, but a tragically misleading one.

". . . any attempt to deny instinct is to deny identity," observes David Mahoney,[13] chairman of the Norton Simon conglomerate, in a 1979 issue of *Fortune*. Robert P. Jensen of the General Cable Corporation relies almost completely on hunches to make the final decisions involving hundreds of millions of dollars in sales and acquisitions. "On each decision the mathematical analysis only [gets] me to the point where my intuition [has] to take over. . . . It's not that the numbers [aren't] accurate, but [are] the underlying assumptions correct?" Then there is the case of Random House chairman Robert Bernstein, perhaps the most blunt believer in hunches. "Only intuition," he says, "can protect you against the most dangerous individual of all—the articulate incompetent."

In 1986 author Roy Rowan published a book called *The Intuitive Manager* in which he documents the admitted reliance on intuitive decision-making, not only by corporate managers, but by prominent intellectuals such as the late think-tank director Herman Kahn and Caltech psychobiologist Roger Sperry; sports figures including John Brodie, Larry Bird, and Roger Staubach; politicians from John Kennedy to Ronald Reagan and Senator Bill Bradley; and even former astronauts like Edgar Mitchell.

There is even an organization in New York City, he reports, called Inferencial Focus, which specializes in scanning hundreds of diverse publications and journals for odd statistics and anecdotes, then attempting to cultivate insights about unexpected developments in various sectors of the economy. They predicted in 1985, for example, that the babyboomers were becoming a generation of homebodies—this on the basis of a rise in champagne consumption, a marked increase in poker playing, and a decline in the popularity of video games. Companies like E. F. Hutton and Chase Manhattan reportedly pay $24,000 a year for this intuitive news service.[14]

And then there is the fascinating case of what happened when Indiana University researcher Richard Cosier and his colleague, John Aplin, took a close look at the relationship between intuitive hunches and effective decision-making.[15] Asking 111 upper-division business students with different intuitive test scores to solve a series of simulated managerial problems, they discovered that the highly intuitive students made such "better subsequent decisions" [that] it was almost as if they had some kind of ESP. "Ruling out luck," Aplin later commented, ". . . it is difficult to interpret [the results] without assuming the possibility that intuitive abilities outside of the traditional five senses may exist."

But the real bombshell in recent years has been the discovery by Harvard Business professor Daniel Isenberg that most successful senior managers in American business today appear to disregard almost completely the so-called rational methods of decision-making.[16]

For more than two years Isenberg conducted an in-depth probe into the private thoughts and attitudes of a dozen of the country's most experienced and competent corporate executives. "I conducted intensive interviews," he recalls, "observed them on the job, read documents, talked with their colleagues and, in some cases, subordinates, and engaged them in various exercises in which they recounted their thoughts as they did their work." Isenberg spent up to twenty-five days studying each manager personally on the job and even read his observations out loud in order to get his subject's reactions.

The one consistency Isenberg discovered was that top executives habitually restrain their need for logical answers in order to let more intuitive solutions percolate up into consciousness. "I think ambiguity can be destroying, but it can be very helpful to an operation," one of Isenberg's successful managers confided. "[Ambiguities] yield a certain freedom you need as a chief executive officer not to be nailed down on everything. . . . The fact is we tie ourselves too much to linear plans, to clear time scales. I like to fuzz up time scales completely."[17]

Indeed, the more Isenberg studied successful managers, the more he found they tended to cultivate intuition in "all phases" of the problem-solving process. "[They] intuitively sense when a problem exists,

. . . rely on intuition to perform well-learned behavior patterns rapidly, . . . synthesize bits of data and experience into an integrated picture, . . . use intuition as a check [on] more rational analysis, . . . [and] use intuition to bypass in-depth analysis and move rapidly to come up with a plausible solution."

Again, these high-powered executives were not trading logic for blind impulse. In many cases, Isenberg's managers used their best rational thinking to sharpen and enlarge their ideas and to explain them to colleagues. What they didn't do was to allow the compulsion for logical answers to override a good hunch or strong feeling. "A lot of people think senior managers just go out and act in the absence of thoughtful analysis," Isenberg says. "Others think they act only after thinking a problem through completely. In fact, the good ones do both."[18]

Of course, one doesn't have to stick to the world of business or public affairs to see the power of intuitive decision-making. Dr. Frances Vaughan has interviewed hundreds of people who, through accident or chance, have learned new ways to apply it. One of her cases was a high school algebra student who had never earned above a B.

"I was confused and ill at ease in the class," the student himself recalls. "I didn't understand what was going on, and each day when I walked into the room I felt painfully embarrassed. Then one day we were given an objective, citywide test, and I scored the highest in our school, and the third highest in the city. When taking the test I was aware that I couldn't figure out the problems and I felt defeated before it began. I resigned myself to failure and decided to go ahead and guess at the answers. As I was guessing I realized that I could just tell which one was the right answer out of three or four possibilities. I felt good and relaxed after I got into the test and decided to give up trying to figure out the answers. I had been extremely tense, and sweating profusely. I relaxed, felt my stomach muscles unknot, and felt almost giddy with laughter."

"When the test results were announced I was shocked, embarrassed, and pleased. I felt confused and scared at the results. How could I have guessed that well . . . ? I did learn that when I didn't know answers on tests I could just let go, relax, and guess or write down whatever came into my head, and I often was right. I began to realize almost unconsciously that the answers are all there already if I can just tap into them somehow. I have never counted on being able to get practical answers of facts, but I do sometimes try to just let go and let the right answer for what I ought to do or decide come to me. If I don't listen to the answer that comes to me and make a different decision, however reasonably, I often get into trouble."[19]

There is even some evidence that intuitive decision-making improves physical as well as psychological performance. In research at a hospital near San Francisco, Richard S. Lazarus of the University of California at Berkeley found that patients who avoided thinking logically about the surgery they were scheduled to have actually fared the better for it,[20] recovering faster and with fewer complications.

Lazarus' colleague, Frances Cohen, discovered that some patients scheduled for gall bladder surgery were extremely vigilant about what would happen—and what might go wrong—even reading medical texts to discover the fine details of the procedure. Others completely ignored such facts, relying instead on their faith that things would probably go right. The intellectualizers, it turned out, recovered more slowly after the surgery and with more postoperative difficulties. In a similar study, researchers at the University of North Carolina have found that patients who avoided intellectualizing about scheduled dental surgery healed more rapidly afterward.

There is one last step to becoming more reliant on our intuitive decision-making and that is simply to discipline the kind of unethical habits which tend to diminish the frequency, clarity, and authority of our instinctual perception.

If this sounds like something vaguely akin to the last chapter's strategy for nurturing enthusiasm, be assured that the parallel is quite intentional. Ever since Plato first described the expression of inner potentiality as the ascension of the winged goddess *Eros*— the stem of our modern word *erotic*—ethical therapists have argued that natural enthusiasm and intuitive intelligence are one and the same. This is why even centuries after doctors had located certain cognitive functions in the cerebral cortex of the brain, most philosophers still considered the heart to be "the seat of the soul."

University of Chicago psychologist Eugene Gendlin has developed a remarkably illustrative technique he calls *focusing.*[21] Taking people who are playing with some new idea or interest, he urges them to take a few minutes to close their eyes and see how their intuitive impulse feels physically, especially in the emotional center of the body around the "stomach and chest." Quite often there is an abrupt adrenal response, the energy of the insight manifesting itself as physical excitement. The reverse is also true: quietly meditating on a blocked emotion in the center of the body will frequently produce a creative insight.

What this means then is that the same techniques which counter-act boredom—disciplining our unethical habits, finding solitude in places where we are less tempted to control others, and the direct petition for spiritual guidance—will ultimately give us the strength of our intuitive convictions, amplifying over time what at first may seem uncertain hunches or wishes into a firmer sense of direction. In fact, it is this kind of reaching within ourselves which is the one characteristic common to all dynamic people, regardless of their particular religion or philosophy. To withdraw temporarily from the world and come back in some new ethical capacity, to seek inwardly for solutions without resorting to familiar judgments and deception is, in the words of histo-rian Arnold Toynbee, "like a rocket that has a second boost."[22]

Frances Vaughan speaks for all ethically aware therapists when she says, "there is a strong connection between integrity and personal power."[23] The willingness "to face self-deception and to be honest with yourself and others is essential," she adds. "Creating any kind of smoke screen interferes with clear vision. Giving up pretenses is a big step in awakening intuition."[24]

Even in cases where our first attempts leave us where we thought we started, with no new sense of direction, there is at least the enlight-ened realization that our indecision is itself a decision: an unconscious choice to stay where we are for however much longer our deeper wis-dom deems it necessary. This is, of course, the most profound and powerful decision of all, to know that where we are, at least for the time being, is exactly where we need to be.

# Chapter 7

---

## *BEYOND WORTHLESSNESS*

. . . it is better to respect one's self than even perfect people.

GALEN[1]

Under the title of "consciousness-raising" many fall into the error of becoming more and more unhappy and discontented just to keep up with the times.

DR. THOMAS HORA[2]

Hailed in his own time as a brilliant poet and revolutionary political thinker, he was a popular speaker in chapels and lecture halls throughout his native England. He could claim credit for accomplishments ranging from educational reform to the founding of two innovative literary journals; and when seen monopolizing some conversation at a fashionable London gathering, the enthralled observer could only wish this man named Coleridge to talk on forever.

Yet to his own way of thinking Samuel Taylor Coleridge was anything but an admirable figure. A grouchy and dissatisfied husband, physically flabby and awkward, he openly criticized himself as unattractive and ill-tempered. "I am nothing, but evil," he once confided to the privacy of his notebook, adding in a moment of dark self-loathing, "Help! Help!"[3]

Not even the popularity of his early *Poems* and *Lyrical Ballads* (for which he wrote the immortal *Rime of the Ancient Mariner)* could assuage his growing feelings of worthlessness, and by 1802 the thirty-year-old author was convinced that only some incredible feat—an ambitious history of English prose or a definitive book on poetry—could save his "floundering" career. Friend William Wordsworth and Wordsworth's wife Dorothy noted how Coleridge was always forming "plans and schemes for working,"[4] even proposing to completely isolate himself until forced by loneliness into some kind of creative breakthrough. At one point Coleridge apparently resorted to plagiarism to maintain his image as a productive thinker, giving a series of lectures in the autumn of 1811 which closely paralleled the translations of a German named Schlegel.[5]

Today Coleridge remains a fascinating figure to historians and laymen alike. The mystic mystery of his poetry, his incredibly turbulent personal and professional relationships, his wide-ranging ventures into the realms of politics and philosophy—all combine to make him one of the most engaging characters in the history of English literature.

But perhaps what really intrigues us the most about Coleridge is not his creative uniqueness but his emotional *similarity.* We ourselves may not be struggling to write great poems or intellectual treatises, but clearly we know what it means to apply ourselves earnestly to some valued task such as raising children, establishing a career, or making a community contribution, yet feel completely inadequate for the job.

And if most of us can identify more easily than we would like to admit with Coleridge's chronic sense of worthlessness, we can certainly identify with his frustrating struggle to compensate for his perceived failings by trying to fulfill some perfectionistic ideal. How often, after all, do we reach for the prescriptions of the latest child rearing bestseller whenever we sense something wrong at home or respond to setbacks at work by playing chameleon to the whims of the boss or fret over a few extra pounds by struggling to imitate the Hollywood figure of some impossible model?

And how often do these responses persist, sometimes evolving into such merciless obsessions that we become emotionally drained by the very preparation to be better? The old jokes about the housewife whose entire sense of worth rises or falls on the cleanliness of her house or the man whose day is destroyed by a scratch in his newly waxed car are sad metaphors for a very common syndrome.

Unfortunately, the consistency of our perfectionistic striving is no guarantee of its effectiveness. Perfectionism may seem such a compelling answer to low self-esteem that even a genius like Coleridge can be taken in by it, but the practical result of this self-judgmental solution is only to aggravate the very feeling of worthlessness we are trying to eliminate.

Perfectionists are living a "no-win scenario," observes Asher Pacht of the University of Wisconsin psychology department. "They are constantly frustrated by their need to achieve, [yet] . . . often totally oblivious to the fact that they are reaching out for an unobtainable goal."[6]

Pacht cites the case[7] of a talented man who was highly successful in his field, yet plagued for years by feelings that he had never lived up to his real potential. The remedy, he came to believe, lay with getting a Ph.D. If only he could earn the "doctor of philosophy" title for himself, this would somehow compensate for all the "wasted time" and "mediocre work" in his life.

The only trouble with this perfectionistic solution was that none of the papers he wrote were ever "good enough" to submit for a thesis. Like many perfectionists, this man's standards were so high he became a constant procrastinator, unwilling to be judged and exhibiting an overwhelming fear of failure. The supposed answer to his problems had become, after so many years, the most egregious example of his agonizing self-doubt.

Dr. Mark Snyder of the University of Minnesota has studied hundreds of perfectionistic men and women—what he calls "high self-monitoring" personalities—and confirms this pattern of diminished self-esteem. People who "are chronically striving in chameleon-like fashion to appear to be the kind of person called for by each situation,"

Snyder observes,[8] "tend to be cut off from their inner feelings, chronically insecure, and ultimately dissatisfied with their performance. Unstable emotionally they are also more likely to leave their mates for the sake of a new partner and to adopt an "uncommitted" profile toward serious relationships.[9]

Even people whose perfection leads to considerable worldly achievement never seem to find the sense of worth they are seeking. This is why so many high achievers think they have fooled people into overestimating their ability. Many use the word *imposter* to describe themselves, believing some day they are going to be exposed for the "frauds they really are."

Most perfectionists are genuinely confused by their plight and continue to believe that the answer lies in striving for an even higher goal, all the while feeling more "anxious" and "confused."[10] After all, the only *logical* way to overcome feeling inferior is to try one's best to be better.

Even those who become angry and rebel against the roles and expectations they grew up with tend to ignore their own complicity in the perfectionistic tyranny and so usually end up repeating the error in another context. Years ago when I lived near a famous meditation center in Big Sur, California, it was not at all unusual to meet some high-powered executives from New York or Chicago who had "chucked the rat race" to lead a more spiritual life at the neighboring retreat. Only now instead of being obsessed with production deadlines and job titles they worry about knowing the "best" chants, getting the "right" mantras, and organizing their contemplative hours to achieve the "highest" state of consciousness.

As ethical therapists down through the centuries have always tried to remind us, perfectionism can never solve the problem of worthlessness because perfectionism *is* the problem of worthlessness.[11] Low self-esteem, inadequacy, chronic worthlessness—all stem from a judgmental attitude in which there is only one criterion for success: complete and absolute conformity to our ideal image. The perfectionist may forge incredible progress in every sphere of his life—he may be a dedicated parent, hard worker, a selfless and conscientious neighbor—yet, since no one can possibly be 100 percent successful at anything, whatever he attains is always experienced as abject failure.

Even if we come to within inches of succeeding beyond our wildest expectations, we are still worthless for, after all, we have only done what was expected. There is no way to see self-improvement, to bask in the light of intermediate success, to build up any kind of self-esteem. We are victims again of the eternal curse of idol worship or what more contemporary therapists like Dr. Pacht charmingly calls the *God/scum* phenomenon.

"For perfectionists," Pacht explains, "only the extremes of the continuum exist. . . . They are . . . either God or they are scum. Despite their striving they find it impossible to be perfect and, as a result, spend a lot of time wallowing at the low end of the continuum. The real tragedy lies in the fact that, for the perfectionist, achieving 95 percent or even 99 percent of the goal is usually seen as a failure because it is not perfect."[12]

Certainly one doesn't have to look far to realize the truth of this observation. The awkwardness and self-doubt that characterize so much of adolescence stems directly from the internalization of impossible peer group standards,[13] just as the downfall of so many dieters is in the adoption of goals that almost guarantee a demoralizing and subversive lapse.

One of the fascinating aspects of bulimia (binge eating), as we will see again in the chapter on addiction, is that the most destructive episodes tend to occur *after* a long period of successful dieting. The slip begins with a mistake that is innocent enough, absentmindedly overeating one day or discovering that a supposedly low-calorie lunch really wasn't all that low calorie. But instead of just writing the episode off to experience, the perfectionistic bulimic decides he or she has failed so miserably that, "what-the-hell,"[14] might as well just keep going.

In cases where the standards are extraordinarily high—the worlds of show business, sports, and Wall Street, for example—the inevitable plunge into the depths of self-loathing can lead to addiction, fraud, and the kind of self-abusive behaviors we have, in fact, come to associate with certain celebrities and other driven achievers.

Going back to our historical example of Coleridge again, here we find a man whose perfectionism left so little room for satisfaction that he became increasingly dependent on solutions of laudanum (opium) to bolster his sagging self-esteem. For almost a decade, from 1807 to 1816, he was a virtual vagrant, forced to live with different London acquaintances for as long as they could tolerate his uncontrollable mood swings.

Of course, the interesting question is, "Why, if our perfectionism generates the very feelings of inadequacy we are trying to overcome, don't we recognize the problem more clearly?"

Part of the answer is that old desire for control. We perfectionists may vary widely in terms of our aspirations. Some of us may strive to be flawless executives; others the perfect wife or lover or artist or teacher. But deep down every perfectionist is motivated by the same secret belief: that he can somehow solve his problems by giving them a precise material definition. There is a magical, almost childlike, belief that by describing our unhappiness in very precise terms we can proceed to engineer some all-embracing solution.

This is why we all so readily identify with the mad scientist of literature and movies who is striving to realize some impossible dream of human perfection. The fact that such efforts produce grotesque results, as in the case of Dr. Frankenstein, or require the implied selling of one's soul à la Dr. Faustus, does not diminish our secret sympathy for such characters.

Regrettably, conventional psychology has actually encouraged us along these lines in recent decades by attempting to sell the public on the idea that perfecting one's personality is a realistic scientific goal. Between the psychoanalytic promise of a sexually liberated Eden as popularized in Robert Rimmer's novel *The Harrad Experiment* and behaviorist B. F. Skinner's prescription for the precise alteration of lifestyles in his famous *Walden Two*, our belief in the utopian fine-tuning of self has been so consistently reaffirmed that it even survives the present decline of the "value-free" therapies which nurtured it.

There is, as well, a widespread confusion between the self-destructive goal of perfection and the far more worthwhile idea of excellence, a mistaken belief that to do something well means we must also do it perfectly. Certainly this is the message of all the books and television programs in which the person cast to play the dedicated hero or heroine also mirrors our fantasies of physical and emotional perfection.

What we have to realize is that real achievement, while it may appear to mimic perfectionism, is really the opposite of it. Genuine excellence means a willingness to *suspend* established standards, to abandon our preconceptions in the service of a deeper wisdom. Just as it is often said that the best artists somehow break with conventional procedure, so the same can be said of the best office managers, the best engineers, even the best parents. "Excellence is the positive side of productivity," says executive-search consultant Jonathan E. McBride,[15] "perfectionism is the negative. Perfectionism is what we try to do; excellence is who we are. It's the people who are not excellent who try to be so perfect."

Dr. Pacht remembers an instructive incident which occurred during a trip to the Southwest a few years ago. He had walked into a store where two belts of turquoise and silver hung side by side. One looked perfect, while the other was full of flaws and inconsistencies.

"Much to my surprise," recalls Pacht,[16] "the imperfect belt cost ten times more than the perfect one. When I asked why, I was told that the perfect belt was machine-made so that each stone and each piece of metal was identical. However, the expensive one was handcrafted by a Native American and was complete with all those imperfections that made it true art."

It was those human quirks, Pacht realized, not the compulsive replication of some ideal, which gave the belt both its true beauty and worth.

Certainly the one consistency in all modern studies of excellence is the importance of siding with intuition over perfectionistic images of how things "ought" to be done. Tom Peters, the Palo Alto, California, consultant and author of the widely acclaimed management text *In Search of Excellence*, recently observed that if there is one thing genuine achievers have in common it is their faith in making what appears to be a complete "mess." Building $100,000 demonstration projects by haphazardly contriving appropriations for hundreds of smaller projects, "bootlegging" spare parts from other equipment, experimenting with new ideas and supporting them through one or two bad years—this disciplined indulgence of ambiguity is the wellspring of excellence in every business, big or small, high tech or traditional.[17]

Daniel Isenberg, whose research on managerial intuition has led to broader studies of how successful executives think and operate, finds that quality managers care much less about living up to preplanned objectives than is generally thought. Our imagined stereotype of the effective executive may be someone who strategizes, quantifies, plans precisely, and then sets out to achieve these objectives in the most efficient way possible; but "in reality," Isenberg says, "specific objectives lurk in the background, not in the forefront of their thoughts."[18]

His subjects' own view of themselves is telling. One top executive of a large firm describes his job as being like a frog on a lily pad, waiting for just the right fly to strike his fancy. Another likens himself to a beachcomber, examining the "spoils of high tide, deciding whether to pick up a piece of flotsam, leave it, or throw it back to be examined another day."[19]

The chief officer of a major bank recently told Isenberg that a good executive tries to take "advantage of the best cartography at his command, but knows that that is not enough—he knows that along the way he will find things that change his maps or alter his perceptions of the terrain. He trains himself the best he can in the detective skills, endlessly sends out patrols to learn greater detail, overflying targets to get some sense of the general battlefield."[20]

Sooner or later, of course, standards do play a role in the manufacture of any excellent product. Industrial goods must be manufactured to consistent and accurate specifications, services must be performed with an eye to customer satisfaction, and even a painting or musical composition must be aesthetically pleasing.

But as Plato himself first observed, a standard of excellence is never something we know at the beginning of a project but something which emerges only as our intuitive efforts unfold. The best a human can produce, he wrote, "spring[s] from the soul . . . flowing out from thence." And elsewhere, that our highest actions "are performed according to their real nature, and not according to our opinion."[21]

Quality-conscious executives and professionals who work day to day trying to produce an excellent car or top-flight legal brief may not think of their work in such profoundly philosophical terms, but it is interesting to note what happened when Dr. Isenberg compared the problem-solving strategies of managers experienced in the rigorous demands of production with that of his intelligent but less experienced Harvard Business School students.[22] Both groups were asked to come up with a business plan for the same product; but the case was presented on a series of index cards, separated paragraph by paragraph, and shuffled randomly.

The students approached the problem by first reading through all the cards quite logically, then rearranging them in chronological order and coming up with a single, "perfect" business plan. The experienced executives, on the other hand, flipped back and forth wildly between the cards, generated possible solutions as early as the third paragraph they read, and eventually developed a flexible business plan with at least one or two contingency options.

Like the English economist John Stuart Mill, the executives disparaged perfectionism, not because they were willing to compromise on excellence, but because they knew perfectionism had so little to do with it.[23]

If there is any connection at all between perfectionism and excellence, it is not that rigid perfectionism leads to greater quality, but rather that excellence grows with a more profound awareness of what it means to be perfect. We are at our "best," in the most constructive sense of the word, when we are being truest to ourselves in the moment, no matter how awkward, irrelevant, confused, dogged, or nonsensical we think our impulses may seem to others.

To see the importance of realization, we could hardly do better than go back to Coleridge.

Here he was in the winter of 1814, desperately ill and long written off as a hopeless morphine addict, when something unexpected happened that surprised even his most disillusioned friends. He was *en route* to deliver some lectures in western England and spending the night in the town of Bath when he was overcome by such severe drug-induced hallucinations that he was bedridden for the better part of a week.

Audiences waiting impatiently in nearby Bristol wrote off his failure to show up as just another laudanum excursion, but over the next two years there began to evolve a startling remission. Accustomed to sponging off others with his adolescent demands for attention and comfort, Coleridge suddenly resumed his writing and lecturing with an industry he hadn't known for years. He began helping to support the family of a friend who had fallen on hard financial times and, by the spring of 1816, had voluntarily placed himself in the hands of Dr.

James Gillman, a retired physician, to begin treatment for opium addiction and a related heart problem. That very same year saw the publication of two of his most famous poems, *Christabel* and *Kubla Khan.*

What happened during those nights in Western England that finally put Coleridge on the road to recovery? What was it that enabled this perfectionistic poet, given up for lost at age forty-four, to suddenly resume a quality of personal achievement he hadn't known for more than a decade?

We know from his letters and public writings that Coleridge had already begun to suspect the negative influence of his judgmental tendencies. He had recently produced a series of articles, for example, about the psychological advantages of disciplining habitual resentments. But it wasn't until his trip to Bristol that Coleridge had finally implicated his perfectionistic attitudes head-on.

"You have no conception of what my sufferings have been," he wrote in his diary at Bath, "forced to struggle and struggle in order not to desire a death for which I am not prepared. . . . Should I recover I will—no—no may God grant me power to struggle to become *not another* but a *better man.*"[24]

*"Not another* but a *better man."*

From the viewpoint of conventional psychology, these words are cryptic at best; indeed, they could even be misread as advocating more perfectionism. But to the ethical therapist they indicate the familiar turning point in the treatment of low self-esteem. Coleridge no longer wished to be "another"—impossible perfect—man, merely a "better," more self-expressive one. He had begun to see that his real value and achievement stemmed, not from the degree to which he imitated some remote ideal of perfection, but from the extent to which he was willing to regard his true inner self as naturally perfect.

"Spiritually we are [already] perfect," is the way a modern therapist like Thomas Hora puts it.[25] "And the more we understand our spiritual essence the more perfect we will be." Family therapist Victoria Brundage views overcoming perfectionism as coming to see ourselves as equal members of the human "fellowship," where every spontaneous person makes a unique and important contribution to the good of the whole.[26]

Fortunately, she adds, the kind of bottoming out experienced by Coleridge is not an inevitable part of therapy. For those torn between feelings of worthlessness, on the one hand, and a stubborn addiction to perfectionism on the other, it is possible to get a convincing glimpse of a more relaxed and authentic life by gradually experimenting with reduced perfectionism in a restricted and relatively nonthreatening area of our lives.

"This is a wonderfully innocent, innocuous, and benevolent way with which to try out new behaviors," she says. It's also foolproof, since being unable to do it perfectly is also good practice at being imperfect.

A perfectionistic woman I knew, whose low self-esteem had been battered down even further by a recent divorce, discovered the benefit of compartmentalized experimentation when the need to support her children forced her to take a part-time real estate job. Had she been less pressed by her busy schedule, she remembers, she probably would have approached the job with the same "crazy compulsion" that she brought to every other corner of her life: dressing immaculately for appointments to show houses, printing stylish business cards, and impressing customers with her spotlessly clean car.

As it was, the only way she could muster the energy to make it through this difficult period was to forget the image for a while and simply act the way she felt, regardless of what potential buyers or sellers might think. The result of this uncharacteristic decision to just show up as herself was that she soon developed a reputation as an exceptionally helpful and competent broker, someone who listened to customers' needs and offered the benefit of her honest opinion.

A similar discovery was made by a hard-driving executive named Steve who was advised by his therapist to stop playing his twice-weekly game of tennis with colleagues from the office: "Use the time for yourself. Go to a different racket club and play with people you don't have to prove yourself with." Not only did Steve find the absence of pressure more enjoyable, but the quality of his game gradually improved.

I am a special fan of this kind of compartmentalized experimentation for the role it played in helping me to develop my own technique as a writer. Certainly during my high school years my own perfectionism had created a very real difficulty in this area. Eager to get into a good college and a workaholic by nature, I was able to satisfy my teachers' expectations in most of my math, science, and history courses. In the area of English, however, my tendency to get bogged down in questions of grammar and style completely inhibited me from developing or expressing a coherent point of view.

The more I tried to improve, the worse things got. I frequently scored near the bottom of the class on composition; and when I took the writing sample portion of the Scholastic Aptitude Test, I flunked it. I am told I was the only person admitted to Princeton in 1964 on an early decision with the provision that he take remedial English.

For three years I studiously avoided courses in literature, creative writing, or any other field that would put me up against all my would-be Scott Fitzgerald classmates. It was only my involvement with some experimental courses in the psychology department and a friend's urging me to write a history of these seminars which led me to spend evenings one summer simply writing out my thoughts without catering to what I imagined to be some professor's rigid standards. I deliberately did this in my spare time without any expectation of what the result would be.

Only a paragraph of my thirty-plus page manuscript was ever published; and even then with so many changes and deletions that it was hard to recognize what I had created. Yet the experience of letting go of my thoughts without having to please my inner critic effected a permanent change in my ability to compose.

Now some will say that it is one thing to practice being less perfect in some quiet little corner of our lives, quite another to extend this practice to a job or relationship where we are so public and have so much at stake.

This would be true if the lesson of compartmentalized experimentation were limited to the area where we practiced it. But the interesting thing about perfectionism is that once we begin to see through its false promises in one corner of our lives, the insight tends to spread almost automatically. The dawning awareness that being true to one's self liberates qualities which are not only superior to perfectionism but, by their spontaneous nature, are far easier to sustain over the long run, becomes a powerful force for conscious and unconscious change.

When I asked Dr. Isenberg, for example, how the successful senior managers he studied had learned to become so fearless in "fuzzing things up," he explained that it was often only a single event—sometimes just an accident—which changed their lives.

"The ones who were eloquent about it," he replied, "said they had a salient experience. [They] paid attention to it and made the right move and [just continued] based on years of cumulating experience."[27]

Even in cases where the perfectionism is severe enough to require clinical attention, the process of recovery seems to be self-perpetuating beyond a certain point. Dr. Pacht, for example, does not believe a thorough modification of the patient's life is necessary or even helpful. "Once the road is laid out and the basic process established, therapists need to trust the patient's ability to complete the process. Therapy beyond that point is not only wasteful but is not in the patient's best interests."[28]

For anyone who suffers from feelings of worthlessness, the end of self-condemnation in the whole of one's life begins with the courage to express genuine excellence in but the least part of it.

# Chapter 8

---

# *BEYOND FEAR*

The inferior man . . . attempts a hundred intrigues
in order to save himself, but finishes only in creating
a great calamity from which he cannot run away.

WANG YANG-MING[1]

Ascend to some sort of partnership with fate . . . go
to meet it, work it to our needs, instead of dodging it
all our days, and being run down by it at last.

WILLIAM JAMES[2]

Fear is the most unique emotional problem in that we really couldn't
afford to be completely rid of it, even if such a thing were possible.

We can imagine living well enough without ever being depressed
or guilty again, and certainly we could do without any more boredom or
feelings of worthlessness to plague us. But fear has a certain practical
utility. To the extent that our apprehensions alert us of real world
pitfalls or serious obstacles to some goal, they are absolutely necessary
for our survival. The part of our mind which spins out gloomy projec-

tions of possible dangers based on its assessment of the current facts is an essential form of social radar.

When we talk about fear as a problem, then, we're not talking about every instance of fear, only our tendency toward overreaction—imagining a problem where none really exists, worrying about things over which we have no control, or turning a reasonable cause for concern into something much worse. An American president once said that we have nothing to fear but fear itself; but it is probably more correct to say that we have nothing to fear but our hand in exaggerating it.

What this excessive fear does have in common with other negative emotions is the irony of being perpetuated primarily by our unethical attempts to be rid of it. Just as our sense of worthlessness stems from our perfectionistic response to a lack of self-esteem . . . our depression from a resentful response to feeling wounded . . . so our worst apprehensions tend to grow out of our *evasive* response to a much smaller threat.

Pretending a false intention we think will ward off some perceived danger, in other words, is precisely what exaggerates our sense of vulnerability. ". . . although often due to intelligent calculation," observed William James, "and the dread of betraying our interests in some more or less definitely foreseen way, [such deception] is quite often a blind propensity. . . ."[3]

James knew whereof he spoke. Plagued from his earliest years by a domineering father who wanted him to become a physicist or chemist, he had always relied on a certain measure of evasion to cope with these domestic pressures, either secretly disobeying his father's wishes or, when unable to do so, deceiving *himself* into career compromises that did not reflect his real interests. The only problem with this deceptive strategy was that James fell victim to long periods of panicky self-absorption which became increasingly frequent after he entered Harvard College in 1863.

For the better part of the next decade James vacillated between protracted leaves of absence to secretly travel and study what really interested him—at one point pretending to his family that he was enrolled in a science course he'd actually withdrawn from—and returning to Harvard with new rationalizations to justify following the academic program laid out by his father. But whether deceiving his family or misleading himself, his fears only grew worse. Increasingly he began to think he was going insane.

Had not James' interest in philosophy begun to take a turn toward ethical self-therapy—particularly the essays of a now obscure Frenchman named Charles Renouvier—there is no telling what might have happened. For by the time he had graduated from medical school the years of alternating secretiveness and self-deception had finally culminated in a nervous breakdown. Walking into his dressing room one night, he saw the image of an epileptic patient he had once observed in an asylum, entirely idiotic with greenish skin, and feeling himself merge with it, "became a mass of quivering fear."[4] He "awoke morning after morning with a horrible dread at the pit of my stomach, and with a sense of the insecurity of life that I never knew before, and . . . for months I was unable to go out into the dark alone."

Fortunately for James, what came very close to precipitating a suicide attempt evolved into the dawning realization that something about his fearful state was due to a lack of ethical conviction. "Today I about touched bottom," James wrote to his diary, "and perceive plainly that I must face the choice with open eyes: shall I frankly throw the moral business overboard, as one unsuited to my innate aptitudes, or shall I follow it, and it alone, making everything else merely stuff for it?"[5] Although it would take some years to verbalize the precise connection between evasion and fear, his general awareness of the need to take a stronger ethical stand had an immediate tonic effect and marked the turning point in what would ultimately prove to be an inventive and courageous career.

How does something as seemingly subtle as an evasive habit have such a powerful psychological effect, amplifying normal apprehensions and concerns into the kind of hallucinatory fears James himself experienced?

In the first place there is nothing mild about deceit. The next time you are tempted to tell a lie, do what Jon Davidson once suggested to me and take just a moment to become aware of your insides. Notice the distortion that accompanies your intention to deceive, the actual breakdown of consciousness which occurs each time you attempt to mislead others or to rationalize a decision you don't really believe in to yourself. The manipulative part of us is literally assaulting our vital center, scattering awareness like some powerful radio jammer.

This diffusion of mind is compounded by a frightening physiological transformation. Breathing accelerates, our heart rate shoots abnormally high, and there is a sharp rise in levels of electro-dermal tension. This is why even the slightest evasion can produce such wild gyrations on the meter of a polygraph, or what they call in detective movies a *lie detector*.

James Pennebaker, professor of behavioral medicine at Southern Methodist University, has found evidence to suggest that the effort required to sustain a false intention places an enormous stress on the body's nervous systems. Experimental subjects who were instructed to give deceptive answers to a psychological test, for example, experienced significant autonomic and respiratory changes.[6]

If the deception occurs in the context of an ongoing relationship, such as a friendship, marriage, or business partnership, the vigilance required to sustain it only compounds the turmoil. Pennebaker has found that people who habitually withhold critical information about themselves, such as a traumatic event or the death of a loved one, become sufficiently unnerved that they are far more susceptible to contagious diseases than those who confide such events.[7] More recent immunological studies at Harvard confirm this finding.[8]

Of course, it would be one thing if the disquieting effect of deception were strictly a physiological matter, completely unrelated to outside events. If that were the case, we might reasonably seek some tranquilizing pill or injection to quell our sensitive body chemistry and simply go on with the business of cleverly evading life's troubling problems. Unfortunately, habitual evasion has a *psychological* effect as well, insuring that no matter how cleverly we have disguised our real desires from others—or, in the case of self-deception, from ourselves—the unsettling situation we think we have diffused has a way of soon looming more ominously.

To see how this happens, let's take the common situation of a young man who fears that his girlfriend will lose respect for him if he shows any sign of doubt or weakness. Every time there is a crisis of confidence, when he feels he can't afford to be open about his feelings, he simply withdraws into himself for a while until the situation blows over. His perceptive girlfriend may ask "What's wrong, dear?" But he just says "I don't feel well. I think I'll just go and lie down."

Now the man may be completely off about how his girlfriend would really have reacted to his insecurity, but the fact that he has successfully avoided the reaction he *imagined* would happen provides such a temporary sense of relief that he becomes convinced his fear must have been real. Over time, he tends to repeat the evasion, each escape from the imaginary threat only further strengthening his conviction of its ultimate truth. This is what some ethical therapists call a "built-in protection for the credibility of the threat." In plainer language, it means that every time we successfully manipulate our way out of an uncomfortable situation we actually increase our fear of it, even when *no* real threat exists.

The same thing happens, of course, when we attempt to deceive ourselves. Take the case of a woman who works in a hairdressing shop and wants to set up her own business, but is so intimidated by the legal and financial paperwork that she decides "it's not worth the headache of owning your own store." A few months of this, and the original obstacles which frightened her assume a life of their own all out of proportion to what really would have been demanded. She may even find herself talking others out of risking similar ventures and secretly reveling in newspaper accounts of failed start-up companies.

Unfortunately this tendency to psychologically exaggerate fearful prophesies not only alienates us from the people and situations that could prove a source of great comfort, it invariably alienates *them from us.* Without getting too technical, there have been a number of scientific experiments in recent years[9] which demonstrate quite convincingly that what we expect from other people leads them to like or dislike us accordingly. Evasive people even antagonize their own therapists,[10] closing off what for many is their best chance for learning to form a trusting relationship.

The sad and paradoxical result, as Theodora Wells points out, is that evasive people tend to end up socializing with the very treacherous people who are most likely to take advantage of them. "When a person acts out of fear," she explains, "the other person can sense that . . . at some level they smell fear and they know you're vulnerable."[11]

Anthropologists frequently note this phenomenon when they

compare neighboring cultures with radically different personality traits. The Eskimo tribes of the Northeast, for example, are well known as a warm, communal people, friendly and self-assured, while the Ojibwa just a few miles away are a sullen and hypersensitive lot with suspicions that border on the pathological.[12]

There are no geographic factors to explain this incredible difference—both tribes have to cope with the same severe climatic and food shortages—yet the child-rearing practices are telling. From their earliest years the Eskimos are taught to be forthright and openly emotional, not ashamed to ask each other for help or to admit weakness. Young Ojibwa, on the other hand, are taught to be secretive, mistrustful, and to expect the worst from any forthright behavior—which is exactly what they get.

Indeed, one of the fascinating discoveries to emerge from the trend toward family and group counseling in recent years is the recognition that a good percentage of the people who suffer from chronic fear in some sense "invite" the anxieties of which they complain the loudest. The institutionalized old man who claims that his kids would do anything to get his money is very often generating the kind of suspicious atmosphere which makes people want to act behind his back. The wife who fears her husband might be running around on her has become so emotionally withdrawn that he is becoming tempted to do just that. And the employee who says he's being deliberately overworked may only be suffering the reaction to his own secretiveness.

Now understandably, it is one thing to realize that much of our fear is a product of evasive reactions to lesser or imagined threats, quite another to just stop being deceptive. This would seem especially true in the case of self-deception where, almost by definition, we really don't quite know what's going on. The very phrase seems to imply an essential lack of knowledge. If by self-deception we mean that we are justifying to ourselves a course of action which is somehow different from what we really want, then surely any awareness of our true intention must be buried at a very deep level of consciousness. How else, after all, could one be deceived?

The best answer I can give is to repeat a conversation I had some years ago with a woman who, after fifteen years of marriage, had finally gotten divorced from her husband.

"When did you know it was over?," I asked.

"The day we were married," she confided. "I guess I just didn't want to admit to myself I was doing the wrong thing."

I have repeated this conversation to a number of people over the years who, when approached with the appropriate sensitivity, will concede that they, too, have always known when they were rationalizing themselves along the wrong path, usually because what they really wanted seemed "dangerous," "risky," "embarrassing," "hard to explain," or just "too much to hope for." Only years later did it become obvious that what seemed, objectively, to be the safer alternative proved in fact the path of greater fear and suffering.

Ethical therapists tend to emphasize this point—namely, that self-deception is much less a problem of knowledge than of faith in our intuitive wisdom. In some real sense, there is no such thing as the unconscious, only the unwillingness to believe that expressing who we really are will be rewarded by the world at large. "What will people say?," we worry to ourselves. "What if I fail?" "Who'll try to stop me?"

Why are we so intimidated by this kind of internal dialogue? Why do we so often behave as if the only way to cope with an intimidating situation is either to rationalize a less desirable course of action to ourselves or, if we do remain true to our intention, to do it covertly, hiding our real motives from others?

The answer, of course, is trust. Or more correctly, the lack of it. We feel we have to evade the gaze of other eyes because we think that being ourselves is going to get us clobbered somehow, if not physically than certainly emotionally.

Now the interesting thing about this assumption is that it has very little validity in the world at large. That is to say, when we approach people in the right way, most can be trusted a great deal; and those who can't be trusted stand out in a pretty obvious way.

Psychologist Julian Rotter and his colleagues at the University of Connecticut have demonstrated this in a rather elegant way with their development of what Rotter calls an "Interpersonal Trust Scale"—a series of statements which, taken together, measure a person's general openness toward the world. For example, someone who agreed "people are more hypocritical than ever" would be considered less trusting in his outlook, while a person who thought washing machine repairmen "are honest" would get a higher score.

The revealing part of Rotter's work is his discovery[13] that it is the *high* trusters who do better in the world and get more love and support from the people they meet. High trusters are better adjusted, have more friends, are more attractive to the opposite sex, and more socially active—all without being any more gullible than the low trusters. As a matter of fact, low trusters are usually the ones more likely to be abused and taken advantage of.

Why, then, have we learned to become so untrusting and evasive?

Regrettably what is true of the world at large may not necessarily be true of our particular social universe. Many of us grew up in families where evading certain sensitive issues may have been the only way to survive; and having once become accustomed to our deceptive habits, we proceeded to attract a network of friends, business associates, and even lovers whose untrustworthy habits were, if nothing else, familiar. If we now live with family members who are as likely to criticize our openness as to be supportive—if we secretly mistrust even our closest friends—then there may be some very legitimate reasons for not saying everything that is on our minds.

Fortunately, indiscriminate openness is not what's really required in order to overcome our evasive habits and the exaggerated fears they sustain. To those we doubt or mistrust, it is perfectly honest to say, "I don't feel comfortable discussing that right now" or "I'd rather not talk about it." As long as our stated avoidance is itself an honest expression of feeling, there is no law which says we have to go into detail.

If pressed, we can even say we're not sure we feel comfortable being open with that person right now. "Dearest Father," author Franz Kafka began a famous letter to his father, "You asked me recently why I maintain I am afraid of you. As usual I was unable to think of any answer to your question, partly for the very reason that I am afraid of you, and partly because an explanation of the grounds for this fear would mean going into far more details than I could even approximately keep in mind while talking."[14] As dramatic as this statement is, one could hardly imagine a more disarming approach.

What is called for is a conscious effort to change the ethical quality of our everyday interactions. Overcoming fear ultimately means taking responsibility for altering our social environment. "You have to create your own circle," says Allen Bergin.[15] Therapist Edward Hoffman agrees. "Over the years," he says, "I find myself emphasizing the importance of a friend."[16] Not a buddy, he adds, but someone with whom "to create a supportive situation. I find myself talking more and more about this lately [because] people are hungry for this kind of thing. What they don't understand is that it's up to them. That's the point of the work, whether you live in Portland or Manhattan."

How is it up to us?

First we must become open to the possibility that the dark reality of present evasion and fear is not the only plane of existence. There exists for each of us a parallel option, a potential universe where honest opinions are valued, not punished; where taking healthy risks is rewarded regardless of the outcome; and where self-expression and success are considered synonymous. Furthermore, this universe is not in some utopian mountain location or in a commune or in an exotic religious cult, but literally as close to us as the people we pass on the street.

Even in the supposedly cold, ruthless world of everyday business and professional competition, the potential rewards of honesty are far greater than generally imagined. "[The] ruthless white-collar villain [you see in the movies] with his fawning executive staff may exist somewhere," says former J. C. Penney board chairman Donald Seibert, "but I've never run into him. . . . Among the people I know at . . . the nation's corporations, the personal quality that is regarded most highly is a solid, unwaivering sense of integrity. The higher a person moves up in business, the more important it is for his peers and superiors to feel they can depend on his word. They have to know he's a 'straight shooter' in every sense of the word, one who won't cut moral corners to further his own interests."[17]

The respected mediator Gerard I. Nierenberg agrees, reminding us that press and television coverage of public events tends to present a highly distorted and unnecessarily paranoid picture of everyday values. Even in the tough world of labor and management conflict resolution, most people do "not play a negotiating game . . . at the earliest possible moment [they] convey to each other [their] maximum concessions and minimum concessions expected in return." All this may be done subtly, Nierenberg adds, but never ambiguously. The artful negotiator simply doesn't have time for deceptive charades that will, in the end, only undermine his confidence and authority.[18]

When the editors of *Business and Society* invited prominent leaders from business and government to comment on the psychological utility of an occasional "strategic lie," the replies were astonishingly critical and to the point. "Honesty is the best policy in international relations, interpersonal relations, labor, business, education, family, and crime control," replied former attorney general Ramsey Clark, "because truth is the only thing that works and the only foundation on which lasting relations can build."

"Honesty isn't the best policy," added Henry Ford II, chairman of the Ford Motor Company, "it's the only policy. When lying has to be described in terms like 'strategic misrepresentation' or 'upgrading,' someone is going to a lot of trouble to deceive himself and, presumably, to fool others."

Once we are willing to at least entertain the possibility of a universe in which it may be safer to be ourselves than we normally imagine, the next step is to take an informal survey of our current relationships. For no matter how few family members or friends we think we can really trust, there is always someone somewhere with whom we know we can risk.

I am thinking in particular of an actress I once knew from a broken home who'd learned to trust none of her relatives and whose history of relationships with violent men had led to a situation where she was once again living tensely with a chronic abuser. Though quite talented, she—we'll call her Dori—was a very fearful person who shared few feelings and had great difficulty making the kind of contacts necessary to further her career. Though she desperately wanted to be more relaxed with other people, she seemed to attract attention from the very manipulative characters she distrusted the most.

The turnaround came when an old acquaintance from college she hadn't seen in almost a decade moved into the neighborhood. Dori really hadn't known the former classmate very well but, feeling she could somehow trust her, began stopping by her new neighbor's house for coffee and chats.

Gradually Dori found herself confiding things in these conversations she was not in the habit of discussing and, with the courage to be more open in this one little corner of her life, found herself feeling less fearful in many of the others. It took some months, but she did begin making plans to get rid of her abusive boyfriend and started speaking up for what she wanted in situations where she had previously felt inhibited and helpless.

If we are married, of course, we must be willing to take whatever steps are necessary to include our mate in our voyage to this new social universe, if this is at all possible. This must naturally be done with some care, as sudden expressions of honest self-disclosure can easily be misinterpreted by someone who has become accustomed to our evasive style.

One helpful technique is simply to be up front about both our intention and our sensitivities. To say, in other words, "It's important to me to learn how to be more open about what I'm feeling and thinking and what I want. On the other hand I don't want to do anything that's radical or that's going to scare you. I want us both to grow from this and to grow as partners." This, in turn, may lead to a joint decision to experiment with being honest in certain areas, leaving other issues alone until a certain level of confidence is achieved.[19]

Having taken our trust inventory of existing relationships, we now have the foundation to begin extending our social network along explicitly ethical lines. The easiest and often the most helpful way to do this is by putting a brake on our evasive habits in situations which feel least threatening.

Someone who works in a large corporation, for example, might find it easier to try being more himself when he is lunching informally with people from another department than in a conference with his boss. Similarly, a man or woman who lives in a small gossipy community might be more comfortable initiating this experiment while visiting friends or relatives in another town.

Now even in such comparatively safe circumstances, the discipline of evasive habits is going to feel awkward at first. From inside it will seem that we are not only more vulnerable and more easily embarrassed, but that our speech is disjointed or that we've run out of things to say. Yet just as our evasion has had the effect of drawing untrustworthy people into our lives, so our new attempts to overcome the habit will begin attracting the opposite.

One way to appreciate the psychological dynamics involved is to recall those times in our lives when we have been thrown together for several days with a large group of strangers—perhaps at a professional training institute or a long seminar or during a vacation at a resort community. Remember how we always seemed to discover the people we liked the most toward the end of our stay, even if we'd bumped into them several times earlier on? This was because it was not until we knew our time was limited that we felt comfortable lowering our normal defenses, finally letting our natural attractions take over.

The trick in terms of building a more ethically supportive social network is to force our evasive barriers down sooner and to do it in a context not so far removed from our daily life that any new relationship is impractical to sustain.

Another way to extend our social network along ethical lines is to join one of the many local self-help groups proliferating across the American landscape.

In every state of the country, there are literally thousands of so-called "support groups," each dedicated to helping people resolve a particular kind of problem. Some are dedicated to assisting members to overcome a temporary crisis—mourning the death of a close relative, for example, or being a newcomer in a strange community—others address themselves to a special psychological situation such as being an adopted child. There are support organizations which focus on spiritual or educational development, overcoming different physical illnesses, even groups to help high-level executives cope with the pressures of decision-making. In the state of Connecticut alone there are more than 200 completely different types of support groups, while total national membership is estimated at over fifteen million.[20]

What all these gatherings have to offer is a fellowship of potential friends and associates, who not only provide helpful information relevant to the particular focus of the group, but who, by their very involvement, tend to share the kind of ethical values which encourage more honest self-expression. Indeed, an early study of self-help groups, published in the journal *Psychotherapy: Theory, Research, and Practice*,[21] found the opportunities they afforded for cultivating a supportive network of personal relationships to be unmatched anywhere. Adding that many group members had gone to "therapists to whom they paid thousands of dollars for help they needed but did not receive," the author of the report concluded by confiding how "moving, thrilling, and inspiring [it is] to participate in a meeting in which . . . members describe the help they have received from their fellowship."

Previously I quoted Donald Seibert, the former J. C. Penney executive. I mention him again because of the credit he gives his own involvement with an executive support group for helping him operate with greater integrity and courage over the years, especially when making tough career decisions.

". . . these 'silent partners' . . . may not work beside you and may have no direct say in whether you get the next promotion that comes along," he says. "But the strength they can inject into your life may be more valuable in the long run for your career than all the business guidance you could glean from any corporate colleague or mentor."[22]

(There are more than forty-three regional non-profit clearing houses across the United States which keep track of many self-help groups in their areas and will be more than happy to help you match your own particular interests with the right group in your area—or perhaps join with others to start one of your own. A list of these regional clearing houses is available by writing the National Self-Help Clearing House, 33 West 42nd Street, New York, NY 10036.)

However we cultivate a more authentic social network—by selectively emphasizing existing relationships, attracting others through greater honesty in relatively safe social situations, joining a support group, or some combination of the three—the effect is a dramatic reduction in the frequency and intensity of our fearful thoughts. Our perpetually suspicious attitudes and sense that life is an endless series of pitfalls dissolve automatically over time and, with their disappearance, many of the tensions and nervous pressures we had almost come to accept as a normal way of life.

The impact of ethically improved relationships on the incidence of fear may still be news to conventional psychiatry, but in the related field of behavioral medicine it is interesting to note the increasing emphasis on bolstering the moral tone of a patient's social life as a means of treating stress-related disorders, such as insomnia, asthma, ulcers, and phobias. According to this approach, sometimes called Social Support Intervention,[23] someone who suffers any of these psychosomatic symptoms is encouraged to examine the quality of his relationships with family, peers, teachers, and business associates. Therapy, in turn, includes not only the usual prescriptions for rest and medicine, but a deliberate effort to cultivate a more trusting and supportive social environment.

In fact, treating fear and its psychosomatic symptoms through the ethical refinement of one's personal life is one of medicine's oldest treatments. Plato himself was so convinced of the relationship between fear and what we today would call "lifestyle" that he advocated corrective education at the earliest age.[24] Plato's twelfth-century successor, Moses Maimonides, advised the "perplexed" of his own time to remember how much his "character traits and actions are influenced by his neighbors and friends,"[25] while Francis Bacon said that the best way to clear the "wood of suspicions" is to cultivate the art of "frank communication," which separates man's "base" relationships from those that are "true."[26]

These sages also knew that the courage which flows from the ethical reconstruction of our personal relationships extends well beyond the boundaries of this newfound community, even to the company of people with whom we once felt the need to be most evasive. Part of this clearly stems from knowing that we have established a psychological base camp, to which we can always turn for support and sympathy whenever we feel under attack in the larger world. A part, too, stems from the extra measure of confidence that automatically comes with investing less of our energies in evasive deception.

But there is also the discovery that no one—save ourselves—can really stifle the genuine expression of our honest intentions and that every attempt to be true to ourselves is ultimately rewarded, though in ways we cannot always predict.

What can be predicted, to paraphrase Dickens, is that our life contains as much potential for great joy as it does for paralyzing fear. And whether we finally see ourselves living in "the best of times" or "the worst of times" will depend, in the end, on our willingness to be seen.

# Chapter 9

----

# *BEYOND FRUSTRATION*

His own manners will be his punishment.

CICERO[1]

The employer generally gets the employees he deserves.

SIR WALTER BILBEY[2]

The well-dressed gentleman has been reduced to tears.

He has spent months trying to interest his "good-for-nothing" nephew in a real job; but just at the moment when a position has opened up at a nearby plant where a friend has an in, everything has suddenly fallen apart. Not only didn't the nephew show for his scheduled interview, he managed to get in trouble by making a pass at the boss's daughter. And now there's news that the nephew has cracked up the uncle's car—into the back of a police car. No one is optimistic that the boy will be able to pay for the repairs anytime soon: the checks he wrote last week have just bounced at the bank.

Seen from the safe distance of a movie screen or the pages of a novel, such a chaotic scenario is easily the stuff of comedy. We could easily imagine John Hillerman or Colonel Hall from the old Bilko television show playing the incensed, if well-intentioned, uncle.

But when we ourselves are reduced to a gnashing of teeth by a colleague who has spoiled our best-laid plans or by friends who don't live up to expectations or by a spouse who consistently disappoints us or children who don't respond to our enlightened parenthood, our own reactions are anything but humorous. We've all felt the constricted chest pains and helpless rage that go with a chronically frustrating relationship.

The great therapist Plato was certainly no stranger to this feeling. Between the obstruction of politically minded rivals and the many students who failed to live up to their early promise, he probably experienced more than his share of indigestion.

Plato had come to see rather early on, however, that the real cause of our most frustrating situations lies, not in the failings of others, but in our own misguided attempts to change and persuade them through dishonest manipulation. He had once witnessed the ruler of a country foolishly try to cajole some friends of an enemy into giving up their leader, only to end up being captured by them;[3] and the incident left a profound impression.

Plato's seventeenth-century successor, the English politician and philosopher Francis Bacon, was even more explicit on the causes of personal frustration, perhaps because he had witnessed—and experienced—so much of it during his own long rise to political office under Queen Elizabeth and, later, as Lord Chancellor under James I. The failed intrigues of the queen's niece Mary Stuart, the eventual imprisonment and execution of the infamous charmer, the Earl of Essex, Bacon's own brief jailing in the London Tower on charges of fixing a court case—all resulted from backfired schemes for personal advancement. Bacon came to see that any form of flattery, cattiness, or intimidation was a "base" art, for while it gave the illusion of advancing our interests, the end result was usually to mobilize greater resistance.[4]

"Base art" probably is a bit too gothic for today's ethical therapist. Most prefer phrases like *game playing, covert manipulation,* or simply *manipulation,* though this last label could apply to any of our judgmental or deceitful habits. The word *scheming* is the most descriptive word, focusing as it does on our deliberate manipulation of someone else's emotions in order to achieve some hidden long-term agenda.

Whatever we call our scheming, we would have to admit that the philosophers' warnings do not diminish its appeal. Hardly a day goes by when we aren't tempted to say or do things for some unstated effect, all the while pretending complete ignorance of our real intention.

The woman who takes her revenge against the person she resents by confiding a piece of gossip to a third person she knows will spread it . . . the man who tells the girl he really wants to date how much money he's spending on his current steady . . . the executive who deflects a rival by deliberately bringing up some embarrassing subject in front of the boss . . . the woman who draws her husband's attention to the newspaper article on "Wives' Biggest Complaints" because she finds it "interesting"—certainly we can identify with at least one of these everyday manipulative scenarios.

The illusion that we can really get away with this kind of emotional prodding is actually encouraged by the persistent journalistic popularization of behaviorist theories, which suggest that any person's desires can be altered through the subtle application of praise and blame. Professional behaviorists are quick to say they do not approve of laymen using such covert methods to secretly condition other people, but the assumption that this is indeed a realistic possibility remains seductively unchallenged.

What is not so clear in our temptation to manipulate others is the hidden flaw in every covert strategy. For no matter how clever our approach, no matter how effectively we think we can coax or intimidate our targets, we can never completely mask our intention. We may be able to play a fine verbal game of emotional pinball, but non-verbally we always betray some hint of a hidden agenda.[5] The high-pitched voice that usually accompanies our dishonest statements[6]—the guarded posture, altered eye movements, and animated gestures—puts any potential victim instantly on alert.

Our manipulation is always doomed to backfire in frustrating failure, because the only people who will continue to play along after such blatant biological warning signs are the very ones who have some inclination to manipulate us, ultimately upsetting our covert intentions.

This is not to say that other people have some kind of ESP which enables them to interpret the exact motives behind our body language. But neither do they play along without at least some unconscious awareness of what we are up to.

One common example of how this works is given by therapist Joel Kanter[7] in describing the common dynamic of a family with a delinquent adolescent. "What you get a lot of the time," he explains, "is that there will be one parent, typically the mother, who'll be generous and read all the books about the [child's] problem." She'll know the technical terms for all the difficulties the son or daughter is going through and will be quite understanding about the slow course of therapy.

The father, meanwhile, takes the tough love approach. He complains that the "kid is just lazy" and thinks the boy ought to be out in the cold, cruel world fending for himself.

Often, says Kanter, the child is quite aware of the struggle between the parents and uses it to his own emotional advantage. Each of the parents thinks they are fighting with each other to control the child, but the child is really controlling them. This can be "quite an explosive situation," Kanter adds, since what you really have is three people trying relentlessly to manipulate each other: the mother by taking the side of the therapist, the father by being fed up, and the child by cleverly being the problem.

Outside the family, habitual manipulators are just as likely to end up attracting the very people—we'll call them *countermanipulators*—who are most likely to frustrate their expectations. Dr. Thomas Hora cites the case of a female client[8] who was continually rejected by the man she was determined to make fall in love with her. Her strategy was to make him like her by constantly boosting his ego, exaggerating the relative worth of everything he did.

Unfortunately, he was the type who was both insecure, yet prided himself on not being taken in by flattery. At first he always enjoyed the compliments, even encouraged them with calculated remarks about not being up to some job or responsibility. But the more she painted him into a superior position, the more his wariness of her support began to make him feel like a "helpless slob." No sooner did she get to the point of spending more time with him, when he would turn around and feel compelled to push her away again.

Even the well-meaning psychologist manipulator tends to attract the most frustrating and obstinate clients. Ethical therapist Jon Davidson, who began his psychological career as a Stanford-trained behaviorist, attributes part of his own conversion from conventional psychiatry to a slow and methodically boring client named Harry.

Jon recalls putting his client through some hypnotic exercises prior to conditioning therapy one weekday afternoon when the next thing he knew it was Jon himself who was being shaken awake. "We deduced that I must have been unconscious for some twenty minutes or so," Jon now admits, "quite asleep on my own hand. . . . I could not repress the meaning of such an incident; . . . I had finally turned off."[9]

Like every other application of ethical therapy, curing frustration begins with the willingness to experiment with the proper ethical discipline. In this case, the next time you get the idea that you can really control what somebody else thinks or does, decide instead to simply keep your mouth shut. Do whatever comes next (as long as it's not another manipulation), but see if you can stop yourself from trying to influence somebody else through covert means.

Don't talk up a vacation you know your wife doesn't want to take; don't try to intimidate your younger brother with terrifying visions of what happens to people who don't finish school; don't hype clients with false flattery or contrived expressions of interest in their well-being. Above all, don't pretend to have abstract intellectual discussions about what you secretly know to be an explosive emotional issue. In the words of Boston psychologist Terry Hunt, "don't just do something, *stand* there!"[10]

Hunt himself remembers working with a woman[11] so afraid of being criticized that she would constantly nag her boyfriend about being insensitive to her feelings as a way to prevent him from really saying what was on his mind. The irony, of course, was that after so much nagging, he became the very critic she feared.

"Basically," says Hunt, "ninety percent of him was supportive of her and only ten percent was critical." But the more she tried to control him by demanding attention for her feelings, "the more quickly he did get sick of her feelings. Believe me, he *really* got sick of her feelings."

Hunt's therapy in this case was literally to tell the woman to be quiet, so her boyfriend could have some space to express what he really felt. What she was surprised to discover was that he really did like her and support her, as long as he wasn't being manipulated into saying so.

A very different illustration, which nevertheless makes the same point, involves a teacher I used to know who was director of the fifth through eighth grade sections of a private day school. As with so many other educators, one of his most frustrating problems was that a certain percentage of students score very highly on intelligence tests, but spend most of their time getting into trouble and teetering on the edge of flunking out.

For years he had engaged in the familiar tactics of trying to change these boys' behavior. He would threaten them with letters to their parents, weekend study detention, and low deportment marks on their records. Finally it occurred to him that since these boys seemed to enjoy the attention of being the worst in their class, his scolding them was, in a very real way, only encouraging the problem. He decided to forget about trying to change these bright delinquents and simply promote them to the more advanced sections of the class. There they would have to either work harder just to stay in school or confront their parents with the fact that they'd finally flunked out. How much of this particular strategy contributed to the teacher's success is hard to measure, but I know that some years later he was made headmaster of an entire school.

We can begin to see from just these two examples that the power of forsaking manipulation to cure frustration lies in the fact that what appears on the surface to be mere passivity is, in reality, our opening the door to powerful corrective forces. "Self-discipline [has come to be] a dirty word in psychiatry," notes Joel Kanter.[12] "People associate it with conformity, restraining the individual, being a cog in a wheel." Yet the unique ability to say "no," he adds, is what sets man off from virtually every other creature on the planet. "That's what human beings do in the final analysis."

A martial arts metaphor might be helpful here. Just as bending with physical blows can often defeat an opponent more decisively than a frontal attack, so forsaking our psychological maneuvering can bring about the very positive outcome we have decided not to force. Instead of butting our heads in elaborate schemes to change an uncomfortable relationship, we stand back from the impulse to control and allow our intuitive wisdom (operating through whatever non-manipulative impulse that comes next) to take care of the situation for us.

Working on the final draft of this manuscript I had the interesting experience of listening to taped interviews with ethical therapists and researchers I had conducted as long as eight and nine years ago. I noticed there were several points in some of these early interviews where I was quietly but persistently pressing these people to give me the answers I wanted to hear based on my premature conclusions about the modern resurgence of ethical therapy. (Believe me, when you hear a recording or see a videotape of yourself trying to manipulate someone else, you'll understand immediately why the only people who will ever go along with it for any length of time are the countermanipulators who want to manipulate you.)

What I didn't discover until years later was that the very chapters which proved the most difficult to organize and execute were the ones where I was using material that came out of these forced interviews. By trying to get people to tell me what I wanted to hear I had only succeeded in wasting months of research and writing. Conversely, I have found in more recent years that my willingness to let research interviews follow the flow of shared interests and excitement will invariably advance my long-term progress, even if the direction appears to go far afield of my immediate concerns.

All this is not to say that forsaking manipulation will get us precisely what we think we're after, although in many cases it is true. Comedy writers intuit this in the familiar scene where some overbearing character—say our fictional uncle at the beginning of this chapter —gets so fed up with trying to change his nephew's incorrigible behavior that he finally gives up, usually in such an abrupt way that it causes the young man to start rethinking the error of his ways. Such fictionalized moments can be quite touching, even inspirational, because they anticipate a profound psychological truth.

But in real life it can also happen that the nephew does not reform right away. He may withdraw into himself or leave town, perhaps even continue acting irresponsibly as if nothing had happened. What can be said is that the ultimate outcome of our refusal to scheme will be as positive *as it is in our capacity to make it,* which in the case of the uncle could involve at least a modification of the nephew's reckless behavior or perhaps the realization that what he wanted from his nephew was really available somewhere else.

At the very least, our willingness to ban our emotional manipulation of others produces an extraordinary lightness and peace of mind. For what at first seems like surrender or inaction ends up restoring an almost forgotten sense of vitality and enthusiasm. All that scheming, it turns out, took up much more time and effort than we thought, energy which is now available for new and more satisfying interests.

A singer I know recalls being involved some years ago with a man who was constantly cheating on her. She did everything she could to make the relationship work. She gave up her career to travel with him, made scenes at parties, even tried tolerating her knowledge of his affairs. It was only when she decided to let him go, she recalls, that "everything turned around."

It wasn't that he suddenly became a better man or said he was now working to keep the relationship together. But in the process of accepting the separation, she found that many other troublesome situations in her life began to resolve themselves almost spontaneously; and people who formerly had aggravated her became mere minor annoyances. Her tendency to become periodically enraged disappeared almost as if by magic, and even physical complaints, such as heartburn and indigestion, started to subside.

And if conquering frustration means understanding that the best outcome is not exactly the one we imagined, it also means understanding that the disengagement can take time, especially when we are trying to break a long-standing manipulative pattern. The countermanipulators in our lives who have grown accustomed to our scheming attentions will not always appreciate the sudden silent respect; and many will try to tempt us back into the game by holding out the hope that just a little more manipulation on our part might finally bring them around to our point of view.

Anyone who has ever worked with a juvenile offender knows exactly the kind of reaction I'm talking about. Just when you've heard all the excuses you can tolerate and you're finally ready to send him to jail yourself, the delinquent minor will often do or say just the right thing to get your hopes up for still one more round of badgering and broken promises.

A really good countermanipulator may even up the stakes by switching from promises to intimidation, suggesting that if we don't persist in our manipulation things may actually get worse. It is not at all unusual for the mother who gives up trying to control her rebellious daughter to see the girl's behavior become still more provocative and outrageous for a time. Similarly, the executive who stops cajoling a malingering employee may find the worker temporarily taking even longer sick leaves. There are even extreme examples where we find we have gotten involved with a countermanipulator—often a jilted lover— who threatens suicide if we do not continue the game.

The important thing in handling a stubborn countermanipulator, many ethically oriented therapists say, is to stand back and take a hard look at the person you're dealing with and what he or she is really capable of. In cases where your desire to end a manipulative relationship is tied up with a legitimate concern for your own rights or property, it is important to set down rules you yourself can enforce without having to depend on the person you've given up trying to control. For instance, the uncle in our fictitious example would do well to get his car back from the wild nephew, just as the man who decides to stop indulging his unpredictable girlfriend should think seriously about canceling the credit card he lent her.

A more relevant example for many people would be the common case of a family with a malingering older son who, though he lives away from home, comes back every few weeks to raid the family refrigerator, sleep around for days, and be generally grouchy. The family may have finally realized that their efforts to coax the boy's rehabilitation have only backfired and that the aggravating inconvenience of their indulgence has got to stop. Yet to really break the pattern someone's got to lay down the rules and say, "Hey, we feel this behavior is rude and inconsiderate. If you would like to come over, call first and see if anyone is home, like anyone else would."

Where the temptation to continue the game is based on the countermanipulator's supposed vulnerability, a closer inspection of all the circumstances will usually allay our doubts. If the person who claims to be helpless without our constant help and attention has no trouble traveling around town when he or she wants to score a dope deal, for example—or the boyfriend who "desperately needs another loan" always seems to have enough cash to bet on the horses—we can feel pretty confident in putting a stop to the manipulative merry-go-round.

Even people who seem incredibly stupid or insensitive will prove remarkably receptive to our firmness over the long run. Dr. Kanter recalls the time he ran a day treatment program for some people who appeared "pretty spaced out."[13] The immediate problem was the mess caused by their chain-smoking.

"They dropped ashes all over the place, burning the furniture," he recalls. "One guy who appeared catatonic, [made] the longest ashes I've ever seen. [He] dropped them most of the time, always missing the ashtray. The others wouldn't put out butts, leaving ashtrays [full] of smoking cigarettes."

Because the patients seemed so unable to cope, Kanter tried the whole gamut of manipulative strategies, at first asking sweetly, then finally nagging people to do it; but nothing worked. Finally Kanter announced that the "slightest violation of smoking etiquette—dropping any ash or butt" and the offending patient would have to go home for the rest of the day. "I had to do it once every six months," he remembers, "[but] I did it, even though the guy [I sent home] usually protested that 'it was just an ash.' It was just incredible to see how people who seemed unable to control this behavior suddenly seemed able to control it."

(It is not recommended that we unilaterally face down the helplessness or suicidal threats of a relative who is institutionalized or diagnosed as severely mentally disturbed. Although we may suspect that part of the supposed illness is really countermanipulative footdragging —and such intuitions are often correct—the situation is potentially unstable enough to benefit from outside guidance. One of the few excellent resources along this line is *Coping Strategies for Relatives of the Mentally Ill*, available from The National Alliance for the Mentally Ill.[14]

Of course, there are times when we will be genuinely unsure of the line that divides the self-frustrating manipulation of others from legitimate domestic and executive responsibilities. Is it scheming when a parent tries to divert a child's attention from a painful wound or the picture of a pornographic scene? Does a factory manager manipulate when he sets up a graded schedule of incentives to improve worker productivity?

It is impossible in the space of a book to distinguish every downright manipulative scheme from an honest parental duty or responsible motivational strategy, but there are four telltale questions which we can ask ourselves in almost every ambiguous case.[15]

First, and most important, "What is my priority in this situation —to do what feels appropriate, regardless of the outcome, or to engineer a particular result?" A responsible action always reflects the former, because being true to our own needs and perceptions is the only thing over which we really have any real control. Manipulation, on the other hand, places its primary emphasis on enforcing our expectation of how others should behave . . . the one goal over which we have the least influence and, therefore, leads to the most disappointment.

Second, "In trying to persuade this person, am I relying on arguments that I myself believe?"

Third, "Am I giving this person options or orders?" Covert manipulation is always recognizable from the tendency to rush others into quick decisions; the responsible motivator allows people an opportunity to think things through for themselves.

Finally, "Am I respecting confidences?" Whether in business or private life, the willingness to betray confidences is an excellent indicator that our intention is manipulative.

As we begin to practice asking ourselves these questions, it can also be helpful to take some time and reflect on the history of our most frustrating and difficult relationships. Who were these people and how were we attracted to them—as friends, lovers, business associates? What kept us going even when we knew we were no longer getting anything out of the relationship?

What we usually find is that our temptation to manipulate follows a predictable pattern. Some of us prefer to control others by playing the role of insightful helper; others by intellectual browbeating or feigning helplessness or by complaining or through guilt or by being overly responsible or even by physical intimidation.

Such is the appeal of our favorite manipulative strategy that it has an almost magnetic quality and can be repeated through a long series of frustrating and destructive relationships. No sooner does a plant manager have to fire a basically intelligent engineer who, despite all the manager's efforts, "just never quite got it together to do the job" when the first man he hires to fill the post is another smart guy "just down on his luck." The same thing frequently happens to women who find themselves going from the failed reform of one "lost puppy-dog" man to another.

Fortunately it is possible to break these patterns[16] if we are willing to be honest with ourselves about what our preferred manipulation is. Such insight gives us the power to stop a potentially frustrating manipulation before it begins, or at least before it ever reaches the point where it begins to backfire. Simply by "becoming aware of your character," says Hunt,[17] "you have some hope of avoiding acting it out. . . . [You'll] get to know other people in a new way and to bring a little more adventure into your life, rather than [making] life into a project."

Finally there is the inevitable question of what we do about the challenge of the benevolent lie. It is one thing to give up covert manipulation if our motives are strictly selfish. We can see that any personal gain we hope for is more than offset by the inevitable aggravation and decide, whatever the consequences, it is better to be honest.

But what if our manipulative motives are altruistic? What do we say to an actor friend, for example, who has just bombed on his stage debut at the community theatre? Do we really tell him what the audience was whispering between the acts? More to the point, what would we tell that same friend if we knew he had a serious illness, but feared revealing our secret opinion of his chances could make things worse?

What makes such choices so difficult, of course, is the purity of our intention. "What could it hurt to lie," we legitimately ask ourselves, "if it makes someone else feel better? It's not as if we're playing on their emotions for personal gain, at least not the kind of gain we need to be ashamed of."

Many ethical therapists have tried to address this question over the years, although few with greater clarity than the eminent Harvard physician Richard C. Cabot. Practicing medicine during the early part of the twentieth century, Cabot was increasingly disturbed by the willingness of colleagues to use placebos, bread pills, colored water, or hickory ash powders, to give the illusion of medical cures. However effective such treatments might be, he argued, they were still calculated lies, with all their subtle pitfalls.

At first, many well-meaning physicians were offended by Cabot's criticism. After all, there was no doubt that placebos could treat a wide range of symptoms, at least for a time; and in this early period when pharmacology was still an infant science such manipulation was not only one of the few reliable medical treatments—in some cases, it seemed the *only* treatment available.

Cabot replied calmly that his criticism of placebos had been misunderstood. The issue wasn't *whether* to take advantage of the patients' mind but *how*. Was it really more compassionate to employ a deceptive placebo he asked, when, for all the times it worked, it could just as easily backfire when patients discovered the ruse? ". . . for us as professional men to have our reputations rest on the expectation of not being found out," he explained, was to invite the disastrous situation where a suspicious public would respond as negatively to a legitimate treatment as it once responded positively to water solutions and sugar-coated pills.[18]

The very same might be said of any modern altruistic dilemma. For us as would-be helpers to prop up a friend with falsehoods is to invite a situation where the other person will eventually respond as negatively to our honest feelings as he or she once seemed to appreciate our phony encouragement.

The measure of authentic altruism is not the ability to tell white lies but the willingness to communicate our concern and honest perception in a constructive way: in the case of the failing actor friend to provide the criticism he needs to improve his stage technique or, for the person who is sick, to extend the kind of support, empathy, and understanding he or she really requires. As Cabot reminded his own colleagues, "No patient whose language we can speak, whose mind we can approach, needs a placebo."[19]

In helping others, as in helping ourselves, the key to success lies not in manipulating the outcome we think we want, but in discovering the subtle blessings that always flow in the direction of ethical discipline.

# Chapter 10

---

## BEYOND LONELINESS

Will I never cease setting my heart on shadows and
following a lie?

ST. AUGUSTINE[1]

The worst thing that ever happened to me was when
I was eighteen years old and read Dale Carnegie's
book, *How to Win Friends and Influence People.* I
memorized his principles and began to use them very
successfully. But . . . this approach led to a tremendous sense of isolation, because I could see I was
using a technique on my friends. . . . That was a
real trap where social success was existential failure.

ANONYMOUS[2]

Loneliness is the quiet killer.
Quiet because so few of us ever complain of it, at least not openly.

In a society that prides itself on the instant companionship of singles bars, town meetings, and retirement communities, we are ashamed to admit that we ourselves can be the victims of what is, in fact, a very common problem. One in six Americans,[3] if the demographers are right, do not have even a single friend in whom they can confide their personal problems; and 40 percent of us would describe ourselves as suffering from shyness and feeling isolated.[4]

Loneliness is a killer because it is such a determining factor in the health and longevity of anyone who suffers from it. For years it has been linked to ulcers, high blood pressure, asthma, colitis, migraines, and skin rashes;[5] but newer studies have expanded this list to include virtually all stress-related disorders.[6] That smoldering rage at being left out of things[7]—"imprisoned in glass," as one therapist put it[8]—has even been implicated in higher cancer rates[9] and mortality following breast cancer diagnosis.[10]

The typical response to loneliness is to think we should be spending more time with other people. Americans part with literally billions of dollars every year just to be in the midst of a noisy group. We go on cruises, join racket clubs, take field trips, stand in crowded streets on New Year's Eve—we even marry people we don't really love just to have the sense of someone else being close to us.

If all this togetherness seems to have a frenetic quality, it is largely to mask the fact that merely being physically close to another person does not do much to solve the problem. College students tend to be among the loneliest people of all social groups, even though they are daily exposed to large numbers of potential friends and without any of the conventional social or vocational restrictions.[11] Many wealthy and powerful men and women are surrounded by people all the time, yet still wonder to themselves, "Is that all there is?" And surely there is as much isolation within "empty shell" marriages as there is among singles.

If the solution were simply a matter of having company, then everyone who suffered a divorce or death of a spouse would be equally damaged by the loss, yet this is clearly not the case. Although virtually all divorced and widowed people do experience an initial period of grief,[12] some continue feeling lonely for years while others rebound in just months. "There may be a prolonged adjustment period to something like divorce," notes Columbia University researcher Jeffrey Young,[13] "and we don't know at exactly what point [the initial] loneliness becomes a life pattern or problem [for some people] . . . but in general we are talking about two different animals."

We might also expect that elderly people, many of whom have lost friends and family and who are retired from the stimulation of a daily working community, would suffer the most from loneliness. Yet one of the striking findings of recent years has been a New York University study which found that "elderly respondents were significantly *less* lonely than young respondents."[14] Older people, moreover, tend to be close to the friends they do have, are more satisfied with their friendships, participate in more social activities, watch less TV, and are far less reliant on drugs and alcohol than virtually any other group.

We make a final mistake when we try to pin our loneliness on urbanization, the decline of the extended family, and all the other supposed ills of modern civilization. In spite of the popular romantic idea that we could somehow eliminate isolated feelings by returning to a simpler past, studies suggest little difference in the loneliness of people in small households versus those from larger families or the loneliness of city dwellers versus those who live in the country.[15]

Indeed, one of the most striking descriptions of loneliness comes, not from modern sources, but from the Carthaginian bishop Augustine[16] (354–430) who, in recalling the years before his famous conversion, tells of feeling increasingly isolated. There was one day in particular, while preparing a speech in praise of the Roman emperor, "intending that it should include a great many lies," when he noticed a cheerful beggar in the streets. Contrasting their two attitudes, the beggar's so happy and his own so miserable, Augustine could not help but "realize how utterly wretched [he] was."

What makes Augustine's account so remarkable is not only the honesty of his emotion but the clarity of his self-diagnosis. Writing in his *Confessions,* he tells how from his earliest years, he had learned to get ahead by mimicking the expectations of social authorities. By his thirties he had parlayed his position from an obscure teacher in the backwaters of Carthage to a prestigious appointment at the University of Milan. He was consorting with nobles, laying plans for an expedient marriage to a wealthy Roman heiress, lobbying for still higher office—all the while painfully aware of the empty "tumult in [his] breast."

This identification of role-playing as the chief cause of loneliness, is one of the strongest themes in the history of ethical therapy and can be traced all the way back to Plato's condemnation of the sophists, those traveling teachers of ancient Greece who specialized in providing rhetorical skills to the children of the wealthy. Plato also went as far as to warn against the influence of theatrical productions, because he felt they encouraged people to substitute imitation for genuineness.[17]

Even during the recent reign of twentieth-century "value-free" psychoanalysis and behavior modification, there have always been sensitive and perceptive therapists who spoke out against what they considered a neglected cause of patient suffering. In 1942, the innovative Boston psychoanalyst Helene Deutsch coined the phrase *as-if personality disorder* to describe clients whose "relationship to life has something about it which is lacking in genuineness and yet outwardly runs along 'as if' it were complete."[18] According to Deutsch, as-if behavior was typified by extreme conformity to social expectations, frequent substitution of one close relationship for another, lack of strong feelings (coupled with an ability to simulate the appearance of strong feeling), easy suggestibility—all culminating in a persistent sense of social isolation.

The case against role-playing was taken up again in the mid-1960s by University of Florida psychologist Sidney M. Jourard, who argued that intense loneliness could be directly attributed to a person's hiding behind restrictive domestic and professional masks—masks that may be supported and approved by family, schools, and a variety of social institutions, yet roles which never do justice to the person beneath it. "Broadly speaking," Jourard said, "if a person plays his roles suitably, he can be regarded [by others] as a more or less normal personality. *Normal personalities, however, are not necessarily healthy personalities.*"[19]

The only reason we have any trouble seeing the problem, he added, is that habitual role-playing "is a sickness which is so widely shared that no one recognizes it."[20] Indeed, many people actually see role-playing as a *cure* for loneliness, thinking that others will love them more for behaving in a certain way. They are completely unaware of how (as we saw in the last chapter) all such manipulation tends to backfire over the long run—in this case, pushing the people we want to have closer further and further away from us.

Today it has become clear, even to many conventional therapists, that lonely people are characterized by an obsession with social norms and expectations.[21] Teachers and social workers who complain of feeling isolated and "without meaning in their lives," for example, are inevitably wedded to some rigid image of their professional role. The same can also be said of troubled adolescents, particularly chemically dependent drug and alcohol abusers. Family therapists increasingly report finding that the loneliest people they have to deal with are teenage children caught up in trying to play out some rigidly defined family role.

When lonely people do experience some warmth in their lives, it tends to come through some unexpected event—a promotion, a move, a family illness—that forces an unexpected lowering of the guard.[22] Sometimes it takes being temporarily trapped in an elevator or witnessing an accident for the habitual role-player to feel any sense of intimacy with the people he sees every day.

But the most interesting evidence of all comes from the testimony of lonely people themselves. For most who enter therapy already *know* the cause of their problem, even before they walk through the door. Many complain in the very first sessions about the personal price they have to pay for hiding behind their "safe" domestic or professional masks.

"I'm anxious and depressed, and I get depersonalized," said one intelligent twenty-nine-year-old woman who presented herself for therapy.[23]

"I'm dying on the inside, but all my students think I've really got it together," said a professor who had just won the Teacher of the Year Award.[24]

A man I know who frequently complains about feeling alienated and out of place is quite articulate about the circumstances which brings on his sense of isolation. "It's whenever I put a hat on . . . whenever I think of what a father or husband or businessman is supposed to be."

Unfortunately, just knowing the cause of the problem is not

enough to cure it, for most of the roles we have learned to play over the years do have a payoff. The workaholic may find a good performance report less satisfying than a real relationship, but at least he has a fat paycheck to fall back on. Similarly, the model student who discovers that good grades do not always compensate for empty weekends can console himself with the perception that he is making some kind of academic progress. Even the negative role of the class buffoon or dumb bimbo or wimp or loser at least provide the player with an ability to predict and control certain uncomfortable social situations.

Indeed, those who do seek professional help for their loneliness are quite up front about looking for a way to either continue their act or, if they are a little more daring, to get a better part.[25] "[Lonely] people aren't looking for change," says Victoria Brundage. "They're looking for relief."[26] Family therapist Harold Goolishian agrees that with loneliness, as (he believes) with most psychological problems, "people are looking for reinforcement of their position."[27]

The therapist says, in effect, "You don't like your symptoms, and you know they are connected with your role-playing. So if you want to feel better, you're going to have to drop that mask."

To which the lonely client invariably answers: "I'd rather have the tranquilizers, please, so that I can go on with what I'm doing."

Even people playing one of the most demeaning roles of all, the psychiatric inpatient, resist any opportunity to get rid of their masks. Therapist Jon Davidson recalls his own experience as a resident in the Palo Alto VA hospital. The patients there "were ineffably lonely. I had never felt that sort of thing before, and I've never felt it since. [Yet] I cannot, in truth, recall a single incident where a patient wanted *contact* with a doc. To be sure, patients would initiate, would knock on a doctor's door. But inevitably the reasons were pragmatic: they simply wanted something the doctors had, (a pass or pill), but never was it love."[28]

In this sense, our lonely role-playing is very much like our insecure perfectionism, which is why the two traits so often appear in the same person. Just as the perfectionist in us thinks if we were just a little better we could feel more worthwhile, so we constantly embellish our roles in the hopes of finally getting them right. If only we could appear the kind of person we think others expect—more amusing, more domestic, more attractive, more competent—then all the rest of our needs will be met, or at least enough of them to compensate for the lack of genuine warmth and intimacy.

Unfortunately, much of this tends to get rationalized in very respectable language. We're not role-playing, we're just meeting our responsibilities as providers and loyal workers.

A thirty-five-year-old attorney whose superficial mannerisms left him feeling "weak, dependent . . . inferior and helpless" nevertheless took great pride in being recognized as the most charming and popular performer of his firm. Even when his growing dependence on amphetamines and increasingly destructive arguments with his wife made it clear that something about his life was a charade, he still clung to the trappings of his superficial facade.[29]

A therapist friend of mine, Claudia Sissons, notes that it is psychologists, social workers, and physicians who are particularly susceptible to this kind of rationalizing. "Because we're in a position of helping others," she says, "it's easy to hide behind the position that we're always working when we are with other people, even when we're supposed to be relaxing. I've got to admit I can get that way myself."

What no role-player really understands until his loneliness has become unbearable is that the emotional cost of hiding one's true self behind an elaborate script cannot be maintained at a constant level. At some point we must either surrender our roles or risk sinking further down into the depths of isolated despair. Like that character in Oscar Wilde's *The Picture of Dorian Gray* who exchanges his identity with the portrait of his youthful charm, every year that we continue to carry off some phony role, the picture of our inner life becomes more hideous and grotesque. The truth is that no man who looks upon himself as a thing can feel safe from the depths of desolation.[30]

The cure for loneliness begins with our taking a moment to distinguish more clearly between being responsible and using the idea of responsibility as a cover for needless role-playing. For giving up our social masks does not mean doing a less effective job at work or refusing to do our civic duties or abandoning our children every time they misbehave.

Indeed, it is quite possible to surrender all our superficial pretenses, yet remain completely faithful to our job description or the fundamental commitments of a personal relationship.

How is this possible?

As the American sociologist Erving Goffman once observed, people not only assume social responsibilities, they also play *at* their responsibilities, fulfilling personal and professional commitments with varying degrees of style.[31] Take the case of two nurses. One nurse responds stoically to patients' complaints, always wears a neatly pressed uniform, and knows every hospital regulation by heart; the other takes time to be sure her charges are comfortable, doesn't mind being rumpled by a friendly hug, and bends the rules if it means everyone is going to be a little happier. Both do the same job, both get the same pay, yet their day-to-day conduct is as different as night and day.

The point to be made is that the responsibilities implied by any position, even the requirements of being a surgeon or a high public official, still provide us with an enormous amount of leeway. Whether we take this freedom as simply the context for greater self-expression or decide instead to mimic safe, stereotyped expectations is strictly a personal decision completely unrelated to duty, professional competence, or anything else . . . save our own sense of isolation.

Indeed, it can even be argued that the concept of responsibility not only allows for a great deal of self-expression, but actually requires it. What does the concept of responsibility mean, after all, but the *ability to respond.* Respond to what? In part to the explicit commitments we've made to the people we love and to our jobs; but it also means the ability to respond to ourselves—to the wisdom we derive, not from any job description or traditional role model, but from our intuitive connection to a deeper intelligence.

We've already seen in the chapter on perfectionism how so much of what we call job *excellence* stems from a willingness to go beyond rigid rules and stereotypes. While most of the research on this is still confined to entrepreneurs and senior executives, there are still enough anecdotes about secretaries who develop an "instinct" for their bosses' needs—or about some off-duty policeman who prevents a bank robbery because he "sensed" something was wrong when he happened to gaze from the street through the lobby window—to demonstrate the importance of spontaneous initiative at all levels of responsibility.

Another way to appreciate the intuitive side of responsibility is to look at the parody of its opposite. One of the most crippling and destructive tactics, often used with great effect by civil rights and labor organizers, is the so-called "Rule Book" slowdown. This is when groups engage in a protest, not by quitting their jobs, but by obeying every single rule and regulation they're supposed to be operating under. It only takes a few people doing exactly what they should be doing to bring an entire business or government bureau to its knees.

Clearly in the realm of personal relationships it is hard to imagine that we can be responsible to those we love without responding to the unique insights and intuitions for which no prefabricated role or social expectation could ever adequately prepare us. At least that's the factor which, more than any other, appears to contribute to the longevity of most marriages. Reporting on their study of "Marriages That Last" in the 1985 issue of *Psychology Today*[32], for example, researchers Jeanette and Robert Lauer found that the most enduring relationships were those in which partners tended to ignore conventional stereotypes of how a husband or wife ought to act and placed a greater emphasis on being responsive to their inmost selves.

Based on interviews with just over 350 couples who had been married for at least fifteen years, the Lauers found that men and women in successful marriages not only felt freer to be themselves, but were greatly valued for it. One typical comment came from a man, married for thirty years, who said his wife had grown so much during that time it was like being married to a series of different women. "I have watched her grow and have shared with her both the pain and exhilaration of her journey. I find her more fascinating now than when we were first married."

There is finally, and most importantly, the responsibility we have to ourselves, to our likes and dislikes, loves and hates, to the pace and style with which we resonate. These inner preferences are not some psychological sideshow, but the very incarnations of our spirit, the conscious expression of who we are.

Not coincidentally, it is in being responsible to ourselves that we finally begin to conquer loneliness, for it is only by revealing our true personality that we have any chance of achieving genuine intimacy with another person. Any attempt to dress ourselves up, no matter how much praise or attention it appears to engineer from others, only succeeds in showering these benefits on the image of a self that doesn't really exist. How many times have we heard of a famous rock star or millionaire executive who committed suicide for want of one real friend?

Or to rephrase the point in more traditional terms, "What doth it profit a man, if he gain the whole world, and suffer the loss of his own soul?"[33]

Having seen that the removal of our phony masks is really quite compatible with our social responsibilities and that both are essential to the conquest of loneliness, we come to the heart of corrective therapy, which is our willingness to risk greater self-expression, both at work and in personal relationships. To begin this section on the positive note it deserves, let me pass on portions of an interesting clinical transcript that was brought to my attention years ago when I first began my research for this book.

It involved a forty-three-year-old engineer we'll call Ralph,[34] who remembers becoming isolated to the point where "my entire life was very much out of balance and not really worth living. I was scared. I felt I was drifting hopelessly toward a vast, merciless void."

Ralph knew that he had been basically dishonest about feelings most of his life, that he "expressed only the safe, positive type of thoughts and feelings, always burying the negative, dangerous, conflict-producing ones." But Ralph was afraid to give up the nice-guy image he secretly knew was "a powerful weapon" for winning arguments with his wife and boss. He felt it was better to stay lonely than to disturb the safe control he had over family, coworkers, and friends.

Then one day, in the midst of an argument with his wife, something in Ralph let go and he spontaneously "told her things I had kept inside myself for many long years. I knew I was taking a terrible risk; yet it felt good and right as I was saying these things for the first time. When I had gotten them all out, she said, 'Don't you think I didn't know those things already. By your actions, your innuendos, your silence?' I was amazed! Being totally honest with her did not destroy her or me; in fact, it brought us closer than we had ever been." For the first time, Ralph had let down his passive mask and the results, in his own words, "were amazing."

Turning to his job, Ralph again was hesitant. "I was risking, I thought, my entire economic security. But try it I did. I started by telling my boss in short simple terms that recent organizational change was increasing my workload beyond reason and that I couldn't operate under the situation. Two weeks later it changed significantly for the better. I also began to say 'No' at work to people asking me to do things which I didn't have to, or shouldn't have to do. I placed a large knife on my work desk, as a symbol of cutting out unnecessary trivia."

In less than a few months' time, Ralph's entire work situation changed dramatically. He was "not overburdened or overpressured. . . . The short-term payoff [allowed me] far more time for planning and creating, better relationships with co-workers and customers, better attitudes toward the job, and, perhaps, coincidentally, amazing successes in new sales."

I have included Ralph's story to illustrate the kind of unexpected intimacy we can begin to experience when we trust the undiluted expression of our intuitive thoughts and feelings. People we used to irritate become surprisingly accommodating, while others we might have feared are more open to our opinions.

This is true even at the top of the highest corporate towers. CEOs and business leaders may not "make a point of promoting it publicly," says executive-search consultant Jonathan McBride,[35] "but senior people know that those who act from the heart make better decisions."

At the same time it must be said that the results of Ralph's sudden and comprehensive self-therapy were unusually smooth and trouble-free. We all know stories about friendships that fell apart when one of the buddies decided to say what he really thought about some sensitive issue or women who got the silent treatment when they sought more closeness from a lover or bosses who acted resentful when they were no longer being flattered by subordinates; and such reactions *are* real possibilities in many situations.

But this is not the same as saying that overcoming loneliness is some kind of unpredictable crapshoot. For most of us have a pretty good intuitive sense about who we can open up to and who we can't; and those who get hurt by trying to be themselves with certain people almost always knew in advance something unpleasant was going to happen.

The real problem is that anyone who has been hiding behind a social mask for some length of time has attracted the very friends and business associates who themselves are resistant to intimacy. The intuitive fear we have that just "being ourselves" might cause more problems than it solves is a legitimate one that deserves to be respected, for our sudden refusal to play out the habitual role of dutiful son, obedient wife, omniscient professional or whatever else may very well aggravate the other actors on our stage who have become accustomed to playing off our part.

What is important to remember is that what is true of our immediate social universe is not true of the world at large. Indeed, even our own lonely world contains within it at least one or two people with whom we can begin to be more ourselves. Just as overcoming fear requires us to take an inventory of our existing relationships, deciding with whom we can safely risk revealing our true intentions, so overcoming loneliness, means taking a similar inventory to see with whom we can safely risk becoming more spontaneous. Not surprisingly, we will likely come up with the same list of names.

Once we know where to start, the only trick is to start small, resorting if necessary to some kind of regular plan. One therapist I know who used to live alone and whose work habits inclined her toward long hours with very taxing clients began to overcome her loneliness by actually scheduling regular conversations with one or two friends. With each call, she then made a point of revealing some personal problem or thought she might otherwise dismiss as "trivial" or "unimportant."

There was often some resistance before making these calls, she remembers. She would say to herself, "it can wait" or "it's not a good time." But it was her willingness to continue sharing the "stupid" and "dumb" things about herself on a regular basis which began to heal the empty feeling in her life.

"[My own] great breakthrough came," she says,[36] "[when I] realized I could share a part of myself that was different from what I grew up thinking and that it was right for me and that I could do that. I never knew [until then] that . . . there was a difference between a role and a person!"

Psychologist Charles Gourgey, a student of Dr. Hora's, describes such discipline as "the willingness to be embarrassed." It is "the only medicine that can heal a pretender," he adds. "If we are pretending, we are trying to preserve an image of ourselves that we know is false. If we are willing to be embarrassed, we become free of the tyranny of this false self-image."[37]

Fortunately, it doesn't take long to discover that what we have given the negative label of embarrassment is really the heat generated by a profoundly liberating psychological transformation. The tremor we feel in our voices whenever we begin sharing our true selves with a receptive listener is simply another word for excitement.

Connecticut therapist Donald Cohen[38] once told me the story of a young graduate student who had complained of feeling lonely ever since she could remember. It wasn't that she lacked people in her life. She came from a large family, lived with several girlfriends, and was dating an attractive if somewhat overbearing classmate.

The only problem was that everyone had cast her in the role of "the comedian, the one who made everyone feel good . . . she was never supposed to cry or have any feelings other than . . . bubbly enthusiasm." No one she knew was even aware of the late hours she spent writing short stories and serious essays or of the thick portfolio of sketches she had produced over the years.

Cohen's strategy was simply to have the girl bring some of her work into the office. He saw her sketches, read some of her stories, and encouraged her to see that there were other people in her life who would be as equally receptive to her serious side as he was. Once she got over this initial embarrassment of exposing her hidden self, there was a "tremendous" outburst of energy. "She asserted herself more . . . wrote more . . . ended the relationship with her boyfriend . . . [found time for] volunteer work in a hospital . . . she even stopped smoking."

As with overcoming fear, reaching out for the support of an ethical community—a church or synagogue fellowship, a support group organized around some particular interest or personal problem, or creating your own values focus group—is also enormously helpful. "Any one of them," says therapist Victoria Brundage, "can be a safe place for people to be trying out new things and getting good responses and discovering that different things do work."[39] The exact nature of the community is less important than our willingness to use it as a context for experimenting with more open self-expression.

How we expand our sense of intimacy from our initial inventory of friends and fellowship to the world at large is difficult to describe, for this is an intuitive process which varies from person to person. In some situations, it will mean letting our guard down a little more often than usual, in others it may mean making some well-considered changes in our work and relationships.

What can be said is that every time we stop role-playing in one sphere of our lives, we receive not only the courage to go on to the next, but the instinctive wisdom to do it right. To make those first small steps beyond lonely role-playing is to discover that the personality we tried so desperately to camouflage is really a magnet which, in fuller view, can attract boundless love and support.

# Chapter 11

---  ⤶

# *BEYOND ANXIETY*

How we respond to [anxiety] is what's important. It can be a signal about what's going on that we need to pay attention to. The question is how do you respond to it. Do you investigate it? Do you really pay attention to what's going on internally? Usually when you turn around and face it, it's like any fear   it'll diminish. The fear gets less and you'll discover what's there.

FRANCES VAUGHAN[1]

Sell your cleverness and buy bewilderment; cleverness is mere opinion; bewilderment is intuition.

JALAL-UDDIN RUMI[2]

Of all psychological problems, anxiety is probably the most misunderstood.

In the strictest sense, anxiety is not a problem at all, but a sign that we are in touch with our intuitive powers. In previous chapters we saw how the discipline of any judgmental or deceptive habit, no matter how beneficial, was often accompanied by apprehensive feelings and the temptation to backtrack. Whether we were trying to break resentment or arrogance or evasion or manipulative scheming, our first attempts were always accompanied by a certain anxious doubting and confusion.

The fact is that anyone who wishes to cultivate their intuitive wisdom must endure at least occasional anxiety over loss of control, for that is exactly what we are doing—surrendering conscious control of our lives to deeper powers. This is why Plato himself considered the confusion *(aporia)* of his students to be a positive sign and why so many of the great physicians who followed him over the centuries—Galen, Moses Maimonides, William James—all subscribed to his theory that "the greatest blessings come by madness, indeed by madness that is heaven-sent."[3]

This is also the reason why the great religious teachers have always advised their followers, in the words of *Ecclesiastes,* to "be not fainthearted in thy mind."[4] "If thou art in a state of perplexity," say the ancient stages of the Near East, "hasten not to cling to anything."

Unfortunately, "value-free" psychiatry has little positive to say about anxiety, for to admit some virtue in apprehensive doubt would be to undermine the objective approach common to all conventional therapies. Today's clinical graduate students are taught next to nothing about the ancient Asclepian healing temples of Plato's time, where patients were encouraged to indulge their anxious thoughts, or about the Greek Corybantic rites which resolved emotional conflicts in a catharsis of agitating music, or about the importance attached to anxiety by the generations of Near Eastern philosophers, doctors, and poets who kept Plato's therapeutic ideas alive during the long dark age from the fall of Rome to the Renaissance.

Jalal-uddin Rumi (1207–1273), the greatest of these Islamic ethical therapists,[5] became world famous for verses in which he extolled anxious bewilderment as "revelations of the Heart,"[6] "the ruin where [our treasure] lies buried,"[7] and the sea which, just when we think we are "drowned in [it] . . . carries [us] up to the surface. . . ."[8] Rumi's belief in anxiety as a gateway to higher wisdom is generally credited with inspiring therapeutic movements throughout the Mediterranean; and when he died his funeral was attended by representatives from every major religious and theological school of his day. "We esteem him as the Moses, the David, the Jesus of the age," said one Christian mourner. "We are all his followers and his disciples."[9]

If anything, conventional psychology only adds to our misunderstanding of anxiety by treating its very existence as a sign of pathology. Someone who says he feels "anxious" is automatically considered to be worse off than when he was free of the symptom. Yet even the carefully controlled world of "value-free" psychology occasionally betrays some unexpected evidence of the positive role anxiety can play in our emotional development.

Consider the embarrassment of the Kaiser Foundation Hospital in Oakland, California, a few years back when their psychiatric clinic was unexpectedly flooded with an unusually large number of requests for counseling. Because twenty-three applicants had to be placed on a six-month waiting list, staff psychologists decided to highlight the benefits of the hospital's program by comparing the progress of the 127 who had been treated against those who had been temporarily put on hold.

To everyone's surprise those who received no help in tranquilizing their anxieties, either through drugs or the assurance of regular counseling, improved at least as well as those in therapy. For all the supposed advantages of professional support and guidance, the experience of having to wait out one's anxieties proved at least as therapeutic as the most comforting psychiatric care the hospital could provide. "The therapy patients did not improve significantly more than did the waiting-list controls," the study's own authors had to admit.[10]

Then there was the case of British psychiatrist Ronald Laing, who shocked his colleagues during the mid-1960s with his unorthodox treatment of supposedly hopeless schizophrenics at London's Tavistock Clinic. Instead of trying to talk them out of their anxious delusions or drugging them into numbness with tranquilizers and anti-depressants, Laing actually encouraged his patients to indulge their disturbing thoughts, even living them out if they felt like it.

It was a courageous approach, to say the least. Some who had been suffering severe hallucinations became even more withdrawn; others yelled and carried on for hours at a time. But in the end the patients who gave in to their anxieties were much more likely to get better than those who kept trying to blank out disturbing thoughts.[11] (Roughly concurrent studies at Yale, the University of Washington, and other universities found that psychiatric inpatients who accepted their inner turmoil were the *most* likely to recover from debilitating emotional problems.)[12]

The late sixties and early seventies also saw a series of so-called "sensory deprivation" experiments, which required volunteers to lie quiet for long periods in closed laboratory environments that screened out all light, sound, and other external stimulation. Knowing that such isolation would automatically amplify any underlying anxieties the subjects might have, many researchers at first worried that some of them might be harmed by the experience; yet precisely the opposite happened. Not only did the initial results suggest a reduction in phobias and certain addictive habits,[13] but later "sensory deprivation" experiments proved helpful in treating disorders ranging from muscle tension to high blood pressure.

Predictably most of "value-free" psychiatry continues to ignore such incidents, treating anxiety as something that needs to be drugged, hypnotized, or otherwise psychologically mugged. But today's more sensitive counselors have learned through experience that anxiety is not the terrible threat we imagine. Connecticut psychologist Bruce Levi is just one of many therapists who, when patients complain of feeling anxious, will sometimes advise that they actually try feeling more anxious. Levi himself has suggested that clients schedule time for anxious thinking or take an anxious obsession and deliberately blow it out of proportion as a way of defusing the apprehension.[14]

Many others, like Jon Davidson, have come to see anxious thoughts as a positive development, an indicator that some kind of intuitive wisdom is knocking on the door of objective consciousness. Being told "one's anxiety responses are in fact unnecessary, irrelevant, and perhaps absurd," he believes, is a form of spiritual psychosurgery.[15]

Indeed, for all its stonewalling of traditional values, one of the few behavior modification techniques which has ever proved itself therapeutically effective is a treatment for phobias which relies heavily on the patient's deliberate acceptance of anxious thoughts. Called *system-*

*atic desensitization,* this method encourages subjects who panic at the sight of spiders, heights, closed spaces, or some other common fear to undertake a two-stage "phobia-reduction" program. First they are helped to calm down through a series of simple muscle relaxation techniques, then told to imagine fearful scenes which increasingly approximate the thing or situation they dread.

A typical series of sessions would involve a woman who is bothered by an overwhelming fear of snakes. At first she would be told to imagine just seeing the snake in a safe situation such as a glass cage. When this fantasy became comfortable enough, she might imagine a larger snake or begin looking at photos, first of small garden snakes and then of slithery anacondas. Finally she might make a trip to the snake exhibit in the local zoo, eventually being able to physically touch one of the reptiles without even flinching.

This kind of phobia therapy is quite common; and, of course, it is all neat and "value-free," at least on the surface. But a closer look at this unusually successful conventional therapy betrays two interesting features. First, the very process of therapy requires a radical suspension of judgment—about the meaning of the phobia, about our vulnerability at different stages of the process, and about the paradoxical nature of the therapy itself.

Second, while the preliminary relaxation does help patients to accept their anxious thoughts, relaxation alone has absolutely no effect on the reduction of phobias. The key to overcoming anxiety is the willingness to accept it, to endure the threatening thoughts and images until their power simply—and inevitably—dissipates.[16]

Of course, to say that anxiety is healthy is not to say that anxiety is fun. Certainly we should not be trying to cultivate any more of it than necessary or to make it last. "[We] have to be careful about not glamorizing anxiety," warns therapist Vaughan. "There's plenty of it around and I don't think we need to worry about getting rid of it."[17]

Unfortunately, this is what most of us are already doing. Much of what we call anxiety is really *hyperanxiety,* the attempt to arrest anxious thoughts with alcohol, drugs, prescription relievers, objective psychiatric analysis or, worst of all, by reverting to some old judgmental or manipulative habit. Because this only increases the separation of our controlling mind from our intuitive intelligence, our healthy anxiety becomes frustrated, and the disturbing undercurrent we thought we were avoiding becomes a chronic obsession.

As Carl Jung suggested to a group of ministers in 1932, most of our complaining about anxiety is really our complaining about the cumulative stress brought on by repeatedly balking at the crest of some intuitive breakthrough and retreating into familiar patterns of resentment, guilt, arrogance, or some other controlling manipulation. "Acceptance of [one's inner self]," he said, "is the essence of the moral problem and the acid test of one's whole outlook on life."[18]

One way to understand this is to remember how as children we played the game of tightly clenching our fist, then opening our hand to an uncomfortable tingling sensation. Now just as we learned that keeping our hand clenched to avoid this tingling only starves the capillaries and condemns us to even greater suffering when our grip finally tires, so preventing our normal anxiety from working its way through the system at the time it arises only condemns us to a more difficult psychological adjustment down the line.

Plato himself drew the famous analogy of a cave dweller slowly emerging from an underground prison to confront the light of day. Approaching the surface, he has the choice of retreating from the dazzling brightness or gradually letting his eyes adjust. If he responds to every encounter with a shaft of light by running all the way back into his hole again, his eyes might find some temporary relief in this white-knuckle retreat, but the net effect will be that he will always be living in a cave.

Fortunately, hyperanxiety is a reversible state.

The first and quickest medication is to share our disturbing thoughts with another person: a friend, minister, rabbi, psychologist, anyone else we feel we can trust to listen with a sympathetic and nonjudgmental ear. This has been a basic tenet of every religion, medicine, and folk wisdom throughout the ages, and for good reason. The very act of confiding anxious thoughts, regardless of the advice it elicits, has the immediate and automatic effect of terminating whatever unethical controls we have used to keep our anxious energies at a distance.

Dr. James Pennebaker, the Southern Methodist University psychologist whose research on deception and stress I referred to in the chapter on fear, has demonstrated the tranquilizing power of confiding anxious thoughts in a number of interesting ways. In a 1984 study, for example, Pennebaker and his associate Robin O'Heeron used coroners' files to contact thirty-one surviving spouses of recent suicide or accidental death victims.[19] Each was mailed a two-page questionnaire designed to measure the respondents' obsessive anxiety over the loss (i.e., the degree to which they constantly thought about the spouse's death), as well as their current state of health and the extent to which they had already confided their thoughts to some other person, such as a close friend. Attached to the survey was a personal letter requesting help in understanding how people cope after the unexpected death of a loved one.

Of the nineteen people who responded, Pennebaker and O'Heeron found a striking correlation between those who had kept their thoughts bottled up and the frequency of anxious rumination about the death. Even in cases where the survivors reported the same number of friends and other options for social support, those who refused to share their feelings actually suffered more anxiety for the effort. They also reported a greater number of stress-related health problems, such as pneumonia, vomiting, ulcers, and weight change.

What happens to such people when, having tried to control their anxiety for a period of months or even years, they suddenly decide to confide their feelings to someone else? And if they do experience relief, to whom do they confide in order to get the most tranquilizing effect?

Pennebaker and O'Heeron could not in good conscience go back and press these kinds of questions on grieving spouses, so joining with colleague Cheryl Hughes, they devised an entirely new series of experiments[20] in which subjects were given an opportunity to volunteer on a publicly posted sign-up sheet. Attached to the sheet was a note saying that volunteers "might be required to talk about traumatic or stressful events that had occurred in their lives."

Later, on the night before the experiment, one of the three psychologists would call the volunteer and explain that on the next day he would be asked to sit in a darkened room and either talk into a microphone or to a nearby anonymous confessor about some event or experience in his life that was "extremely traumatic or stressful . . . preferably this should be something that you have not discussed much with anybody else." At this point each was given the opportunity to withdraw from the experiment, though none did so.

The experiment itself was conducted with a number of elaborate controls. The volunteers were wired to measure skin conductance levels, systolic blood pressure, diastolic blood pressure, heart rate, finger temperature, and corrugator muscle electromyography. They were also given an opportunity to talk about an emotionally trivial subject, such as their plans for the day, so that the researchers could compare the physiology of confiding a stressful event with a neutral baseline.

The results themselves were fascinating. Not only did Pennebaker and his colleagues discover that confiding the anxiety of a long-repressed event had the effect of raising the measure of skin resistance (which is inversely related to stress), but this seemed true regardless of whether the confessor was a real person sitting behind a curtain or just a tape recording to be heard by an anonymous researcher at some later point. Even more interesting was the fact that the act of confiding itself, far from being the taxing effort we imagine, was often associated with the lowest stress readings. Experimentors were also surprised to discover the subjects would divulge "as much intensely personal information in so short a time."

If there is any implication from this scientific study of ethical therapy it is to confirm the ancient wisdom that sharing a hyperanxious thought with anyone we trust is better than keeping it to ourselves or waiting around for the perfect confidant. If there is no one immediately available we feel comfortable opening up with, there is always the option of walking into the local church or synagogue and simply asking for someone to talk things over with.

Once we have confided a worry we have previously attempted to control or ignore, we can hasten our recovery by taking time to look back on the events leading up to our attack of hyperanxiety and try to identify the judgment or deception we used to repress our original healthy anxiety.

What were we doing when we first started feeling more anxious? Whom were we with? What were we trying to accomplish? What were we thinking about and what tactics were we using?

The advantage of pinpointing the manipulative source of our increased anxiety is twofold. First, we may still be contributing to the problem. One obvious example would be the spouses of the accidental death victims who were still keeping a lid on their experience by pretending to friends as if nothing were wrong. A less dramatic example which makes the same point would be the case of a free-lance advertising copywriter whose anxieties about being rejected by a new client lead him to censor his most inventive thoughts. Once he realizes that keeping a lid on his ideas is causing more anxiety than expressing them, he has the freedom to change the situation by taking the risk to be more creative.

Even if the option to change the source of the particular anxiety is no longer open—if in the case of the copywriter, for example, the commercial he was trying to write has already been filmed—it is still worth noting for future reference how certain habitual manipulations that seem to quell our anxiety in the moment can wreak so much emotional havoc down the line.

I can still remember years ago when I was in therapy with Jon Davidson how every time I found myself suffering from some anxious problem, he would lead me back through the events of recent days, stopping at the first sign of a major lie, resentment, perfectionistic self-judgment. He did not always use explicitly ethical language, but the tranquilizing effect of drawing my attention to the ways I inadvertently manipulated my healthy anxiety into hyperanxiety was quite remarkable.

In the years since, my research and writing in psychology has given me the opportunity to see some of the country's most highly regarded therapists in action, and I am always struck by the degree to which the success of their treatment for extreme anxiety usually involves getting the patient to address some unethical response to a less anxious state.

This isn't to say that all these therapists are deliberately using ethical discipline as a form of therapy. Many would see themselves as doing conventional psychoanalysis or behavior modification. But unconsciously there seems to be a second level of communication where the therapists' basic good character shines through the superficial limits of his or her "value-free" technique. It is almost as if there are two therapies going on at the same time: the overt seemingly rigorous and objective, the covert paradoxically quite spiritual. Certainly a behaviorist can both highlight and discourage quite a bit of self-defeating manipulation if he appraises his client's "conditioned responses" in a perceptive way, just as a sensitive psychoanalyst can attentuate a lot of patient perfectionism through a sympathetic probing of his past. Indeed, I would even venture to say—and I'm not the first to suggest this —that the reason why a very few therapists in every conventional school are astonishingly successful, even while the techniques they use are never particularly helpful in the hands of other colleagues, has to do with the subtle ethical bias of their personal style.

The third and ultimately most effective solution to hyperanxiety is to make a regular practice of absorbing our anxious feelings as they arise, allowing their excitement to transform us gradually rather than build up to a crisis of obsessive tension. This is what Jung meant by his famous observation that "we cannot change anything unless we accept it. Condemnation does not liberate, it oppresses. . . ."[21]

The modern geologist who studies earthquakes would know exactly what I'm talking about. He knows that the best alternative to some devastating seismic tremor is not the absence of any earthquake at all, but a regular series of small shocks. The absence of any movement for a long period of time only means that tension is building up on the friction-locked plates below the surface. A series of occasional small quakes, on the other hand, while it may shake the dishes, is what prevents the day from ever happening when it feels as if our house is going to fall down.

How we go about the process of absorbing our small psychological tremors is partly a matter of sharing our experience with another person. But we must also spend some time alone with it, going some place where we have a chance to sit or lie quietly and simply pay attention to the constricted feelings in our chest, the tension in our arms and legs, and allow whatever associated thoughts to jump around a little bit until they settle.

Now the first time we consider doing something like this, we are naturally a little wary. What if our thoughts should get out of control? What if we start thinking about something we don't like and can't stop?

Once we have some experience surrendering to our anxiety, we learn that these are exactly the kinds of states that our quiet absorption prevents. Nevertheless many of us find it helpful to begin this practice, not by closing our eyes, but by sitting down at a desk and writing out our anxious thoughts in longhand on a sheet of paper. This introductory practice can itself be divided into two stages, the first and less threatening being to write only an objective description of our anxious thought. Then, once we are comfortable with this kind of surface treatment, we can begin to describe some of the feelings associated with our disturbing images.

Interestingly, Dr. Pennebaker has found that having volunteers merely write about their anxieties for brief periods appears to have the same healthful effect as confiding the thoughts to a real person. Subjects who spent fifteen minutes each day writing about a traumatic event in their lives, for example, made fewer trips to the doctor for the next six months than other volunteers who only wrote about trivial matters.[22]

As our step-by-step approach to anxiety would suggest, those who described only the superficial details of their disturbing thoughts experienced practically no difficulty describing even the most upsetting events and ideas. ". . . having subjects write about the objective aspects of the traumatic events alone was neither arousing nor particularly upsetting," Pennebaker found. "Indeed, these findings are reminiscent of . . . studies . . . wherein hearing a nonemotional and/or intellectual description of an upsetting scene greatly reduces physiological responses to that event."[23]

When we begin to sense that our anxious feelings are not the devils we imagined, we are ready to close our eyes and give these anxious energies more liberty to express themselves. If our thoughts seem to spin in circles, for example, we allow them the ride; if our chest seems lightly pressed by an invisible weight, we breathe into it.

There will always be some resistance to this: apprehension at first, annoyance as we become more accustomed to the practice. After all, if normal anxiety really is a message from our higher self, our conscious mind, so eager to stay in control, is always going to put up a bit of a fuss.

But instead of identifying with our resistance, trying to deny our anxious feelings or pushing them away, we invite them inward, reminding ourselves that our resistance to anxiety is more of a problem than the anxiety itself. Confronted with a choice between opening ourselves to a deep and spontaneous transformation we do not objectively comprehend or attempting to live within the confines of our conscious understanding, we choose to risk faith in our deeper self and to be inspired in ways we cannot always predict.

Which is precisely what happens. For just at the moment when the fog of our confusion threatens to grow darker, something happens. It may be a feeling, an insight, a new sense of direction, or some combination of the three, but there is always a transformation and, with it, a sudden sense of peace.

Once we become accustomed to this technique, we find that the most anxious thoughts and even nightmares can become a source of unexpected insight and tranquillity. Let me clarify what I mean with a specific example from my own experience.

Some years ago I was writing portions of a college textbook when I was overcome by a whirling sense of dread that lasted for several hours. I went to sleep that night and had the following dream.

I was standing on a remote tropical island where an atomic bomb had just ignited. Although the center of the blast was a few miles away from me, I knew that I could be killed by the expanding fireball and the shock waves radiating from it. Terrified, I ran from the mushroom-shaped cloud, but as I looked over my shoulder, I could see trees and boulders shattering in the wake of the explosion's concussion. Finally, I reached the edge of the island and ran onto a glass bridge that spanned over turbulent waters and into a fog bank miles away. As I raced across the bridge, the shock waves roared in behind me, shattering glass in all directions. The portion of the bridge under my feet dissolved and I fell toward the churning sea and what seemed to be a certain death.

At this point I woke up sweating. I could not remember a more vivid or frightening dream. Nor did I want to experience such a thing again. Yet something within me, a strange but compelling intuition, told me that I should lie back and let the dream complete itself in the fantasy of near sleep. With trepidation, I closed my eyes and rested my head against the pillow. Within minutes . . .

. . . I was falling into the sea, drowning I thought. At least it seemed that way at first. But then I bobbed to the surface. The waves subsided, the winds calmed, and soon I found myself enjoying an effortless swim.

Later that morning I got up with an enthusiasm for writing that I hadn't felt in weeks. By embracing my anxious dream I had not just defused a particular nightmare, I had spontaneously worked through some major problems with the book.

Admittedly such a powerful self-therapy appears on the surface to be quite at odds with society's current view of anxiety. Certainly most of what we read and see on television is not calculated to bolster our faith in the therapeutic value of accepting inner turmoil. Aspirin commercials warn us daily that anxiety is intolerable; the soap operas predict that unchecked nervous tension will lead to emotional collapse; even the news documentaries seem to automatically regard anxiety as some kind of threat.

Yet the notion of surrendering to anxious thoughts, while not openly advocated, is very much implicit in a number of popular self-development techniques of recent years, including meditation, yoga, biofeedback training, and many relaxation therapies. Indeed, the willing and nonjudgmental acceptance of one's inmost thoughts is probably the one feature they all have in common.

Surrender to anxious thoughts is so necessary for our serenity and long-term peace of mind, in fact, that even the media must inevitably confirm it, if not directly, then in the myths of heroic fiction and children's stories. A Walt Disney movie a few years back described the adventures of a lost spaceship orbiting a "black hole" in a remote part of the galaxy. Unable to imagine that this fiery rim had the power to do anything but destroy them, the frightened crew spent most of the film trying to avoid its powerful gravitation pull. It was only at the end of the story when, finally sucked into the heart of it, the astronauts discovered that what appeared at first to be a chaotic maelstrom was the very shortcut home they had been looking for all along.

# Chapter 12

---

# *BEYOND ADDICTION*

If, indeed, you use the word *[self-denial]* in the sense of some weak sour moralists, and much weaker divines, you'll have just reason to laugh at it. But if you take it as understood by philosophers and men of sense, you will presently see her charms and fly to her embraces . . . ; for self-denial is never a duty, or a reasonable action, [but] a natural means of procuring more pleasure than you can taste without it. . . .

BENJAMIN FRANKLIN[1]

There is only one way to cope with life, namely, to find that system of values which is not subject to fashionable trends, . . . which will never change, and will always bear good fruit in terms of bringing us peace and health and assurance, even in the midst of a very insecure world.

DR. THOMAS HORA[2]

There is an old saying among scientists and engineers that defining a problem is halfway to solving it.

Certainly this is true of compulsive drinking, drug abuse, overeating, chain-smoking, habitual gambling, or any other self-destructive addiction. Writing from the perspective of someone who considers himself a recovering substance abuser—my addictions were alcohol and hashish—and who has spent almost four years counseling recovering addicts of all kinds, I can say that anyone willing to read a chapter on addiction has already made substantial progress. This is not to minimize some of the challenges that lie ahead of you, but simply a recognition that what makes addiction such a difficult psychological disorder to treat is the reluctance of so many of us to admit to ourselves that we do indeed have a problem.

As we do come to grips with the fact of our abuse, it is a pleasant surprise to discover that addiction is the one topic in contemporary psychology which is least distorted by the outmoded "value-free" theories of conventional psychology. Having long ago discovered that neither behavior modification nor psychoanalysis is very effective at treating addictions of any kind, scientists in this field have shown a remarkable willingness to experiment with everything from hypnosis and encounter groups to ESP and even electrical stimulation of the brain. Psychologists have also experimented with the one-shot administration of powerful psychedelic drugs, such as pure LSD, to radically alter the consciousness of habitual alcohol and heroin abusers.

One result of this unusually wide-ranging research is a growing consensus that addictive behaviors have a lot in common. In 1979, the National Institute on Drug Abuse brought together leading researchers in alcoholism, obesity, smoking, and drug abuse and found striking agreement about the definition and treatment of these once seemingly varied problems. Similar conclusions appeared in a later, more extensive study by the National Academy of Sciences. While the problem of alcoholic drinking may on the surface appear very different from, say, binge eating or the abuse of street drugs or out-of-control gambling habits, both reports noted the underlying psychological dynamics to be very similar.[3]

"Until a few years ago," observes the widely respected University of New Mexico addiction researcher William Miller, "these were thought of as relatively independent and separate problem areas. Psychologists, psychiatrists, social workers, and other mental health professionals . . . specialized in the treatment of *one* of these behaviors, but few (extended) their therapy and research efforts to cover more than one or two of these disorders. . . . (In) the past few years, however, . . . there is an increasing awareness that workers in each of these areas have much to learn from one another. . . ."[4] Once familiar labels such as *alcoholic, drug addict, bulimic,* and *compulsive gambler* are increasingly replaced by more comprehensive phrases, such as *addictive personality* or *substance abuser;* and the latest academic journals go by the widely inclusive titles of *Addictive Behavior* and *International Journal of Addictions.*

And what is it exactly that our self-abusing habits have in common?

One interesting, and hopeful, denominator of addiction is that its physical grip on us is not nearly as strong as we imagine. While a few heavy drinkers, smokers, and drug abusers do experience severe symptoms as they attempt to drop their consumption of psychoactive chemicals—indeed, even a recovering gambler must suffer the lower adrenaline levels that come with reduced gaming excitement—the supposed severity of addictive withdrawal is largely the myth of melodramatic novelists and Hollywood directors.[5]

"In a supportive setting," writes Harvard-trained physician Andrew Weil of his own experiences as a volunteer physician at the Haight-Ashbury Medical Clinic in San Francisco, ". . . a heroin addict can withdraw without medication other than aspirin and have little more discomfort than that of a moderate cold. I saw this in San Francisco in 1968 in men with $70-a-day habits."[6]

Similarly, the notorious "d.t.'s," which we associate with alcohol detoxification, inflict only mild discomfort in the majority of cases. Of the total number of patients who present themselves to clinics or family doctors for the treatment of acute alcoholism, less than half require any formal detoxification program at all. And of those who do, at least

81 percent seem to be able to do it safely and effectively on an outpatient basis.[7]

Even protracted withdrawals, such as the chronic compulsions experienced by abstaining cigarette smokers or cocaine abusers, are greatly exaggerated as a barrier to recovery. There is no evidence, in the case of smoking, that heavier users have any more difficulty giving up their habit than those accustomed to smoking far fewer cigarettes or that the intensity of residual cravings is the primary cause of relapse.[8]

As for the supposed chemical intractability of cocaine, the observations of Dr. David Musto, professor of psychiatry and the history of medicine at Yale University,[9] are especially revealing. Drawing a parallel between today's cocaine epidemic and the late nineteenth century, when a combination of permissive laws and quack medical fads made "coca cigarettes" and "coca inhalants" as popular as today's street drugs, he notes that it took just a few years for public awareness of increased crime and other harmful side effects to culminate in near universal abstinence. This widespread turnaround required no massive detoxification program or methadone-like substitutes but occurred, according to Dr. Musto, because "peer pressure, so often given as the reason for the spread of drugs, can be just as potent a force against drug use, once the image of the drugs effects has changed from miraculous to destructive."

Why, then, if the physical bonds of addiction are less formidable than we've come to believe, is it so difficult to overcome what we now concede is a self-destructive habit?

Let us consider the typical case of the busy executive who finally decides he's going to quit smoking. After a week of successfully abstaining from cigarettes, he encounters a whole series of unexpected setbacks: a big client is flying into town on one hour's notice, the secretary is out sick until further notice, and his teenage daughter has threatened to drop out of college—all in one afternoon.

At first he takes just one cigarette to calm himself; but no sooner does the butt touch his mouth when he tells himself, "Well, I've completely blown this little non-smoking campaign, I might as well just finish the pack." Which he proceeds to do, finally deciding at the end of the day that he's just not ready to break the habit.

Any of us who've ever tried to break an addictive habit on our own know it's not just the chain-smoker who experiences such dichotomous all-or-nothing flip-flops. Whether we are trying to abstain from alcohol, drugs, binge eating or gambling, most failed attempts can be traced to some unexpected emotional stress. First comes the flush of anger, frustration, jealousy, or fear, then the attempt to tranquilize these negative feelings with "just one" drink, joint, snack, or spin of the roulette wheel.[10] In the space of minutes, the firmest resolution can slip into what seems like distant memory.

If every addict can identify with this emotional barrier to recovery, he can also feel a kinship with those substance abusers who speak of a void at the center of their being, what Carl Jung called "the spiritual thirst of our being for wholeness."[11] For some the experience has religious significance—the sense of having lost the simple faith of one's youth—for others there is just the nebulous sense of not expressing a deeper potential, of being cut off from one's inmost abilities.

However we describe the state, we know that something vital is missing and that getting high on alcohol, drugs, compulsive eating, or whatever other addiction seems the only way to fill the gap. There's no doubt that many addicts are trying to find "God in a bottle," observes Dr. Charles Whitfield, Medical Director of the Resource Group in Baltimore. They're trying to "celebrate God [though] it's not working, not very well."[12] Dr. Howard Clinebell, professor of pastoral counseling at the Claremont School of Theology, agrees that alcoholism and other addictions are primarily a response to unfulfilled spiritual potential, what he called "unlived life."[13]

This need to quell our inner void does not perpetuate our addictive behavior in as obvious a way as the onset of intense negative emotion, but it is striking just how many recovering drug addicts, gamblers, or alcoholics attribute their success to finding a substitute sense of spiritual fulfillment. Those who have recovered, notes Clinebell, "have been those who have begun growing again, often after many years of blocked growth caused by the downward spiral of addiction."[14]

It is not at all unusual to read in the scientific journals about a pill or drug abuser who after years of bouncing in and out of various treatment programs, losing his wife, his children, his job, and his good health, finally has what he calls a "spiritual," "religious," or "transcending" experience and becomes straightened out virtually overnight.

Jung himself reported "many experiences with [patients] of this kind."[15]

(It is interesting to note that when LSD was first tested on substance abusers in the early 1950s to see if it could simulate the psychotic-like effects of severe dependence, patients who reported having "mystic" or "cosmic" experiences on the drug were the ones who later had the easiest time abstaining from their addictive habit. It was as if the chemically simulated spirituality had temporarily filled some void and, by doing so, reduced the need to escape reality in the usual way.[16])

The apparent role of spiritual hunger in the persistence of addiction is demonstrated by the fact that so many successfully recovered addicts make a concerted effort to sustain what they would call a "spiritual," "elevated" or "idealistic" state of mind. Some do it by joining a church or synagogue, others by seeking more meaningful friendships or taking jobs that allow for more reflection and creativity.

Dr. Ron Stall, a medical anthropologist who has made an extensive study of spontaneous remission in alcoholics finds that continued abstinence seems to depend, first and foremost, on a conscious cultivation of the "inner" self. "To know I've found a person inside me that I didn't know existed," that "I was a pretty nice person and that I liked the person I found there," that "I was capable of doing more than I thought I could"—these are typical of the reasons given for staying sober.[17]

Even among populations of non-addicts there appears to be a strong relationship between the need to experiment with addictive substances and one's state of spiritual development. When Rutgers University education psychologist Carol Turner and her colleague Robert Willis surveyed a thousand students at a private New Jersey day school, for example, they found that the boys and girls with deep spiritual beliefs were far less inclined to experiment with marijuana, barbiturates, amphetamines, or hallucinogenics than their more cynical and worldly-wise classmates.[18]

A similar study by Jeffrey David Fisher and Amerigo Farina at the University of Connecticut found that even the spiritual orientation of a college social science course can influence the desire for substance abuse.[19] Undergraduates who had signed up for the more conventionally oriented psychology class finished the semester feeling relatively empty and confused and more willing to experiment with drugs, even months after the last lecture had ended. Those who had studied under professors with a more elevated concept of human nature, on the other hand, were comparatively happy and drug-free.

Having identified the inability to cope with extreme negative emotions and the sense of inner void as the primary causes of our addictive behavior, it is important to remind ourselves that these are not really two separate motives, but two aspects of the same controlling personality. Just as the judgmental and manipulative strategies that we habitually substitute for a more intuitive life inevitably give rise to emotional pain, so the onset of depression, loneliness, guilt, or feelings of worthlessness erodes even further our faith in some kind of inner wisdom.

Certainly in my own volunteer work with substance abusers attempting to recover, their reports of strong negative emotion and feelings of spiritual emptiness almost always occur simultaneously. This double-strength causation explains why the desire to indulge a habit can feel so desperate and spiral so quickly out of control.

The real challenge of overcoming addiction, then, is not deciding which of these problems, negative emotions or inner void, contributes the most to our particular habit—or even which should be treated first —but how we can most effectively attack them both at the same time. The bitter professor who compulsively drowns his depression in a nightly sea of highballs must learn to curb his resentments *and* find inner guidance. The perfectionist housewife who anesthetizes her low self-esteem with eating binges must stop demanding so much of herself *and* strive for deeper awareness. The angry man who tries to forget his frustrations in some Atlantic City casino must learn to take his chances on less manipulation *and* his intuitive wisdom.

If treating addiction begins to sound like a major psychological undertaking, it is.

Not only must we became fairly sophisticated in mastering a wide range of negative emotions—all the while risking greater dependence on our intuitive powers—but we frequently find ourselves limited in unexpected ways. A high percentage of we addictive personalities, for example, tend to come from families with a history of substance abuse, if not our preferred indulgence, then one of its sister addictions. Indeed, many of us were introduced to our habit by our own relatives.[20] And because this is the kind of atmosphere where we feel most comfortable, we also tend to associate with friends and fall in love with people who in one way or another support our self-destructive behavior (even at the same moment they may be verbally complaining about it).

What this means is that any serious attempt to change the attitudes which encourage our addiction often meet with considerable resistance from even well-intentioned parents, spouses, and children. Anyone like myself who works with recovering addicts frequently meets people who have had to go through hell just to get to the point where they can admit to themselves that they have a substance abuse problem, only to have friends and relatives try and talk them out of this lifesaving perception. One recovering alcoholic I know had to experience eight drunk-driving accidents, the last of which left him in a hospital bed for six months, as well as lose his wife and children, before finally admitting to a drinking problem. Even then his ex-wife would say, "Oh, dear, you don't have a drinking problem; you've just got to control your anger." The man's parents and friends also tried to talk him out of his self-diagnosis.

Addicts fortunate enough to benefit from the support of friends and family will still have too many blind spots to implement effective self-therapy without some kind of help. This is why it is not at all unusual for highly motivated recovering addicts to think they are making progress, only to switch from one addiction to another (e.g., from alcohol to pills) or to remain uncomfortably abstinent until a major crisis some months or years down the line triggers a relapse. The old story about the alcoholic minister at the local church, while certainly not typical, does betray the fundamental truth that even people whose education and temperament would incline them toward an understanding of ethical therapy are not, in the case of addiction, always capable of administering it to themselves.

Luckily, addiction is the one emotional problem for which there is more sound help available than all the others put together . . . and at the incredible cost of practically nothing, save the time and energy we are willing to invest in our own sanity.

I am referring to the growing nationwide network of so-called "anonymous" organizations for the treatment of addiction: Alcoholics

Anonymous, Narcotics Anonymous, Cocaine Anonymous, Overeaters Anonymous, Gamblers Anonymous, and most recently Debters Anonymous. These independently organized groups, which nonetheless are very similar to one another, provide regular meetings in local communities across the country, sponsored and run by recovering addicts themselves for the purpose of assisting any addict in his ethical-intuitive approach to recovery.

Now, there are some bizarre stereotypes which persist in the public mind about these programs, particularly about Alcoholics Anonymous, which is the oldest. I myself had the image of a bunch of Bowery bums huddled together in some dingy soup kitchen mumbling religious hymns. Part of this stereotype, I suspect, comes from the fact that many candidates for these programs do feel like bums by the time they are ready to admit their addiction.

But the real culprit in generating this unappealing stereotype has been the tendency for conventional psychologies to variously neglect and denigrate any form of ethical self-help or, even worse, to interpret its effectiveness in an unflattering way. Until recent years, it was quite common for psychoanalysts to "explain" the anonymous programs as "24-hour mothering" or playing the "maternal role . . . in the life of the [addict]."[21]

What you do find when you enter an anonymous meeting is a group of warm, friendly, and understanding people who are dedicated to an ethical way of living which is summarized in twelve therapeutic principles or "steps." These include making "a searching and fearless moral inventory of ourselves," making "direct amends to such people [we have harmed]," and practicing spiritual principles "in all our affairs."

At the heart of all these twelve steps is the attempt to replace our failed manipulative habits with the kind of intuitive self-reliance that alleviates both negative emotion and spiritual emptiness, and with them, the compulsion for addictive escape. "[This] is not a mysterious procedure," a Narcotics Anonymous member reassures beginners. "Often it means simply listening to those hunches and intuitive feelings that we think would benefit others or ourselves, and acting on them spontaneously. . . . We are then able to make decisions based on principles that have real value to ourselves."[22]

The parallel between the anonymous programs and ethical therapy is not a coincidence. At the time of its founding in the mid-1930s, A.A. was heavily influenced by the Oxford Movement, a nondenominational spiritual self-help program which, during the early twentieth century, became a haven for many lay and professional opponents of "value-free" behaviorism and psychoanalysis.

Narcotics Anonymous was started in 1953 by two California drug addicts who had been attending A.A. meetings and decided that maybe a separate group would be more appropriate to their needs. Gamblers Anonymous, which took its inspiration from the two previous anonymous programs, was next in 1957. Overeaters Anonymous came three years later when a California woman drove a friend to a meeting of G.A. in Los Angeles and, liking what she heard, founded the first weekly meeting for people with food compulsions. The more recent anonymous programs, as the names suggest, have continued to follow the original A.A. model.

Interestingly, the many values-oriented therapists I interviewed for this book, no matter what their particular interest or specialty, were virtually unanimous in praising the anonymous programs. "They are very close to us," says Dr. Hora. "[It is] very beneficial to large numbers of people, regardless of education and background, and that's the [great thing about it]."[23]

"What they do essentially is that they bring in a spiritual element," explains Frances Vaughan. "It's the one therapeutic program which brings in spirituality without making it a religious issue [and] one of the few things in our society which is widely accepted and lets you get in touch with the spiritual dimension without belonging to organized religion."[24] "I think it's great," adds Allen Bergin. "That's what the community psychiatry and psychology movements were supposed to be about in the early and late sixties, but they kind of blew it."[25]

Dr. M. Scott Peck, author of the *Road Less Traveled,* has gone so far as to suggest that the twentieth century will be remembered for two pivotal events that profoundly changed the nature of human relations: the Holocaust and the founding of the first anonymous program.

Even many conventional psychologists, who remain hostile to any discussion of ethical or spiritual values, have had to concede that addicts with the greatest chance of recovery are those who have participated in the appropriate anonymous group. In 1980, for example, the Rand Corporation completed the most extensive study of alcoholism to date. Tracking the lives of more than 920 patients for a period of four years, the researchers concluded that participating in regular A.A. meetings automatically increased one's chances of remaining abstinent by 32 to 47 percent, regardless of what other therapy the patients had tried.[26]

Translating these findings into a time perspective, the probability of an alcoholic staying sober two years, given one year of A.A. sobriety, appears to be about 70 percent, while the probability of staying sober for a third year given two years of sobriety is an astonishing 90 percent.[27]

But perhaps the most telling fact about the effectiveness of anonymous programs is the extent to which they have been incorporated into standard hospital programs for the cure of alcohol, drug, and prescription pill abuse. More than 1,100 treatment centers across the country now sponsor one or more of the anonymous groups,[28] though many of the doctors and psychiatrists who run them would claim to be dedicated behaviorists or psychoanalysts in good standing.

Even in more compulsory treatment settings, where many patients are sometimes motivated less by a genuine desire to quit substance abuse than by the threats of an irate employer or the hope of softening the heart of a traffic judge, recovery rates can still be remarkably high. "Overall results indicate that A.A. treatment can be a highly effective approach in treating alcohol-dependent patients," says Geary S. Alford of the University of Mississippi Medical Center.[29] In the same year as the Rand report, Alford and his colleagues completed their own study of fifty-six alcoholics who averaged thirty-eight days of inpatient treatment based on Alcoholics Anonymous principles and who were then followed for two years after their discharge from the hospital. Almost half (49 percent) were productively employed by then, had good social relationships, and were completely abstinent.

Locating the relevant anonymous meetings in your own area is as simple as looking up the number in the white pages of your local telephone directory. Volunteer receptionists will give you the time and location of meetings scheduled for the day you called or for any other day of the week, and someone will even give you a lift if you're a bit nervous. As of this writing, there are more than 4,000 regular weekly Overeaters Anonymous meetings in the United States, over 600 Gamblers Anonymous meetings, 6,600 Narcotics Anonymous gatherings, and at least 67,000 weekly meetings of Alcoholics Anonymous.

(Although anonymous groups for smokers are still too new and few to be readily accessible, many of the better smoking clinics have adopted such anonymous strategies as promoting a personal inventory of ethical habits and using a buddy system, which encourages clients to call each other between treatment sessions and after the program has ended. To check out a clinic in your own area, simply call and ask them to mail you a comprehensive brochure of their treatment methods and philosophy.)

As for any worries that you may have about being "exposed" to an employer or gossipy neighbor as an addict, remember that the shared title *anonymous* exists for a reason—so that participants may feel free to practice a new way of living without fear of public embarrassment. Membership does not even require giving one's full name—which is why I have deliberately avoided giving names in this chapter—and all meetings feature the reminder that confidences are to be kept that way.

During the first few weeks of attending anonymous meetings, you'll make some remarkable discoveries. You'll learn that drinking, drugging, or whatever your self-abuse is not a necessary part of a life, that business and personal relationships devastated by your addictive compulsion can be rectified, and that the combined therapeutic power of a few recovering amateurs dedicated to mutual self-help is worth more than all the conventional psychologists put together.

"When I came on the N.A. program," says one recovering drug addict, "I had identified my problem—I had the desire to stop using, but couldn't see how. . . . My whole personality was geared toward getting, using, and finding ways and means to get more. . . . Totally self-centered, I tried to manage my life by manipulating people and circumstances to my advantage. . . . My willpower could not change my diseased body that craved drugs compulsively. My self-control could not change my diseased mind, obsessed with the idea of using mood changers to escape reality. . . . With the help of the recovering addicts at N.A. meetings, I abstained a minute, an hour, a day at a time. . . . I saw hope. I met addicts recovering from their disease. I came to believe I could learn how to live without drugs [and] at this point I have stopped using drugs. . . ."[30]

A bus driver who is 5'10" and once weighed 320 pounds recalls being brought to O.A. by a heart attack. "This time my doctor didn't say, as he had for years, 'I think it would be a good idea if you lost weight.' He said, 'Lose weight or die.'

"When I got out of the hospital I called O.A. and went to a meeting. I was unprepared for what I saw. The people were smiling. They seemed to be happy. They looked relaxed. They didn't look like they were fighting food. . . . I've lost 134 pounds but, best of all, the compulsion has been lifted. I no longer have cravings."[31]

But the most remarkable discovery of all is that the fact of your compulsion, which at this moment probably seems a bitter *curse*, is really a tremendous blessing in disguise. The problem so intractable that its treatment has forced you into an alliance with fellow sufferers has also put you on the fast track to mastering virtually all aspects of the ethical therapy. The idea of intuitive self-reliance, once a vague and fanciful dream, very quickly becomes a living reality; and the chronic fears of emotional turmoil, shattered relationships, and even financial insecurity will slowly but surely be lifted.

I have heard recovering addicts in the anonymous programs describe their habit in many ways. But from the oldest and wisest, one word seems to stand out among the rest: *gratitude*.

# Chapter 13

## THE FAMILY BAROMETER

The greatest and fairest sort of wisdom by far is that which is concerned with the ordering of states and families.

PLATO[1]

And a man's foes shall be they of his own household.

MATTHEW[2]

No other therapy even comes close to the ethical refinement of our intuitive powers. Unlike psychoanalysis with its murky investigations of childhood memories or behavior modification with its pseudo-scientific schedules of reward and punishment, ethical therapy seeks, not merely to analyze or modify, but to *unleash*. We discipline our judgments and deceptions, not to impose controls, but to lift them; beyond the limited vision of the conscious mind is the endless vista of the liberated spirit.

In the very first chapter I tried to give some idea of the extent to which many conventionally trained therapists have spontaneously converted to ethical therapy through the trial-and-error research of their own practice. Such a radical departure from the "value-free" education most of these therapists received in graduate school should really not surprise us. "Value-free" psychiatry can promise to alleviate pressing emotional problems only so long before the disillusioned public will simply refuse to listen, and what Lincoln said about government is proving equally true of therapy: you can fool all of your patients some of the time and some of your patients all of the time, but you can't fool all of your patients all of the time.

Already the enrollment in university psychology courses, once the most popular subject in the undergraduate curriculum, has fallen off precipitously—replaced not coincidentally by an increased interest in ethics, history, philosophy, and religion. "Fortunately," observes Stanford University's Dr. Carl Thoresen,[3] "the wisdom of the ancient Hippocratic era is reemerging: [we are seeing that] mind, body, and spirit act in concert to determine health and well-being."

Yet the very power of ethical therapy is such that our initial use of it can seem to yield wildly erratic results. Even our best efforts at greater ethical discipline will seem awkward, hesitant, and certainly incomplete; and it will be easy to misinterpret the first anxious signs of remission as mere floundering. Multiply this to get the effect of trying to discipline more than one unethical habit at a time, and there will always be days when we wonder if we are making any progress at all.

The most confusing sign of all may well be the reactions we get from certain members of our own families. The world at large may work best according to ethical principles; but, in the narrow confines of every family universe, certain judgments and evasive practices can assume a certain legitimacy, which is why many of us grow up feeling we have to control our environment in the first place. If such habits, and the assumptions which support them, are not corrected by early adulthood, we find ourselves attracted to partners who consciously or unconsciously support these unethical habits, thus extending the manipulative outlook we inherited from previous generations horizontally to wives or husbands, as well as downward to our own children.

What this means is that the more we succeed in renouncing judgments and lies, the more likely we are to irritate certain relatives who've grown comfortable with the attitudes and even the emotional problems that surround our behavior. Our refusal to continue old patterns of guilty rumination, malicious gossip, blaming diatribes, mistrustful evasions, or covert meddling will test their patience;[4] and if we are really working at ethical therapy, we will quite soon find ourselves labeled everything from "dreamer" and "too idealistic" to "out of it" and possibly worse.

Simon[5] had always been at odds with his father. From childhood, Simon was the family star, excelling at school, later in business, and always attracting the most attention. The father was so jealous that he constantly did little things to sabotage his son's success: he made jokes about Simon behind the boy's back, purposely made discouraging remarks, and deliberately showed up late for special celebrations.

Simon avoided the father's hurtful comments by indulging in a few of his own. He often stopped dinner conversations by accusing the father of being "narrow-minded" and "stupid." Privately, Simon spent considerable time fantasizing revenge.

This defensive strategy worked well for many years, but around his twenty-third birthday Simon began feeling "uncontrollably" anxious and listless. He was having second thoughts about his career, and he was also overeating.

The "therapy" in this case was the very weight of Simon's depression. He simply lost the energy to be vengeful, even his taste for imagining it. He just stopped talking with his father when the conversations became painful, either finding something else to do or just politely excusing himself.

The father did not take kindly to this development. Without a butt for his verbal slings, he became extremely irritable and even more abusive, accusing his son of being "silly," "not himself," "ungrateful," or anything else that might goad him back into the old game of shared resentments. Like all relatives who become upset with another family member's sudden reliance on ethical discipline, Simon's father used every verbal trick he could think of to fill the void that might force a reevaluation of his own ethical priorities.

Such reactions are quite familiar to family therapists who frequently find that the ethical-intuitive recovery of one patient is accompanied by agitated symptoms in a close relative. Eve Chevron, formerly of the Depression Research Unit at Yale, remembers seeing a patient who at the end of treatment said, "I'm certainly less depressed, but I'll tell you one thing—I'm fighting [with my spouse] a hell of a lot more."

"It's a paradoxical," observes Chevron. "Although the patient's less depressed at the end of treatment on all those standardized depression measures, in terms of marital fighting or adjustment she would look worse."[6]

Interestingly, when Chevron and her colleagues at Yale tested their values-oriented version of psychoanalysis (Interpersonal Psychotherapy) as a part of the NIMH's Treatment of Depression Collaborative Research Program, they did a separate "Marital Study" to measure the impact of therapy on the husband or wife of the identified patient. The majority of spouses, it turned out, were in favor of the treatment; but in two cases (10 percent), what proved healthy for the patient only ended up aggravating the other partner.

In one of these two negative outcomes, the wife of the depressed patient actually became depressed herself as her husband began to feel better. In the other situation, a wife who had participated in group therapy sessions with her husband became so agitated that she pulled both of them out of therapy prematurely.

If some kind of family antagonism is a possible result of our therapeutic progress, we certainly can't be blamed for wondering if the benefits of ethical therapy are worth the price. "What's so great," we'd like to know, "about a treatment that only appears to add to our problems?"

Fortunately, the resistance of certain relatives is not as bleak or as formidable as it first appears. One of the great ironies of family life is that the tendency to arouse discomfort through greater ethical discipline is matched only by our increased immunity to whatever protest we may engender. Some relatives may complain openly, others may grumble or pass provocative remarks or allow their symptoms to become exaggerated for a time, but the continuation of such criticism in the face of persistent sincerity is surprisingly slight. As Dr. Hora puts it, "Nobody can encroach [on someone] who is a beneficial presence in the world."[7]

The protest of a parent may seem particularly threatening because we approach the challenge of greater integrity from the viewpoint of the child who still fears he or she is going to get "clobbered" for breaking some ancient family taboo. But as adults, we discover that the values we thought would make us so vulnerable turn out to empower us in the most unexpected ways.

"I believe there's a tremendously powerful undertow in . . . families," says family therapist Victoria Brundage, "that the old habits and the old tricks are very, very powerful, but I don't think they're all-powerful. I think people have some room to move. And people may try new behaviors and succeed and then turn around and get back into the same old garbage; but then the next day be able to try a new behavior and succeed. . . . [Even the most difficult] families have room to move and potential."[8]

Consider the case of Kay,[9] a thirty-three-year-old West Coast public relations executive, who was still tied to her New England family by a gnawing sense of guilt. Ever since she was a little girl, Kay played the role of conciliator whenever her mother became upset with her father or with Kay's older brother, Frank. Kay was the one who listened to all the mother's complaints and then manipulated the men into making some kind of restitution.

As time went on, however, Kay experienced her role as a growing burden that seemed to demand increasingly ennervating sacrifices. Whenever her mother was angry with her father for some hapless comment, for example, it was Kay who called him at the office 3,000 miles away to urge that he apologize with flowers. When Frank married an Oriental girl that the mother disapproved of and went to live in Florida, it was Kay who flew to Miami and lectured her brother on the need to make things right. Then, too, Kay herself had disappointed her mother: instead of marrying a successful professional and providing the family with grandchildren, she had moved across the country to pursue an independent career.

Eventually the weight of Kay's manipulative role began to take its toll. Kay's enthusiasm for work declined sharply, and she became more isolated, a fact which frustrated and alienated her fiancé, George. When he tried to talk with her about it, Kay went into a fearful rage and hid in a closet. Later, when George brought up the subject during a drive to the grocery store, Kay stopped the conversation abruptly by ramming her Buick into a neighbor's fence.

No one was seriously hurt, but the "accident" was a message that even Kay could not ignore. With George's support, she started resisting her manipulative responses to the mother's prodding. The next time her mother called with a complaint, Kay listened sympathetically but declined to play intermediary. She also declined to spend Thanksgiving at home, deciding instead that her life in Los Angeles *was* home.

Kay's mother noted the change, shedding a few tears about her "loneliness," yet over time the reaction was far less dramatic than Kay had imagined. Kay's depression began to lift and, as it became clear she was not going to play conciliator any longer, the mother protested less and less. In a strange way, the mother seemed to respect her daughter's newfound independence; and Kay's next visits East were unique in that, for the first time, she seemed to enjoy herself.

What Kay discovered through her persistence was that facing down a relative's initial negative reaction to our self-therapy does not mean that we are condemned to endless rows with the agitated parent, child, wife, or sibling. Quite the contrary, by renouncing the judgmental and deceptive controls in our life, we begin cultivating an inner wisdom that becomes harder and harder to attack. Quietly, almost unconsciously, we assume an authority that, while not always acknowledged, is always respected—and secretly admired—for it honors the highest potential in everyone.

Even relatives with whom we have a long history of antagonism may surprise us with an abrupt and unexpected change of heart. Therapist Joel Kanter[10] tells of a divorced woman who had been consistently abused and exploited by a young adult son. When she finally decided she was fed up with the guilty stance she had always taken within her family and wasn't going to allow herself to act that way any more, the son's sullen and withdrawn behavior changed almost overnight. He even became an active member of a religious service organization.

One tip which seems to help enormously in facilitating our ethical transformation within the family is remembering to keep our communication with difficult relatives on a person-to-person basis. In other words, we should do our best to insure that our conversations stay focused on issues and problems of mutual concern and do not stray into gossiping about other members of the family.

The power of this remarkably simple guideline stems from the fact that virtually all judgmental and manipulative communication within

THE FAMILY BAROMETER    163

the family occurs when two parties are discussing a third. If we feel resentful toward a parent, for example, we rarely express it directly, but rather tell a sibling, mate, or the other parent about it. Deception is also usually a collaboration between two or more sympathetic family members against a third party. Doing our best to see that conversations with difficult relatives are "between us" and "about us" has the ability of refining our ethical self-discipline almost overnight.[11]

Dr. Robert Isrealy,[12] a Port Chester, New York, psychiatrist I interviewed in 1979, told me of a particular incident which radically changed his entire approach to psychology. He was practicing therapy in Washington, D.C., and leading an encounter group whose members included an Air Force sergeant. The soldier was very unhappy and complained about a number of problems: arguments with his wife, his child's sickness, and his anger at having grown up with a negligent, philandering father. For months, Dr. Isrealy tried to help the sergeant, but nothing really seemed to work.

Then, without any instruction from Dr. Isrealy, the sergeant began visiting his parents, who lived in nearby Baltimore. He would talk with each of them separately, deliberately forsaking old battles and directly expressing opinions he had long kept secret. He was able, in Isrealy's words, to "bring himself to his parents."

The result of the sergeant's brave, if unsolicited, attempts at sincerity was a pronounced elevation of self-esteem. His parents hadn't done anything to change, but the soldier was noticeably more cheerful and active. His marriage improved, and soon he was ready to terminate therapy. Isrealy himself came to see that no theory he had learned in graduate school was anywhere nearly as effective as a client's willingness to relate directly, honestly, and confidentially with difficult relatives.

The side benefit of relating person-to-person is that it enables us to take an ethical stand without having to go into an elaborate and potentially provocative explanation of our motives. It is one thing to say we don't want to discuss other family members because we feel such conversation is manipulative and we're trying to contain this kind of behavior, quite another to say, "Let's just talk about us." There is an intrinsic persuasiveness to this kind of request; and, however much it might be resented at first, it is one of those precious statements which says everything without anything else having to be said.

This point is illustrated again in the story told me by Connecticut therapist Bernard Raxlin and his colleague Mimi Leuba.[13] It concerned an artistic woman who had come into therapy complaining of a miserable home life. She was burdened by caring for two young children, especially the older and more rambunctious son, and she'd had no sexual relations with her husband for over a year. She felt frustrated at having no time to paint and constantly blamed her husband for "getting her pregnant in the first place" and "destroying her career as an artist."

The first attempts to change the habitual patterns of communication were difficult emotionally. Not only had she become a hardened female chauvinist by the time she entered therapy, but the other family members had become accustomed to the emotional battle lines, with the wife and daughter typically aligned against the father and son.

Gradually, however, the woman learned to stop complaining to different family members about how some other had "sent her selfhood down the tube" and deal with each directly. The husband sulked at first and her daughter was shaken by the new approach, yet the mother's increased directness eventually began to have an effect.

Looking back after some months of progress at what had seemed to be an impossible challenge without even token support from her family, the woman felt an unexpected sense of achievement, not only for having recovered her values in the midst of such a conflicted environment, but also for having set a good example in the process. Indeed, her son, who had become a heavy marijuana smoker under the pressure of family tension, suddenly kicked the habit.

"This was extraordinary," her therapist remembers with a smile, "he stopped smoking entirely and became practically an evangelist . . . among his friends, saying how much better he felt not smoking every day and how much more productive he was. . . . His energy was released as well—[so] was the daughter. [She] had been off in a corner; [but now] she was verbal and open."

Of course, not all difficult relatives respond in such a supportive and joyful way. Although our position is inevitably respected, sometimes the courtesy is limited to silence or, as in the case of Kay's mother, an unspoken and begrudging acquiescence.

The important thing is that we don't depress ourselves by blaming manipulative relatives for their unwillingness to change. For some, the history of manipulation and countermanipulation may be such that they don't yet believe any other way is possible. No matter how much our own lives may improve as a result of our ethical-intuitive self-therapy, they will find a different way to interpret our progress. Others may be severely damaged by alcohol and drugs or simply feel so guilty that they do not see how they can live with a more truthful way of being.

Regardless of the reasons for their lack of enthusiastic support—and we may not know what all the reasons are—we must always remember the basic assumption of ethical therapy, which is that everything is not what it seems. What may appear on the outside to be stubborn stagnation can, in context, be very real progress; and just because someone is not ready to trade manipulation for faith in his or her intuitive powers does not mean this will always be the case.

One surprising consolation for our patience will be that the resistance of some family members is quite often accompanied by the unexpected blossoming of others. Just as breaking our unethical patterns in the broader world outside the family leads to social dividends from unexpected quarters, so we find ourselves developing creative new relationships within our very family.

Certainly this is true in cases where the agitated relative is someone who already uses extreme behavior, such as violence or the threat of suicide, to intimidate others in the household. People who take the lead in demanding responsible limits to such behavior—calling the police, for example, when anger gets out of control—find they are setting an example which is supported and often emulated by more ambivalent family members.

In my own work with relatives of drug and other substance abusers, I frequently see cases where a sober family member's decision to stop playing manipulative games—say, to stop covering up for the mess created by a spouse's addiction—generates an interesting split within the family. The active alcoholic or drug abuser himself may condemn the unexpected ethical stand, but often finds himself more isolated as other family members respond to the new example.

One recovering alcoholic I worked with had been separated from his wife, who was also an alcoholic but still drinking, and together they had custody of their two children. The older daughter seemed to adjust well enough to the separation, but the boy had few friends and was having a great deal of difficulty with his school work.

The wife wanted nothing to do with her husband's ethical self-therapy, particularly his interest in relating more honestly about difficult issues and his attempts to find a more peaceable alternative to the usual arguments about money and how the kids should be raised. The son, however, became remarkably open to his father after a few months. They were able to take regular sailing trips together, which had never happened before, and the son himself suggested remedial steps to improve his grades.

A similar situation[14] involved a forty-two-year-old woman I'll call Mrs. J., who finally agreed to start letting up on the resentment she had always displayed toward a neglectful, alcoholic mother. At least the woman agreed to start calling her mother on Mother's Day and organizing a few holiday get-togethers.

Although Mrs. J.'s mother made even these small steps seem as painful as possible, Mrs. J.'s relationship with her own daughter, which had grown strained in recent years, took a surprising turn for the better. What at first appeared to promise only a burdensome obligation with respect to her alcoholic mother proved instead to be a healthy realignment of the broader family's emotional network, with Mrs. J. and her daughter growing so close over the months that the problem of the drinking grandmother simply dwindled by comparison.

A second consolation for the resistance of certain relatives comes from the fact that our commitment to ethical self-therapy—especially our demonstrated willingness to suspend resentful judgments—creates a situation where parents feel freer to share a bit more of their personal history. Even a parent who is resisting our self-therapy can be encouraged to apply less self-censorship when it comes to reconstructing pieces of his or her own past. Although this doesn't sound like a major breakthrough, the impact on our emotional and even physical well-being can be enormous.

Allen Bergin relates the case[15] of "one young woman [who] had a bitter relationship with her father and expressed all of her negative feelings about him during therapy. The connections between his behavior and her problems seemed clear; . . . [but] she was encouraged to go back to visit her father and, instead of confronting him with the pain he had caused, to invite him to tell her about his history and to [tape] a family history interview. She was not to ask about his dynamics or disturbances and their consequences but about his identity, experiences, and so forth.

"The result of doing this, including tape-recording and writing [out] the interviews with her father, caused a dramatic reconciliation between them, a merging of perceptions of painful events that had occurred. It stimulated her father to face certain realities he had never faced. This was, however, a gentle experience occurring in a forgiving atmosphere. As a result, he was able to lower his defenses, apologize, and seek to make up for his past conduct. The changes in both client and father as a result of this encounter appeared to be dramatic and more profound than the changes that had been occurring via regular treatment."

A similar story was related to me by a family therapist who had gone back to visit her own mother after a series of two miscarriages left her anxious about the possibility of ever having a child.

"I had a lot of anxiety about getting pregnant again," the family therapist told me. "I [felt] I needed to learn about my mother's experience of pregnancy and about [what it was like] during the birth of my brothers and sisters."

The therapist wasn't sure how her mother would react to the request, but she decided to go home in the spirit of "gathering information" and simply sharing her own problems. "I experienced [my mother] being really open with me [and] I was able to put some pieces together. For example, I found out that my youngest sister, who is fourteen years younger than me, was born two months after my grandmother died. So I learned that my mother was dealing with [death] two months after she had my sister, who for me was like having my own baby, because I was fourteen and helped raise her."

Just the very act of getting this information "began to make a difference," she now recalls. "What I experienced was that my anxiety went down and I was ready to try again. . . . Today, I've got my little boy."

It is important to emphasize that creating a situation where we can benefit from our parents' history is not an analytical process. Indeed, any attempt to interpret what we hear only puts us in the position of appearing to judge, with the likely result that we will not hear much more.

Our healing comes from "the truth" itself, explains the therapist who went to her mother. "It's emotional. It frees you up. It's not analytical; it's faith in the process."

Relief from the negative emotions which accompany our manipulative habits, the unexpected blossoming of troubled family members, the option to be healed through family history—certainly these more than compensate us for the initial resistance of a few antagonistic relatives and for the fact that some may not be able to come around for years to come and, even then, not to the degree that we would like.

But there is, in addition to these compensations, the final reward of contributing to something which is at once very personal and yet transcends time as we know it. For by deliberately renewing our values in the family context, we are doing more than asserting our right to personal happiness; we are breaking the "curse" of a controlling mentality that has been passed on from one generation to the next, perhaps for centuries.

We become, in the words of Allen Bergin, a "transitional figure"[16] in the history of our family. By choosing to absorb a small amount of pain in the short run—refusing to vent resentments, abstaining from the usual family game playing, tolerating a measure of criticism from agitated relatives—we give those we love and those who may come after a new chance at a more satisfying way of life. We reconcile with our forebears, reach out to spouse and siblings, and become a generator of positive change in the minds and hearts of spirits yet to be born.

# EPILOGUE

---  ⤜

# HELPING

The character of the physician may act more power-
fully on the patient than the drugs employed.

PARACELSUS[1]

This above all, to thine own self be true,
And it must follow, as the night the day,
Thou canst not then be false to any man.

SHAKESPEARE[2]

I certainly could not end a book on ethical therapy's approach to self-
help without saying a few words about helping others, for much of life's
greatest pleasure comes from giving to those in need.

It is interesting that toward the end of his own life Plato was
called upon to address this very problem in the most serious of circumstances. Years of civil warfare had reduced the island kingdom of Syra-
cuse into a nation of bitter rivalries; and the exhausted adherents of one

faction had finally decided to write Plato and seek his advice on how to restore peace and prosperity to their homeland.

"I would give the same advice to you as I [gave to your king]," Plato replied.[3] "This was in the first place to conduct his daily life on such a plane as to give him the highest possible degree of mastery over himself and to win him loyal friends and associates."

Here we see the outline of the psychological principle which has characterized all successful helping from ancient times right down to the present: namely, that helping others and helping oneself through the refinement of one's own personal values are intimately connected. This is not merely to say that helping others is a form of virtue. It is to suggest that helping is often a subtle process, not easily measured by overt offers of assistance, and that the only way to assure the strength and intelligence necessary to really benefit another person is by placing our highest priority on the ethical cultivation of our own intuitive powers.

This is true even when our help is provided on a professional basis, as a doctor, for example, or as a lawyer or social worker. In the case of wanting to be an effective psychotherapist, observes Dr. Richard Firestone,[4] "the ideal therapist [is] a person of unusual personal honesty and integrity. . . . The therapist's personal life is very important, because if a therapist is defensive in his personal life, he will necessarily be limited in the amount of help he is able to offer his patients. . . . With his patients and with his personal friends and family, [the good therapist] would be direct and nonmanipulative."

Of course, it is one thing to equate helping with personal integrity in the abstract, quite another to practice this principle in personal or business situations where we think a little constructive manipulation might actually get somebody else to do what's in their own best interest. How many parents, for example, aren't tempted to "help" their children by withholding information, exaggerating (or minimizing) the importance of certain events, and making promises without really intending to follow through? How many mentors try to build up the egos of the young executives they are shepherding through the business?

What we have to remember is that the most important thing we can ever give a floundering person is not our enlightened manipulation but our courage. Indeed, one of the striking things about people who are struggling with a major difficulty is that they often already know the solution to their problems. Ethically oriented therapists report something I have frequently observed myself—namely, that helpful suggestions are often received with a faint smile of recognition. It is almost as if the patient has been waiting for permission to believe in something he or she suspected could be true, but did not have the faith to act on.

And since most real solutions to difficult personal problems involve taking some kind of ethical risk, what people need from us is neither our detached objectivity nor our manipulative tricks, but our example. They need to see that someone else has taken the kind of chance they themselves are already privately debating and to see that the roof has not fallen in.

This does not mean becoming preachy. There is nothing worse than being preached at, particularly for someone who is genuinely confused. Not only does he know that many would-be helpers will suggest things they themselves have never had the courage to try, but the very act of receiving wisdom from "on high" only reinforces his feeling of incompetence.

To share our courage is to share the fear that went with it: how we tried to be more honest and tolerant, how we backtracked, how we tried again and did a little better, how we still fall far short of being perfect, and how we found being perfect matters much less than simply being true to ourselves. While this may sometime seem like we are conveying weakness, the effect is to minimize the distance between what the floundering person feels he is currently capable of and what he intuits he should try—in other words, to make the risk of bridging this gap seem a realistic possibility.

Sharing any sustenance we have gained from our spiritual beliefs is also enormously helpful. One of the great misconceptions perpetuated by conventional psychology is the idea that spiritual fortitude is intrinsically dangerous for an emotionally troubled person, as if it will be somehow abused or relied on as a crutch. This goes hand-in-hand with the common misconception that psychopathology correlates strongly with religious beliefs. (Statistically, the opposite is true.[5]) A more enlightened guideline is suggested by the fact that the majority of practicing psychologists themselves tend to have very spiritual attitudes—

more than half label themselves religious, for example—and roughly 10 percent hold official positions in various religious organizations.[6]

Beyond expressing our values in a more public way, the basic issue which has to be decided is whether we see the person we want to help as someone who himself *wants* to be helped. We all have friends, relatives, associates, and, if we are professional helpers, clients, who, while they may be suffering from a lack of ethical courage, do not really appear interested in changing. These are the people who attempt to get what they want by loudly complaining about problems or showing themselves to be in a great deal of pain, all the while deriving secret pleasure from their ability to frustrate the very people who would help them.

Unfortunately, distinguishing this obstinate footdragger from the "lost soul" who seems genuinely motivated to change is not something that can always be decided by just asking. Indeed, the person who doesn't want to be helped will often ask for it more often than the one who does, since establishing the need for help is sometimes the best excuse for staying the same. Our decision, therefore, must be an intuitive one, based more than anything else on a reasonable amount of experience with the person in question. Basically we have to ask ourselves, "Am I dealing with someone who *can't* change or someone who *won't?*" Is this a footdragger or a genuine seeker?

It helps to remember that we are not making a moral judgment here. The person who seems to deliberately frustrate our good intentions certainly suffers from his or her stubbornly manipulative attitudes and is as deserving of our sympathy as the one who is responsive— probably more so since, in the long run, he has a harder road to travel.

The distinction between footdragger and seeker is a distinction we make purely to understand how it is that we can be most helpful. In the case of a footdragger we have to understand that we are in a situation where whatever we want for the other person—even what really might be in their very best interest—is precisely what's going to be resisted. Now we might think this kind of reaction is self-destructive and stupid. We might wish our relationship with this person had evolved in a different way. But the essential nature of the relationship is not likely to change in the next couple of days.

This does not mean we give up on helping the footdragger. But it does mean that the only immediately constructive role we can play in his or her life is to take some responsibility for the degree to which we ourselves have inadvertently encouraged the manipulative behavior.

Remember how in earlier chapters we talked about the fact that people raised in an unethical atmosphere will frequently choose friends, associates, and even lovers who reflect and support their distorted emotional reality. If we are at all involved with a footdragger, the chances are that we have extended or compromised ourselves in ways that confirm his unethical perception of how the world works. Our actions may have been very well-intentioned—we didn't want to be hard on someone who's in so much pain—but the paradoxical effect of pretending to be unfazed by manipulative helplessness is to encourage the very behavior which perpetuates the pain.

The only way to help someone who won't get well is to let them know how their behavior really affects us and to draw the line on being abused by them or taken advantage of any longer. This does not mean becoming vengeful or hard-hearted, but simply extending our sense of personal integrity to include *all* our relationships.

Where this gets difficult, of course, is in the case where we are dealing with a relative who has been institutionalized for a psychiatric problem or has been diagnosed as suffering from a major mental disorder. How can we demand respect from someone who has been labeled *schizophrenic* or who suffers from the effects of severe drug abuse or has a long history of emotional problems?

Before we answer this question, it might be useful to review one of the first cases assigned to therapist Joel Kanter while he was interning at a large training facility. The patient was a twenty-one-year-old woman with a history of auditory hallucinations since the age of four, who had such crippling schizophrenic symptoms that none of the senior residents even wanted to treat her.

"My individual psychotherapy sessions with this woman were painful experiences for me," Kanter recalls.[7] "She came regularly to her meetings, but sat mutely in a terrified silence, answering my inquiries in a whispered phrase often five to ten minutes later. She reported being overwhelmed by frightening mental images." Because of her problems in communicating, "it was very difficult . . . to learn what her life was like outside of our meetings. Of the hundreds of clients I've encountered since meeting Martha ten years ago, I have only met a handful who were as actively and painfully schizophrenic in their day-to-day living."

Yet the most interesting thing about Martha was the fact that, for all her psychotic symptoms, she was quite functional. She was never hospitalized and steadily maintained outside employment. "She owned and drove her own car, collaborating with the consulting psychiatrist about what medications would allow her to do this safely. She did not drive her family crazy. She got herself to therapy sessions and paid her own fee. And she got herself better, using treatment to help reduce her anxiety level and, in turn, her psychotic symptoms."

Martha taught Kanter something very important he has never forgotten—namely, that severe physical and emotional handicaps are not synonymous with a lack of personal responsibility. Just because she had psychiatric problems, in Kanter's words, "she did not have to act like a mental patient."

Completing his graduate training and beginning work in a psychiatric aftercare program, Kanter discovered many patients with symptoms much less severe than Martha's who *did* act like mental patients. They did not work or attempt to get jobs, "although they all talked about it." They constantly irritated their families, abused hospital facilities, grossly neglected their physical health, and "no matter how much effort our staff expended trying to help them, little was accomplished."

At the same time there were patients like Tom, who "though grossly delusional, would take a bus and subway with clockwork regularity to participate in a sheltered workshop. Arlene, though hospitalized fifteen times, worked steadily as a hospital clerk and got herself to therapy three times a week. Ned, whose hallucinations continued in spite of considerable medication, [yet managed to] covertly collaborate with his psychiatrist in optimally adjusting his chemotherapy."

Kanter not only discovered that mental patients were capable of responsible behavior, and of improving the quality of their lives in the process, but that the choice to do so could be influenced by family expectations. This latter point became especially clear when he began working with a thirty-eight-year-old man named John[8] who had been diagnosed dysfunctional since adolescence and had been through a series of unsuccessful therapies.

After years of trying every method he knew, Kanter finally terminated treatment with John, saying there was no more he could do and there was "little value in wasting each other's time." It was some months later when Kanter learned that John had been permitted to return to his parents' home with the provision that he obey three strict conditions: that he shower daily, that he not watch television late into the night, and that he stay away from the house each day for a certain number of hours, regardless of the weather.

Not only was John able to live by these values, but he began to get bored with idly wandering around the community and sought out professional help on his own initiative. Eventually he enrolled in a sheltered workshop where he was finally able to make some real therapeutic progress. Kanter could only attribute "this modest step in his improved functioning to his family's increased expectations. . . ."

To get back to the question, then, of how to help a footdragging relative with a history of psychological impairment, the point is not to let a psychiatric diagnosis prevent us from investigating the possibility of a more mutually respectful relationship. I am not suggesting this is something that should be done unilaterally without professional guidance, but neither should we limit ourselves to just one opinion, particularly if we are dealing with a therapist who equates emotional handicaps with lack of responsibility. For readers who are wrestling with this kind of situation, I again recommend Kanter's excellent manual, *Coping Strategies for Relatives of the Mentally Ill,* available from The National Alliance for the Mentally Ill.[9]

Fortunately the process of helping someone who *is* sincerely motivated to change is a much simpler one. Beyond the prerequisite willingness to share the courage of our own struggle, the best thing we can do is to listen with a sympathetic ear and reflect the emotion we are hearing between the lines.

This would mean occasionally punctuating the conversation with phrases like "I sense what you are feeling is sadness" or "You're talking about not caring, but I'm hearing a lot of anger." Someone who is able to do this with continued love and acceptance is, in the words of Frances Vaughan, "a natural healer."[10]

"For the ordinary garden variety abnormality you see in families, neighbors, and friends," explains Allen Bergin,[11] "I think the best approach . . . is where you learn to be a very good listener. And I don't just mean being silent, but where you tune in to the emotional experience of the person and communicate [you] understand the experience you perceive."

Bergin, who with his wife teaches this technique in marriage and family relations classes at a local church, finds it "very healing and powerful" in ordinary helping situations, especially when listeners "practice not judging or evaluating what they hear."

What makes this approach so effective, from the viewpoint of ethical therapy, is the way it helps the person to clarify his feelings and, with time, connect them to variations in ethical behavior. In the case of the motivated "lost soul," it is this lack of awareness which most often prevents him from spontaneously making constructive choices.

Finally we must be willing to acknowledge that helping someone else change is not the same thing as having him do what we think we would do in his or her place. If being helped means anything, it means becoming more responsive to one's intuitive wisdom, which by definition transcends outside opinion.

Does this mean acknowledging unreasonable limits to our power?

Only if we continue to identify with our controlling mind and not with the intuitive wisdom it constantly tries to usurp. Even in helping others we inevitably come back to the old paradox that getting what we want often means giving up what we know. The reward for this enforced humility is the privilege of letting those we love—including ourselves—be seen in a way that conventional psychology can never acknowledge: as free and inspired human beings.

# NOTES

## Introduction

1. T. Maeder, "Wounded Healers," p. 37+.

2. Quoted in T. Edwards, *et al.*, eds., *The New Dictionary of Thoughts*, p. 164.

3. W. James, *Principles of Psychology*, p. 130.

4. Hamlet's advice to his mother.

## Chapter One: The Revolution in Therapy

1. Quoted in E. Hamilton, *The Echo of Greece*, p. 42.

2. Quoted in C. Thoresen and J. Eagleston, "Counseling for Health," p. 78.

3. H. Stupp, *et al.*, *Psychotherapy for Better or Worse: the Problem of Negative Effects*.

4. P. Buckley, *et al.*, "Psychotherapists View Their Personal Therapy."

5. M. Parloff, "Can Psychotherapy Research Guide the Policy Maker?"

6. M. Goldfried, "Toward the Delineation of Therapeutic Change Principles."

7. S. Levine, "Who Should Do Psychotherapy?," p. 61.

8. "Religion in America: 1982," p. 7.

## Chapter Two: What Is Ethical Therapy?

1. Unfootnoted quotes were collected prior to my developing an organized research strategy.

2. A. Bergin, "Three Contributions of a Spiritual Perspective to Psychotherapy and Behavior Change," p. 4.

3. J. Jensen and A. Bergin, "Mental Health Values of Professional Therapists: a National Interdisciplinary Survey."

4. A. Bergin, "Psychotherapy and Religious Values."

5. E. Hamilton, *Witness to the Truth*, p. 31.

6. B. Simon, *Mind and Madness in Ancient Greece*, p. 206.

7. C. Gill, "Ancient Psychotherapy."

8. For more on Franklin's method see his *Autobiography*.

9. Quoted in D. Levin, "The Puritan in the Enlightenment: Franklin and Edwards," p. 32.

10. J. S. Bockoven, *Moral Treatment in American Psychiatry*, pp. 18–19.

11. Quoted in D. T. Campbell, "On the Conflict between Biological and Social Evolution and between Psychology and Moral Tradition," p. 1108.

12. For more on the history of psychoanalysis see B. Bettelheim, "Freud and the Soul."

13. Quoted in B. Bettelheim, "Freud and the Soul."

14. H. Hartshorne and M. May, *Studies in the Nature of Character*.

15. R. C. Cabot, *The Meaning of Right and Wrong*, pp. 5–6.

16. R. Leys, "Meyer, Watson, and the Dangers of Behaviorism."

17. For more on the history of behaviorism see F. Samelson, "Organizing for the Kingdom of Behavior: Academic Battles and Organizational Policies in the Twenties."

18. Quoted in B. Bettelheim, "Freud and the Soul," p. 63.

19. Quoted in F. Samelson, "Organizing for the Kingdom of Behavior: Academic Battles and Organizational Policies in the Twenties," p. 42.

20. For a good example, see O. H. Mowrer, ed., *Morality and Mental Illness*, pp. vii–viii.

21. C. Holman, *The Cure of Souls*, p. 217.

22. D. Browning, *The Moral Context of Pastoral Care*, p. 18.

23. J. Kanter, Interview.

24. For an example of such research, see C. Safran, "65,000 Women Reveal How Religion Affects Health, Happiness, Sex and Politics."

25. G. Mora, "Recent American Psychiatric Developments," p. 32.

26. D. Peterson, "In Memorium: O. Hobart Mowrer: 1907–1982."

27. Quoted in M. Hall, "A Conversation with Abraham Maslow," p. 55.

28. A. Maslow, *Motivation and Personality*, p. 160.

29. C. Jung, *Modern Man in Search of a Soul*, p. 34.

30. For more on Cognitive Behavior Therapy see S. Hollon and A. Beck, "Cognitive Therapy of Depression."

31. For more on Interpersonal Psychotherapy see G. Klerman, *et al.*, *Interpersonal Psychotherapy of Depression*.

32. E. Chevron, Interview.

33. Quoted in D. Goleman, "Confiding in Others Improves Health," p. C2.

34. Interestingly Thoresen does not view his findings as a discovery as much as a rediscovery "of the collective wisdom about health and well-being gathered through the centuries." C. Thoresen and J. Eagleston, "Counseling for Health," p. 15.

35. D. Isenberg, "Field Research on Managerial Thinking: Seven Findings, Seven Puzzles," p. 8.

36. D. T. Campbell, "On the Conflict between Biological and Social Evolution and between Psychology and Moral Tradition," p. 1120.

37. Source: A. A. World Service.

38. H. Goolishian, Interview.

39. E. Hoffman, Interview.

## Chapter Three: Beyond Depression

1. Quoted in A. Beck, *The History of Depression*, p. 15.

2. Quoted in D. Levin, *The Puritan Enlightenment: Franklin and Edwards*, p. 32.

3. H. Schmeck, "Defective Gene Tied to Form of Manic-Depressive Illness" and "2nd Genetic Defect Linked to Illness."

4. M. Gross, "The Psychological Society," p. 133. Also W. Dorfman, "Depression and Its Expression in Physical Illness," pp. 702–8.

5. For women the statistic is an astonishing one in three. M. Scarf, "The More Sorrowful Sex," p. 48.

6. R. D. Hicks, trans., *Diogenes Laertius on Lives of Eminent Philosophers*, Vol. I, pp. 38–39; pp. 310–12.

7. Quoted in A. Brock, ed., *Greek Medicine*, p. 171.

8. T. Hora, *Forgiveness*, p. 2.

9. Reported in C. Tavris, *Anger, the Misunderstood Emotion*, pp. 186–88.

10. Ibid., p. 42.

11. For a detailed description of this study see I. Elkin, *et al.*, "NIMH Treatment of Depression Collaborative Research Project."

12. Quoted in P. Boffey, "Psychotherapy Is as Good as Drug in Curing Depression, Study Finds," p. B11.

13. Quoted in "Talk Is as Good as a Pill," p. 60.

14. J. Brody, "Study Suggests Changing Behavior May Prevent Heart Attacks," p. C1.

15. R. Case, *et al.*, "Type A Behavior and Survival After Myocardial Infarction."

16. C. Thoresen and J. Eagleston, "Counseling for Health," p. 62.

17. T. Hora, *Forgiveness*, p. 8.

18. T. Hora, *Dialogues in MetaPsychiatry*, p. 25.

19. T. Hora, *Forgiveness*, p. 3.

20. Quoted in A. Brock, ed., *Greek Medicine*, p. 169.

21. Quoted in W. James, *Varieties of Religious Experience*, pp. 151–52.

22. Quoted in T. Hora, *Beyond the Dream*, p. 222.

23. H. Goolishian, Interview.

24. Quoted in G. Harkness, *The Dark Night of the Soul*, pp. 58–60.

25. M. Friedman, C. Thoresen, and J. Gill, "Type A Behavior: Its Possible Role, Detection, and Alternation in Patients with Ischemic Heart Disease," p. 95.

26. Quoted in A. Brock, ed., *Greek Medicine*, p. 167.

## Chapter Four: Beyond Guilt

1. Quoted in J. Gardner, *Self-Renewal*, p. 111.

2. O. H. Mowrer, *The Crisis in Psychiatry and Religion*, p. 42.

3. H. Hart, "Displacement Guilt and Pain."

4. E. Chevron, "Adolescent Depression."

5. Quoted in W. Durant, *The Story of Philosophy*, p. 139.

6. T. Hora, *Compassion*, p. 2

7. A. Beck, *The Diagnosis and Management of Depression*, p. 16.

8. D. Goleman, "Research Affirms Power of Positive Thinking," p. C5.

9. M. Buber, "Guilt and Guilt Feelings," p. 121.

10. O. H. Mowrer, *The Crisis in Psychiatry and Religion*.

11. Quoted in O. H. Mowrer, *The Crisis in Psychiatry and Religion*, p. 98.

12. Quoted in P. Vitz, *Psychology As Religion*, p. 93.

13. O. H. Mowrer, *The Crisis in Psychiatry and Religion*, p. 100

14. R. Driscoll, "Their Own Worst Enemies," p. 47.

15. T. Hora, Interview.

16. Quoted in R. Weiss and C. Butterworth, eds., *Ethical Writings of Maimonides*, p. 68.

17. J. Kanter, Interview.

18. Personal communication.

19. J. Kanter, Interview.

20. K. Stewart, "Dream Theory in Malaya."

21. Quoted in O. H. Mowrer, *The Crisis in Psychiatry and Religion*, p. 89.

22. A University of Houston psychologist named Lynn Rehm set up a training program that simply encouraged patients to become more aware of their guilty thoughts, evaluating and rewarding their own behavior with some realistic perspective. Working with small groups of depressed women, meeting roughly once a day for about ninety minutes, Rehm found that any attempt to define the legitimate boundaries of one's guilt tends to shrink those boundaries and lead to an elevation in mood. A. Rosenfeld, "Depression: Dispelling Despair," pp. 32–34.

23. Quoted in G. Brown, *The New Celibacy*, p. 4.

24. "For I have hardened his heart and the heart of his servants." Quoted in J. Melber, *The Universality of Maimonides*, pp. 124–25.

## Chapter Five: Beyond Boredom

1. Quoted in W. Chittick, *The Sufi Path of Love*, p. 33.

2. *Matthew* (King James version) 10:39.

3. Quoted in R. Kuhn, *The Demon of Noontide*, p. 12.

4. S. Keen, *What to Do When You're Bored and Blue*, p. ix.

5. D. Darden and A. Marks, "Teaching Problems and Boring Students."

6. See B. Gunter and M. Wober, "Television Viewing and Public Trust." Also H. Pope and M. Ferguson, "Age and Anomia in Middle and Later Life"; L. Sigelman, "Is Ignorance Bliss? A Reconsideration of the Folk Wisdom"; and L. Lovell-Troy, "Anomia among Employed Wives and Housewives."

7. S. Healy, *Boredom, Self, and Culture*, p. 53.

8. Ibid.

9. See Plato's *Symposium*.

10. See especially A. Maslow, *Motivation and Personality*, chapter 2.

11. T. Hora, *Existential Metapsychiatry*, p. 170.

12. T. Hora, *Dialogues in Metapsychiatry*, pp. 24–25.

13. M. Scott Peck, *The Road Less Traveled*, pp. 291–92.

14. R. Firestone, *The Truth*, p. 117.

15. Ibid., p. xiv.

16. T. Wells, *Keeping Your Cool Under Fire*, p. 226.

17. Adapted from Franklin's *Autobiography*.

18. T. Hora, *Compassion*, p. 20.

19. D. Isenberg, "Field Research on Managerial Thinking: Seven Findings, Seven Puzzles," p. 13.

20. G. Jampolsky, *Love Is Letting Go of Fear*, pp. 100–1.

21. Examples from T. Wells, Interview.

22. T. Wells, *Keeping Your Cool Under Fire*, p. 225–53.

23. Ibid., p. 226.

24. A. Bergin, "Three Contributions of a Spiritual Practice to Psychotherapy and Behavior Change," p. 15.

25. Ibid., p. 14.

26. A. Huxley, *The Perennial Philosophy*, p. 221.

27. Quoted in A. Huxley, *The Perennial Philosophy*, pp. 221–22.

## Chapter Six: Beyond Indecision

1. Quoted in D. B. Phillips, ed., *The Choice Is Always Ours*, p. 4–5.

2. Plato said Socrates was the wisest man in all Greece because he "knows that he does not know."

3. 1976.

4. See Chapter Two, note 1.

5. W. James, "The Sentiment of Rationality," p. 9.

6. See R. Rowan, *The Intuitive Manager*, p. 4.

7. For more on Yang-ming, see J. Ching, *To Acquire Wisdom* and J. Ching, *Philosophical Letters of Wang Yang-ming*.

8. Quoted in J. Ching, *To Acquire Wisdom*, p. 44.

9. Ibid., p. 31.

10. Ibid., p. 68.

11. J. Davidson, *The Buying and Goodbying of Behaviorism's Way*, p. 240.

12. J. McBride, "Some Heady Talk about Gut Feeling."

13. Examples from R. Rowan, "Those Business Hunches Are More Than Blind Faith."

14. R. Rowan, *The Intuitive Manager*.

15. R. Cosier and J. Aplin, "Intuition and Decision Making: Some Empirical Evidence," p. 280.

16. D. Isenberg, "How Senior Managers Think."

17. Quoted in D. Isenberg, "How Senior Managers Think," p. 87.

18. Quoted in D. Sperling, "Best Executives Know Intuition Supplements Logic," p. 2b.

19. Quoted in F. Vaughan, *Awakening Intuition*, pp. 156–57.

20. D. Goleman, "Insights into Self-Deception," p. 43.

21. See E. Gendlin, *Focusing*.

22. Quoted in R. May, *Physicians of the Soul*, p. 31.

23. F. Vaughan, Interview.

24. F. Vaughan, *Awakening Intuition*, p. 204.

## Chapter Seven: Beyond Worthlessness

1. Quoted in A. Brock, *Greek Medicine*, p. 169.

2. T. Hora, *Marriage and Family Life*, p. 9.

3. Quoted in M. Lefebure, *Samuel Taylor Coleridge: a Bondage of Opium*, p. 480.

4. Ibid., p. 339.

5. M. Lefebure, *Samuel Taylor Coleridge: a Bondage of Opium*, p. 469.

6. A. Pacht, "Reflections on Perfection," pp. 387–88.

7. A. Pacht, Interview.

8. M. Snyder and J. Simpson, "Self-Monitoring and Dating Relationships."

9. M. Snyder and N. Cantor, "Thinking About Ourselves and Others," pp. 222–23.

10. D. E. Hamachek, "Psychodynamics of Normal Neurotic Perfectionism," p. 28.

11. Many historians assume Plato was a perfectionist because of his theory of ideal forms. In his *Parmenides*, however, Plato tells us that ideals are models, not to be imitated, but to be realized through self-expression. See J. Wild, *Plato's Modern Enemies and the Theory of Natural Law*, p. 138.

12. A. Pacht, "Reflections on Perfection," p. 387.

13. J. Kizziar and J. Hagedorn, *Search for Acceptance: the Adolescent and Self-Esteem*.

14. See J. Polivy and C. Herman, "Dieting and Binging."

15. J. McBride, Interview.

16. A. Pacht, "Reflections on Perfection," p. 386.

17. T. Peters and N. Austin, *A Passion for Excellence*, p. 175.

18. D. Isenberg, "How Senior Managers Think," p. 84.

19. Isenberg's description. See D. Isenberg, "Strategic Opportunism: Managing Under Uncertainty," p. 32.

20. Quoted in D. Isenberg, "Strategic Opportunism: Managing Under Uncertainty," p. 18.

21. Quoted in J. Wild, *Plato's Modern Enemies and the Theory of Natural Law*, p. 147 and p. 146 respectively.

22. D. Ingber, "Inside the Executive Mind," p. 34.

23. See his speech on *Perfectibility* (1828).

24. Quoted in M. Lefebure, *Samuel Taylor Coleridge: a Bondage of Opium*, p. 477 and p. 479.

25. T. Hora, Interview.

26. V. Brundage, Interview.

27. D. Isenberg, Interview.

28. A. Pacht, "Reflections on Perfection," p. 389.

## Chapter Eight: Beyond Fear

1. Quoted in J. Ching, *The Philosophical Letters of Wang Yang-ming*, p. 85.

2. Quoted in G. W. Allen, *William James*, p. 9.

3. Quoted in H. Feinstein, *Becoming William James*, p. 209.

4. W. James, *The Varieties of Religious Experience*, pp. 135–36. Although attributed to a Frenchman, this account is now believed to be autobiographical.

5. Quoted in M. Shaw, "Paradoxical Intention in the Life and Thought of William James," p. 8.

6. J. Pennebaker and C. Chew, "Behavioral Inhibition and Electrodermal Activity During Deception."

7. See J. Pennebaker, "Traumatic Experience and Psychosomatic Disease: Exploring the Roles of Behavioral Inhibition, Obsession, and Confiding," and J. Pennebaker and R. O'Heeron, "Confiding in Others and Illness Rates Among Spouses of Suicide and Accidental Death Victims." In another and more ominous study of 225 doctors who as young men had taken a test to measure defensive vigilance, the death rate over a twenty-five-year period was some six times greater for the high scorers. See C. Creekmore, "The Death of Cynicism," p. 80.

8. See D. Goleman, "Confiding in Others Improves Health," p. C2.

9. See especially R. Curtis and K. Miller, "Believing Another Likes or Dislikes You: Behaviors Making the Beliefs Come True."

10. J. Rotter, Interview.

11. T. Wells, Interview.

12. S. Parker, "Eskimo Psychopathology in the Context of Eskimo Personality and Culture."

13. See J. Rotter, "Trust and Gullibility."

14. F. Kafka, *Letters to His Father*.

15. A. Bergin, Interview.

16. E. Hoffman, Interview.

17. D. Seibert and W. Proctor, *The Ethical Executive*, p. 6 and p. 37.

18. G. Nierenberg, *The Art of Negotiating*, pp. 25–26.

19. For organized help in reducing marital evasion, many ethically oriented therapists speak favorably of Marriage Encounter. Started in Barcelona, Spain, in 1952 by Father Gabriel Calvo, a Roman Catholic priest, it brings together groups of from twenty to forty couples for a long weekend designed to stimulate one-on-one discussions between the partners.

These structured encounters, which are scheduled at frequent intervals in all parts of the country, usually begin with a lecture, in which a presenting couple talks for a while about the importance of increased honesty and open communication. The audience then breaks up so that each person can reflect on what has been said, write down feelings, and then discuss these reactions in private with his or her mate. After a time, the couples reconvene for a new lecture, and the process is repeated.

What makes Marriage Encounter so helpful is that the technique appears to work equally well with people of all faiths and backgrounds. The same format is followed at a Jewish weekend, a Baptist weekend, an Episcopal weekend, a Catholic weekend, or among non-denominational groups, while the main presenting couples can be clergy or laypersons. By current estimates, (S. Ogg, Interview) roughly 100,000 couples a year in at least twenty-eight countries participate in some form of marriage encounter, with favorable articles appearing in publications as diverse as *Psychology Today* and the *Christian Herald*.

Equally striking is the effectiveness with which it helps even habitually evasive partners begin to communicate with love and trust. The response of one woman named Neville is typical: "The night we drove home from our weekend it was pouring rain. Normally I would have been nervous about the road conditions and the traffic. But that night was different. I felt as though I were in a boat in the harbor while the storm raged at sea beyond, and I felt very peaceful, trusting, loving, and loved." (J. Kenyon, "44 Hours to a Better Marriage.") A male participant put it like this: "[We] experienced the most beautiful weekend of our lives. As we drove away from it on Sunday I had the same feeling I had 20 years earlier as we left our wedding reception." (Ibid.)

People interested in attending a non-denominational weekend in their area should send a self-addressed, stamped envelope requesting further information to Sandy and Chuck Ogg, National Marriage Encounter, 4704 Jamerson Place, Orlando, Florida 32807. Those who feel more comfortable in a more religious context should contact their local church, archdiocese, or Jewish Marriage Encounter, c/o Muriel and Jack Diamond, 3983 Carrel Boulevard, Oceanside, N.Y. 11572.

20. V. Smith, Interview.

21. N. Hurvitz, "Peer Self-Help Psychotherapy Groups and Their Implication for Psychotherapy."

22. D. Scibert and W. Proctor, The Ethical Executive, p. 202.

23. C. Thoresen and J. Eagleston, "Counseling for Health," pp. 74+.

24. See his Republic.

25. Quoted in R. Weiss and C. Butterworth, eds., Ethical Writings of Maimonides, p. 46.

26. See his essay "On Suspicion."

## Chapter Nine: Beyond Frustration

1. Cicero quoted in J. Spedding, et al., eds., The Works of Francis Bacon, Vol. V, p. 77.

2. Bilbey was a nineteenth-century economist. Quoted in C. Hickman and M. Silva, Creating Excellence, p. 127.

3. Epistle VII 348–49.

4. See W. Durant, The Story of Philosophy, p. 96.

5. See especially B. De Paula, et al., "Detecting the Deceit of the Motivated Liar."

6. L. Streeter, et al., "Pitch Changes During Attempted Deception."

7. J. Kanter, Interview.

8. T. Hora, Interview.

9. Personal communication.

10. T. Hunt, Interview.

11. Ibid.

12. J. Kanter, Interview.

13. Ibid.

14. 1200 15th Street, NW, Suite 400, Washington, D.C. 20005

15. For more on questions two, three, and four see M. Feinberg and A. Levenstein, "The Danger in Manipulating Employees."

16. I am indebted to therapist Phyllis Carozza for this discussion of favored manipulations.

17. T. Hunt, Interview.

18. Quoted in H. Brody, *Placebos and the Philosophy of Medicine,* p. 101.

19. Ibid.

## Chapter Ten: Beyond Loneliness

1. Quoted in M. Muggeridge, *A Third Testament,* p. 39.

2. Quoted in T. Hora, *God in Psychiatry,* p. 23.

3. A. Campbell, *The Sense of Well-being in America.*

4. P. Pilkonis and P. Zimbardo, "The Personal and Social Dynamics of Shyness."

5. S. Jourard, "Healthy Personality and Self-Disclosure," pp. 228–29.

6. K. Rook, "Promoting Social Bonding," p. 1389.

7. C. Moustakas, *Loneliness,* pp. 28–29.

8. J. F. T. Bugenthal.

9. D. Kissen, "The Significance of Personality in Lung Cancer in Men."

10. R. Derogatis, *et al.,* "Psychological Coping Mechanisms and Survival Time in Metastic Breast Cancer."

11. W. Jones, *et al.,* "The Persistence of Loneliness," pp. 45–46.

12. See J. Meer, "Loneliness," p. 30.

13. Quoted in J. Meer, "Loneliness," p. 30.

14. C. Fischer, *To Dwell among Friends.*

15. C. Rubenstein and P. Shaver, "Loneliness in Two Northern Cities," p. 326.

16. For more on the life of Augustine see P. Brown, *Augustine of Hippo;* also, M. Muggeridge, *A Third Testament.*

17. See Book Three of the *Republic.*

18. H. Deutsch, "Some Forms of Emotional Disturbance and Their Relationship to Schizophrenia," p. 302.

19. S. Jourard, *The Transparent Self,* p. 20.

20. Ibid., pp. 22–23.

21. V. Sermat, "Some Situational and Personality Correlates of Loneliness," p. 306.

22. K. Rook, "Promoting Social Bonding," pp. 1395–96.

23. Quoted in C. Gardner and S. Wagner, "Clinical Diagnosis of the As-If Personality Disorder," p. 139.

24. Personal Communication.

25. K. Rook, "Promoting Social Bonding," p. 1401.

26. V. Brundage, Interview.

27. H. Goolishian, Interview.

28. Parenthetical amplification mine. J. Davidson, *The Buying and Goodbying of Behaviorism's Way,* p. 217.

29. Adapted from C. Gardner and S. Wagner, "Clinical Diagnosis of the As-If Personality Disorder," pp. 142–43.

30. Analogy suggested by E. Schachtel, "On Alienated Concepts of Identity," p. 127.

31. E. Goffman, *Encounters,* p. 124.

32. J. Lauer and R. Lauer, "Marriages Made to Last," pp. 22–26.

33. *Matthew* (Douay version) 16:26.

34. From E. Shostrom, *Man, the Manipulator,* pp. 223–25.

35. J. McBride, Interview.

36. Personal communication.

37. C. Gourgey, "Integrity and Self-Esteem," p. 5.

38. D. Cohen, Interview.

39. V. Brundage, Interview.

## Chapter Eleven: Beyond Anxiety

1. F. Vaughan, Interview.

2. Quoted in A. Huxley, *The Perennial Philosophy*, p. 141.

3. Quoted in A. Beck, *et al.*, *The History of Depression*, p. 12.

4. *Ecclesiastes* (Douay version) 7:9.

5. For more on Rumi and his times see especially A. Iqbal, *The Life and Thought of Mohammad Jalal-ud-din Rumi.*

6. Quoted in K. Hakim, *The Metaphysics of Rumi*, p. 105.

7. Quoted in R. Nicholson, trans., *Rumi*, p. 146.

8. Quoted in A. Arberry, trans., *The Mystical Poems of Rumi*, p. 55.

9. See Chapter Two, note 1.

10. Quoted in M. Gross, *The Psychological Society*, p. 18.

11. R. D. Laing, *The Politics of Experience*, p. 101.

12. See S. Sheikh and N. Panagiotou, "The Use of Mental Imagery in Psychotherapy"; also J. Singer, *The Inner World of Daydreaming.*

13. P. Suedfeld, "The Benefits of Boredom: Sensory Deprivation Reconsidered."

14. Personal communication.

15. J. Davidson, *The Buying and Goodbying of Behaviorism's Way*, pp. 93–94.

16. For more on systematic desensitization see *Psychotherapy by Reciprocal Inhibition* and other works by Joseph Wolpe.

17. F. Vaughan, Interview.

18. Quoted in A. Watts, *Psychotherapy East and West*, p. 97.

19. Thirty-nine were mailed, but one spouse died and seven were postmarked unforwardable. J. Pennebaker and R. O'Heeron, "Confiding in Others and Illness Rate Among Spouses of Suicidal and Accidental Death Victims."

20. J. Pennebaker, C. Hughes, and R. O'Heeron, "The Psychophysiology of Confession: Linking Inhibition and Psychosomatic Processes."

21. Quoted in A. Watts, *Psychotherapy East and West*, p. 97.

22. J. Pennebaker and S. Beall, "Confronting a Traumatic Event: Toward an Understanding of Inhibition and Disease."

23. Ibid., p. 15.

## Chapter Twelve: Beyond Addiction

1. Quoted in C. Van Doren, *Benjamin Franklin*, pp. 84–85.

2. T. Hora, *Beyond the Dream*, p. 163.

3. K. Brownell, *et al.*, "Understanding and Preventing Relapse," p. 765.

4. W. Miller, "The Addictive Behaviors," p. 3.

5. For an economic perspective on why the image of addictive withdrawal is exaggerated, see W. Miller and R. Hester, "Inpatient Alcoholism Treatment: Who Benefits?"

6. A. Weil, *The Natural Mind*, p. 42.

7. W. Miller and R. Hester, "Treating the Problem Drinker," p. 15.

8. For women only, there is a relationship between craving intensity and failure to complete a "cold turkey" withdrawal program. R. Gunn, "Reactions to Withdrawal Symptoms and Success in Smoking Cessation Clinics."

9. D. Musto, "Lessons of the First Cocaine Epidemic," p. 30.

10. C. Cummings, *et al.*, "Relapse: Prevention and Prediction," p. 304.

11. Quoted in L. W. White, "Recovery from Alcoholism: Transpersonal Dimensions," p. 118.

12. Whitfield is talking primarily about alcoholism. Quoted in T. Prugh, "Alcohol, Spirituality, and Recovery," p. 30.

13. Quoted in T. Prugh, "Alcohol, Spirituality, and Recovery," p. 31.

14. Ibid.

15. Quoted in L. W. White, "Recovery from Alcoholism: Transpersonal Dimensions," p. 118.

16. L. W. White, "Recovery from Alcoholism: Transpersonal Dimensions," pp. 122–23.

17. R. Stall, "An Examination of Spontaneous Remission from Problem Drinking in the Bluegrass Region of Kentucky," p. 203.

18. C. Turner and R. Willis, "The Relationship Between Self-reported Religiosity and Drug Use by College Students."

19. J. Fisher and A. Farina, "Consequences of Beliefs About the Nature of Mental Disorders," pp. 320–27.

20. J. Greene, "The Gambling Trap," p. 51.

21. Quoted in N. Hurvitz, "Peer Self-Help Psychotherapy Groups and Their Implications for Psychotherapy," p. 47.

22. *Another Look.*

23. T. Hora, Interview.

24. Frances Vaughan, Interview.

25. A. Bergin, Interview.

26. For more on the Rand Study, see J. Polish, *et al., The Course of Alcoholism.*

27. W. Miller and R. Hester, "Treating the Problem Drinker," p. 50.

28. *A. A. in Treatment Centers.*

29. G. Alford, "Alcoholics Anonymous: an Empirical Outcome Study," p. 369.

30. *One Addict's Experience with Acceptance, Faith, and Commitment.*

31. *To the Man Who Wants to Stop Compulsive Overeating, Welcome.*

## Chapter Thirteen: The Family Barometer

1. Quoted in W. Durant, *The Story of Civilization,* Vol. II, p. 517.

2. *Matthew* (King James version) 10:36.

3. C. Thoresen and J. Eagleston, "Counseling for Health," p. 77.

4. The family is such a sensitive subject that even famous ethical therapists have failed to comprehend it, although something odd or violent in their opinions betray at least an unconscious awareness of the family's importance. Plato, for example, believed that the one exception to the principle of truthfulness was the "noble lie" of telling political leaders that they were not born of women.

5. Personal communication.

6. E. Chevron, Interview.

7. T. Hora, Interview.

8. V. Brundage, Interview.

9. Personal communication.

10. J. Kanter, "Moral Issues and Mental Illness," p. 535.

11. This technique is often attributed to Georgetown University family therapist Murray Bowen, although Bowen himself believes we benefit most from person-to-person conversation if we have an experienced "coach" to help us. M. Bowen, *Family Therapy in Clinical Practice*, pp. 540–41.

12. R. Isrealy, Interview.

13. B. Raxlen, *et al.*, Interview.

14. Ibid.

15. A. Bergin, "Three Contributions of a Spiritual Perspective to Psychotherapy and Behavior Change," p. 18.

16. Ibid, p. 16.

## Epilogue—Helping

1. Quote attributed to his *Archidoxa* (Arch Wisdom), 1524.

2. *Hamlet*, Act I, Scene III.

3. *Epistle VII* 332 (Hamilton translation).

4. R. Firestone, *The Truth*, p. 225.

5. When in 1970 researcher L. L. Lindenthal and his colleagues at Yale did psychiatric evaluations of nearly a thousand people in the New Haven area, they found a distinctly positive relationship between church affiliation and freedom from emotional impairment. Independent data gathered by Survey Research Center at Berkeley and the National Opinion Research Center at the University of Chicago a year later confirmed this finding. A. Bergin, "Religiosity and Mental Health: a Critical Reevaluation and Meta-analysis," p. 177.

6. Ibid., p. 181.

7. J. Kanter, *Coping Strategies for Relatives of the Mentally Ill*, p. 7.

8. Ibid., p. 8.

9. 1200 15th Street, NW, Suite 400, Washington, D.C. 20005

10. F. Vaughan, *The Inward Arc*, p. 194.

11. A. Bergin, Interview.

# REFERENCES

*A.A. in Treatment Centers.* New York, A.A. World Services, 1979.

Africa, T., "The Opium Addiction of Marcus Aurelius," *Journal of the History of Ideas* (January-March 1961), pp. 97–102.

Alford, G., "Alcoholics Anonymous: an Empirical Outcome Study," *Addictive Behaviors* (Vol. 5), pp. 359–70.

Ali Shah, Ikbal, *The Spirit of the East.* New York, Dutton, 1975.

———, *Selections from the Koran.* London, Octagon Press, 1980.

Allen, F., "Bosses List Main Strengths, Flaws Determining Potential Managers," *Wall Street Journal* (November 14, 1980), p. 33.

Allen, G. W., *William James.* Minneapolis, U. of Minnesota Press, 1970

Amore, R., *Two Masters, One Message.* Nashville, Abingdon, 1978.

Andrae, T., *Mohammed, the Man and His Faith.* New York, Barnes and Noble, 1935

Andrews, L., and Karlins, M., *Psychology: What's in It for Us?*, 2nd ed. New York, Random House, 1975.

*Another Look.* Van Nuys, Calif., N.A. World Service, 1984.

Arberry, A., trans., *The Koran Interpreted.* New York, Macmillan, 1955.

———, trans., *Mystical Poems of Rumi.* Chicago, U. of Chicago Press, 1968.

Arieti, S., "Roots of Depression," *Psychology Today* (New York, April 1979), pp. 54–58, 92–93.

Arieti, S., and Bemporad, J., *Severe and Mild Depression.* New York, Basic, 1978.

Arnold, E., trans., *The Bhagavad-Gita.* New York, Collier, 1910.

Augustine (Ryan, J., trans.), *Confessions*. Garden City, N.Y., Doubleday, 1960.

Ausubel, N., *The Book of Jewish Knowledge*. New York, Crown, 1964.

Baily, J., "Clues for Success in the President's Job," in E. Collins, ed., *Executive Success*. New York, Wiley, 1983, pp. 29–41.

Bakan, D., *Sigmund Freud and the Jewish Mystical Tradition*. Princeton, N.J., D. Van Nostrand, 1958.

Barfield, O., *What Coleridge Thought*. Middletown, Conn., Wesleyan University Press, 1971.

Bate, W., *Coleridge*. New York, Macmillan, 1968.

Bateson, G., *Steps To An Ecology of Mind*. New York, Chandler, 1972.

Battenhouse, R. W., "The Life of Augustine," in R. W. Battenhouse, ed., *A Companion to the Study of St. Augustine*. New York, Oxford University Press, 1955.

Bazelon, D., "Veils, Values, and Social Responsibility," *American Psychologist* (February 1982), pp. 115–21.

Beauvais, P., of Wellspring Intermediate Care Facility, Interview. (Bethlehem, Conn. August 19, 1980).

Beck, A., *The Diagnosis and Management of Depression*. Philadelphia, U. of Pennsylvania Press, 1967.

———, "Role of Fantasies in Psychotherapy and Psychopathology," *Journal of Nervous and Mental Disease* (Vol. 150, 1970), pp. 3–16.

———, *The History of Depression*. New York, Pfizer Laboratories, 1977.

Becker, J., *Depression: Theory and Research*. New York, Wiley, 1974.

Beinfield, M., of Norwalk Hospital, Interview. (Norwalk, Conn., October 1979).

Bellah, R., *The Broken Covenant*. New York, Seabury, 1975.

———, "Civil Religion in America," in R. Bellah and W. McLoughlin, *Religion in America*. Boston, Houghton Mifflin, 1968.

Bentwich, N., *Philo-Judaeus of Alexandria*. Philadelphia, Jewish Publication Society of America, 1910.

Berger, P., and Neuhaus, R., *To Empower People*. Washington, D.C., American Enterprise Institute, 1977.

Bergin, A., "Psychotherapy and Religious Values," *Journal of Consulting and Clinical Psychology* (Vol. 48, 1980), pp. 95–105.

———, of Brigham Young University, Interview by telephone. (Provo, Utah, February 13, 1981).

———, "Religiosity and Mental Health: a Critical Reevaluation and Meta-analysis," *Professional Psychology: Research and Practice* (Vol. 14, No. 2, 1983), pp. 170–84.

———, of Brigham Young University, Interview by telephone. (Provo, Utah, July 17, 1986).

———, "Three Contributions of a Spiritual Practice to Psychotherapy and Behavior Change," *Counseling and Values* in press.

Bettelheim, B., "Freud and the Soul," *New Yorker* (March 1, 1982), pp. 52+.

Bhattacharyya, H., *The Cultural Heritage of India*, Vol. IV. Calcutta, Ramakrishna Mission, 1937.

"The Bill W.–Carl Jung Letters," *A.A. Grapevine* (November 1974), pp. 30–31.

Bishop, J., "Placebos Are Harmless, but They Work, Posing Problems for Medicine," *Wall Street Journal* (Vol. XCVII, No. 39), p. 1 and p. 21.

Blake, W., *Ms. Notebooks* in G. Bentley, ed., *William Blake's Writings*. Oxford, Clarendon Press, 1978, pp. 921–1006.

Block, S., and Reddaway, P., *Russia's Political Hospitals*. London, Futura, 1978.

Bockoven, J., *Moral Treatment in American Psychiatry*. New York, Springer, 1963.

Boffey, P., "Psychotherapy Is as Good as Drug in Curing Depression, Study Finds," *N.Y. Times* (May 14, 1986), pp. Al and Bll.

Bok, S., *Lying*. New York, Pantheon, 1978.

Bokser, Ben Zion, *The Legacy of Maimonides*. New York, Philosophical Library, 1950.

Bonhoffer, D., *Ethics*. New York, Macmillan, 1962.

Bonny, H., *Music and Your Mind*. New York, Harper & Row, 1973.

Booth, R., "Toward an Understanding of Loneliness," *Social Work* (March-April 1983), pp. 116–19.

Borisov, V., "Personality and National Awareness," in A. Solzhenitsyn, *From Under the Rubble.* New York, Bantam, 1976, pp. 193–228.

Bourke, V., ed., *The Essential Augustine.* Indianapolis, Hackett, 1964.

Bowen, M., *Family Therapy in Clinical Practice.* New York, Jason Aronson, 1978.

Boy, A., and Pine, G., "Religion and Psychotherapy: a Humanistic View," *Religious Humanism* (Summer 1979), pp. 115–19.

Branden, N., *Honoring the Self.* Boston, Jeremy Tarcher, 1983.

Brann, N., "Is Acedia Melancholy?," *Journal of the History of Medicine and Allied Sciences* (April 1979), pp. 180–99.

Bratton, F., *Maimonides: Medieval Modernist.* Boston, Beacon, 1967.

Brennan, J., *Ethics and Morals.* New York, Harper & Row, 1973.

Breznitz, S., *Cry Wolf: the Psychology of False Alarms.* London, Lawrence Erlbaum Associates, 1984.

Brock, A., ed., *Greek Medicine.* New York, Dutton, 1929.

Brody, H., *Placebos and the Philosophy of Medicine.* Chicago, U. of Chicago Press, 1977.

Brody, J., "Study Suggests Changing Behavior May Prevent Heart Attacks," *N.Y. Times* (September 16, 1980), pp. C-1+.

Brooks, G., and Aalto, S., "The Rise and Fall of Moral Algebra," *Journal of the History of the Behavioral Sciences* (Vol. 17, 1981), pp. 343–56.

Brown, G., *The New Celibacy.* New York, McGraw-Hill, 1980.

Brown, P., *Augustine of Hippo.* Los Angeles, U. of California Press, 1970.

Brown, T., of Yale Divinity School, Interview. (New Haven, Conn., November 16, 1978).

Brownell, K., *et al.*, "Understanding and Preventing Relapse," *American Psychologist* (July 1986), pp. 765–82.

Browning, D., *The Moral Context of Pastoral Care.* Philadelphia, Westminster Press, 1976.

Bruce, W., *Benjamin Franklin Self-Revealed.* New York, Knickerbocker Press, 1917.

Brundage, V., of the Milwaukee Psychiatric Hospital, Interview by telephone. (Milwaukee, Wisconsin, July 25, 1986).

Buber, M., "Guilt and Guilt Feelings," in M. Friedman, ed., *The Knowledge of Man*. New York, Harper & Row, 1966.

Buckley, P., *et al.*, "Psychotherapists View Their Personal Therapy," *Psychotherapy: Theory, Research, Practice*. (Vol. 18, 1981), pp. 299–305.

Burton, A., *Twelve Therapists*. San Francisco, Jossey-Bass, 1972.

Burtt, E. A., trans., *The Teachings of the Compassionate Buddha*. New York, Mentor, 1955.

Butts, R. F., *The American Tradition in Religion and Education*. Boston, Beacon, 1950.

Bybee, J., Interview. (New Haven, Conn., April 22, 1985).

Cabot, R. C., *The Meaning of Right and Wrong*. New York, Macmillan, 1933.

Calabrese, A., of the Christian Institute for Psychotherapeutic Studies, Interview. (Hicksville, N.Y., December 14, 1978).

Campbell, A., *The Sense of Well-being in America*. New York, McGraw-Hill, 1981.

Campbell, D. T., "On the Conflict between Biological and Social Evolution and between Psychology and Moral Tradition," *American Psychologist* (Vol. 30, 1975), pp. 1103–26.

Carozza, P., family therapist, Interview by telephone. (Kansas City, Missouri, July 23, 1986).

Carus, P., *The Gospel of Buddha*. LaSalle, Ill., Open Court, 1973.

Casady, M., "The Tricky Business of Giving Rewards," *Psychology Today* (September 1974), p. 52.

Case, R., *et al.*, "Type A Behavior and Survival After Acute Myocardial Infarction," *New England Journal of Medicine* (Vol. 312, No. 12, 1985), pp. 737–41.

Chevron, E., "Adolescent Depression," Hall-Brooke Foundation Lecture, June 7, 1984.

———, therapist and author, Interview by telephone. (Saddle River, New Jersey, June 12, 1986).

Ching, J., *The Philosophical Letters of Wang Yang-ming*. Columbia, S.C., U. of South Carolina Press, 1972.

———, *To Acquire Wisdom*. New York, Columbia University Press, 1976.

Chittick, W., *The Sufi Path of Love*. Albany, N.Y., State University of New York Press, 1983.

Clark, R., *Einstein, the Life and Letters*. New York, World, 1971.

Cohen, D., of Fairfield University, Interview. (Weston, Conn., August 9, 1979).

Coleridge, S. T., *The Friend*. London, George Bell and Sons, 1906.

Coles, R., *The Middle Americans*. Boston, Little, Brown, 1971.

Commager, H., *Jefferson, Nationalism and the Enlightenment*. New York, Braziller, 1975.

Cornfield, F., trans., *The Republic of Plato*. New York, Oxford University Press, 1945.

Conze, E., *Buddhist Scriptures*. New York, Penguin, 1959.

————, *Buddhism: Its Essence and Development*. New York, Harper & Row, 1975.

Copeland, E. A., "The Institutional Setting of Plato's *Republic*," *The International Journal of Ethics* (Vol. 34, 1923–24), pp. 228–42.

Cooper, J. C., *Taoism*. New York, Samuel Weiser, 1972.

Cosier, R., and Aplin, J., "Intuition in Decision-Making: Some Empirical Evidence," *Psychological Reports* (Vol. 51, 1982), pp. 275–81.

Cox, R., ed., *Religious Systems and Psychotherapy*. Springfield, Ill., Charles C. Thomas, 1973.

Coyne, J., "Toward an Interactional Description of Depression," *Psychiatry* (Vol. 39, 1976), pp. 28–40.

Creekmore, C., "The Death of Cynicism," *Psychology Today* (April 1984), p. 80.

Crossley, H., trans., *The Golden Sayings of Epictetus*. New York, Collier, 1937.

Cua, A., *The Unity of Knowledge and Action*. Honolulu, U. of Hawaii Press, 1982.

Cummings, C., *et al.*, "Relapse: Prevention and Prediction," in W. Miller, ed., *The Addictive Behaviors*. New York, Pergamon, 1980.

Curtis, R., and Miller, K., "Believing Another Likes or Dislikes You: Behaviors Making the Beliefs Come True," *Journal of Personality and Social Psychology* (Vol. 51, 1986), pp. 284–90.

Cushman, R., *Therapia*. Chapel Hill, U. of North Carolina Press, 1958.

Danish, S., and Smyer, M., "Unintentional Consequences of Requiring a License to Help," *American Psychologist* (January 1981), pp. 13–21.

Darden, D., and Marks, A., "Teaching Problems and Boring Students," paper presented to the Mid-South Sociological Association (October 1985).

David-Neel, A., *Buddhism: Its Doctrines and Its Methods.* New York, St. Martin's, 1977.

Davidson, J., *The Buying and Goodbying of Behaviorism's Way.* Roslyn Heights, N.Y., Libra, 1977.

Dawood, N., trans., *The Koran.* New York, Penguin, 1968.

deBary, W., ed., *Sources of Indian Tradition,* Vol. II. New York, Columbia University Press, 1958.

DeLacy, P., ed. and trans., *Galen on the Doctrines of Hippocrates and Plato.* Berlin, Academie-Verlag, 1978.

DePaulo, B., "Detecting the Deceit of the Motivated Liar," *Journal of Personality and Social Psychology* (Vol. 45, No. 5, 1983), pp. 1096–1103.

Derogatis, L., *et al.,* "Psychological Coping Mechanisms and Survival Time in Metastic Breast Cancer," *Journal of the American Medical Association* (Vol. 242, 1979), pp. 1504–8.

Deutsch, H., "Some Forms of Emotional Disturbance and Their Relationship to Schizophrenia," *Psychoanalytic Quarterly* (Vol. 11, 1942), pp. 301–21.

Diament, B., psychologist, Interview. (New Canaan, Conn., January 5, 1979).

Dorfman, W., "Depression," *Psychosomatics* (November 1978), pp. 702–8.

Doyle, J., President-elect, Association for Humanistic Psychology, Interview by telephone. (Belvedere, Calif., May 28, 1980).

Drake, R., "Comparison of the Moral Value Judgements of Neurotics and Normals," *Nursing Research* (January–February, 1969), pp. 34–39.

Driscoll, R., "Their Own Worst Enemies," *Psychology Today* (July 1982), pp. 45–49.

Dumbauld, E., *The Political Writings of Thomas Jefferson.* New York, Liberal Arts Press, 1955.

Durant, W., *The Story of Philosophy.* New York, Simon & Schuster, 1926.

———, *The Story of Civilization,* Vol. I–VII. New York, Simon & Schuster, 1935–1961.

Edwards, T., et al., eds., The New Dictionary of Thoughts. New York, Stanbook, 1977.

Ehrenthall, O., "The Almost Forgotten Feuchtersleben: Poet, Essayist, Popular Philosopher and Psychiatrist," Journal of the History of the Behavioral Sciences (January 1975), pp. 82–85.

Einstein, A., Out of My Later Years. New York, Philosophical Library, 1950.

Eitzen, Rev. L., "Confrontation Action Psychotherapy with Religious-Moral Values," Journal of Pastoral Care (Vol. XXII, 1964), pp. 26–35.

Elkin, I., et al., "NIMH Treatment of Depression Collaborative Research Program," Archives of General Psychiatry (Vol. 42, 1985), pp. 305–16.

Ellsworth, R., et al., "Self-Esteem and Chronic Pain," Journal of Psychosomatic Research (Vol. 22, 1978), pp. 25–30.

Eysenck, H. J., The Scientific Study of Personality. London, Routledge and Kegan Paul, 1952.

Ezekiel, I., Kabir, The Great Mystic. Punjab, India, R. S. Satsung Beas, 1966.

Fagles, R., trans., The Orestia. New York, Bantam, 1982.

Feinberg, M., and Levenstein, A., "The Danger in Manipulating Others," Wall Street Journal (March 4, 1985), p. 26.

Feinberg, M., of BFS Psychological Associates, Interview by telephone. (New York City, August 12, 1986).

Feinstein, H., Becoming William James. Ithaca, N.Y., Cornell University Press, 1984.

Fingarette, H., "The Ego and Mystic Selflessness," in M. Stein, et al., eds., Identity and Anxiety. New York, Free Press, 1960.

Finkelstein, L., ed., Interview. (London, September 5, 1980).

Firestone, R., The Truth. New York, Macmillan, 1981.

Fischer, C., To Dwell among Friends. Chicago, U. of Chicago Press, 1982.

Fisher, J., and Farina, A., "Consequences of Beliefs about the Nature of Mental Disorder," Journal of Abnormal Psychology (Vol. 88, 1979), pp. 320–27.

Fisher, L., et al., "Types of Paradoxical Intervention and Indications/Contraindications for Use in Clinical Practice," Family Process (Vol. 20, 1981), pp. 25–35.

Fiske, E., "Analysts Win Battle in War of Philosophy," *N.Y. Times* (January 6, 1981), pp. C-1+.

Flach, F., *The Secret Strength of Depression*. New York, Lippincott, 1974.

Frank, J., "The Medical Power of Faith," *Human Nature* (August 1979), pp. 40–47.

Franklin, B., *The Autobiography*. New York, Collier, 1973.

Friedenberg, E., *The Disposal of Liberty and Other Industrial Wastes*. Garden City, N.Y., Doubleday, 1976.

Friedlander, M., trans., *The Guide for the Perplexed*. New York, Dover, 1956.

Friedman, M., and Rosenman, R., *Type A*. New York, Knopf, 1974.

Friedman, M., Thoresen, C., and Gill, J., "Type A Behavior: Its Possible Role, Detection, and Alternation in Patients with Ischemic Heart Disease," in J.W. Hurst, ed., *Update V: the Heart*. New York, McGraw-Hill, 1981.

Fromm, E., *Psychoanalysis and Religion*. New Haven, Yale University Press, 1950.

Fruman, N., *Coleridge, The Damaged Archangel*. New York, Braziller, 1971.

Gallup Polls, 1976.

Gardner, C., and Wagner. S., "Clinical Diagnosis of the As-If Personality Disorder," *Bulletin of the Menninger Clinic* (March 1986), pp. 135–47.

Gardner, J., *Self-Renewal*. New York, Norton, 1981.

Genlin, E. T., and Olsen, L., "The Use of Imagery in Experiencial Focusing," *Psychotherapy: Theory, Research and Practice* (Vol. 7, No. 4, 1970), pp. 221–23.

Genlin, E. T., *Focusing*. New York, Basic, 1981.

Chananda, S., *Sri Ramakrishna and His Unique Message*. London, Ramakrishna Vedanta Centre, 1937.

Gill, C., "Ancient Psychotherapy," *Journal of the History of Ideas* (Vol. XLVI, No. 3), pp. 307–25.

Glasser, I., "Prisoners of Benevolence," in Gaylin, W., *et al.*, eds., *Doing Good: The Limits of Benevolence*. New York, Pantheon, 1978.

Goddard, D., ed., *A Buddhist Bible*. Boston, Beacon, 1970.

Goffman, E., *Encounters*. Indianapolis, Bobbs-Merrill, 1961.

Goldfried, M., "Toward the Delineation of Therapeutic Change Principles," *American Psychologist* (November 1980), pp. 991–99.

Goleman, D., "Confiding in Others Improves Health," *N.Y. Times* (September 18, 1984), pp. C1–C2.

———, "Insights into Self-Deception," *N.Y. Times Magazine* (May 12, 1985), pp. 36–43.

———, "Research Affirms Power of Positive Thinking," *N.Y. Times* (February 3, 1987), pp. C1 and C5.

Goodenough, E., *An Introduction to Philo Judaeus.* Oxford, Basil Blackwell, 1962.

Goodstein, L., and Sandler, I., "Using Psychology to Promote Human Welfare," *American Psychologist* (October 1978), pp. 882–91.

Goolishian, H., of the Galveston Family Institute Interview by telephone. (August 11, 1986).

Gourgey, C., "Integrity and Self-esteem," *P.A.G.L. Newletter* (September 1985), pp. 1–6.

Grant, M., trans., *Cicero.* New York, Penguin, 1971.

Green, J., "The Gambling Trap," *Psychology Today* (September 1982), pp. 50+.

Green, L., and Cruz, A., "Psychiatric Day Treatment as Alternative to and Transition from Full-time Hospitalization," *Community Mental Health Journal* (Fall 1981), pp. 191–201.

Greene, D., and Lepper, M., "Intrinsic Motivation: How to Turn Play into Work," *Psychology Today* (September 1974), pp. 49–54.

Grimsley, R. *Kierkegaard.* New York, Scribner, 1973.

Gross, M., *The Psychological Society.* New York, Random House, 1978.

———, "The Psychological Society," *Book Digest* (May 1978), pp. 129–49.

Gross, S., "The Myth of Professional Licensing," *American Psychologist* (November 1978), pp. 1009–16.

Guillaune, A., *Islam.* Baltimore, Pelican, 1954.

Gunn, R., "Reactions to Withdrawal Symptoms in Smoking Cessation Clinics," *Addictive Behaviors* (Vol. 11, 1986), pp. 49–53.

Gunter, B., and Wober, M., "Television and Public Trust," *British Journal of Social Psychology* (Vol. 22, No. 2), pp. 174–76.

Hadas, M., trans., *The Stoic Philosophy of Seneca.* New York, Norton, 1958.

Haecker, T., *Soren Kierkegaard.* London, Oxford University Press, 1937.

Hajal, F., "Galen's Ethical Psychotherapy: Its Influence on a Medieval Near Eastern Physician," *Journal of the History of Medicine and Allied Sciences* (Vol. 38, No. 3, 1983), pp. 320–33.

Hakim, K., *The Metaphysics of Rumi.* Lahore, Institute of Islamic Culture, 1959.

Hall, M., "A Conversation with Abraham Maslow," *Psychology Today* (July 1968), pp. 34+.

Hamachek, D., "Psychodynamics of Normal and Neurotic Perfectionism," *Psychology* (Vol. 15), pp. 27–33.

Hamilton, E., *The Echo of Greece.* New York, Norton, 1957.

———, *Witness to the Truth.* New York, Norton, 1948.

Hamilton, W., trans., *Phaedrus* and *The Seventh and Eighth Letters.* New York, Penguin, 1973.

Harder, D. *et al.,* "Relationships Among Life Events, Self-Deception and Psychological Impairment," *Journal of Consulting and Clinical Psychology* (Vol. 47, No. 6, 1979), pp. 1117–19.

Hariton, E., and Singer, J., "Women's Fantasies During Sexual Intercourse," *Journal of Consulting and Clinical Psychology* (Vol. 42, No. 3, 1974), pp. 313–22.

Harkins, P., trans., *Galen: on the Passions and Errors of the Soul.* Columbus, Ohio State University Press, 1963.

Harkness, G., *The Dark Night of the Soul.* New York, Abingdon-Cokesbury Press, 1945.

Hart, H., "Displacement Guilt and Pain," *Psychoanalytic Review* (Vol. 34, 1947), pp. 259–72.

Hart, P., and D., retired Marriage Encounter leaders, Interview. (New Canaan, Conn., December 4, 1981).

Hartshorne, H., and May, M., *Studies in Deceit.* New York, Macmillan, 1928.

Harvey, J., and Katz, C., *If I'm Successful, Why do I Feel Like A Fake?.* New York, St. Martin's Press, 1985.

Hatch, N., *The Sacred Cause of Liberty*. New Haven, Yale University Press, 1977.

Healy, S., *Boredom, Self, and Culture*. London, Associated University Press, 1984.

Hein, N., of Yale Divinity School, Interview. (New Haven, Conn., November 11, 1978).

"Help! Teachers Can't Teach!," *Time* (June 16, 1980), pp. 54–63.

Henderson, L., "Physician and Patient as a Social System," *New England Journal of Medicine* (Vol. 212, 1935), pp. 819–23.

Hendin, H., *The Age of Sensation*. New York, Norton, 1975.

Heschel, A., *Maimonides*. New York, Farrar, Straus, & Giroux, 1982.

Hickman, C., and Silva, M., *Creating Excellence*. New York, NAL Books, 1984.

Hicks, R.D., trans., *Diogenes Laertius on the Lives of Eminent Philosophers*, Vol. I. London, Heinemann, 1925.

Hilgard, E., "The Trilogy of Mind," in *Journal of the History of Behavioral Sciences* (Vol. 16, 1980), pp. 107–17.

Hocking, J., and Leathers, D., "Nonverbal Indicators of Deception: a New Theoretical Perspective," *Communication Monographs* (Vol. 47, 1980), pp. 119–31.

Hoffman, E., *The Way of Splendor*. Boston, Shambhala, 1981.

——, therapist and author, Interview by telephone. (East Meadow, New York, May 20, 1986).

Hollon, S., and Beck, A., "Cognitive Therapy of Depression," in P. Kendall and S. Hollon, eds., *Cognitive-Behavioral Interventions: Theory, Research and Practice*. New York, Academic Press, 1979.

Holman, C., *The Cure of Souls*. Chicago, U. of Chicago Press, 1932.

Holmes, C., *Aldous Huxley and the Way to Reality*. Bloomington, Indiana University Press, 1970.

*The Holy Bible Containing the Old and New Testaments*, Revised Standard Version. New York, Thomas Nelson and Sons, 1952.

Hoover, T., *The Zen Experience*. New York, New American Library, 1980.

Hora, T., *Dialogues in Metapsychiatry*. New York, Seabury, 1977.

————, *Existential Metapsychiatry.* New York, Seabury, 1977.

————, therapist and author, Interview. (Bedford Village, N.Y., December 1978).

————, therapist and author, Interview. (Bedford Village, N.Y., June 9, 1979).

————, *Forgiveness.* Orange, Calif., PAGL Press, 1983.

————, *Compassion.* Orange, Calif., PAGL Press, 1985.

————, *God in Psychiatry.* Orange, Calif., PAGL Press, 1985.

————, *Marriage and Family Life.* Orange, Calif., PAGL Press, 1985.

————, *Beyond the Dream.* Orange, Calif., PAGL Press, 1986.

————, therapist and author, Interview. (Bedford Village, N.Y., May 26, 1986).

Hume, D., *An Inquiry Concerning the Principles of Morals.* Indianapolis, Bobbs-Merrill, 1957.

Humphries, R., M.D., of Silver Hills Foundation, Interview. (New Canaan, Conn., August 8, 1979).

Hunt, T., clinical director of the Aqua Retreat Center, Interview by telephone. (Cambridge, Mass. July 29, 1935).

Hurvitz, L., trans., *Scriptures of the Lotus Blossom of the Fine Dharma.* New York, Columbia, 1976.

Hurvitz, N., "Peer Self-Help Psychotherapy Groups and Their Implication for Psychotherapy," *Psychotherapy: Theory, Research, and Practice* (Vol. 7, 1970), pp. 41–49.

Huxley, A., *The Perennial Philosophy.* New York, Harper & Row, 1944.

Immergluck, L., "Determinism-Freedom in Contemporary Psychology: an Ancient Problem Revisited," *American Psychologist* (Vol. 19, 1964), pp. 270–81.

Ingber, D., "Inside the Executive Mind," *Success!* (December 1984), pp. 33–34.

Iqbal, A., *The Life and Thought of Mohammad Jalal-ud-din Rumi.* Lahore, BAZM-I-IQBAL, n.d.

"Is Dishonesty Good for Business?," *Business and Society Review* (Summer 1979), pp. 4+.

Isenberg, D., "Field Research on Managerial Thinking: Seven Findings, Seven Puzzles," Working Paper presented at the International Conference on Thinking (August 1984).

———, "How Senior Managers Think," *Harvard Business Review* (November–December 1984), pp. 81–90.

———, "Strategic Opportunism: Managing Under Uncertainty," Harvard Business School Working Papers (1986).

———, Harvard Business School, Interview. (May 29, 1986).

Isherwood, C., ed., *Vedanta for the Western World.* Hollywood, Calif., Vedanta Press, 1945.

Isrealy, R., therapist, Interview. (Port Chester, N.Y., October 1979).

James, W., *The Principles of Psychology,* Vol. I. Cambridge, Harvard University Press, 1890.

———, *A Pluralistic Universe.* New York, Longmans, Green, 1909.

———, *Varieties of Religious Experience.* New York, Mentor, 1958.

———, "The Sentiment of Rationality," in A. Castell, ed., *Essays in Pragmatism.* New York, Hafner, 1968.

———, "The Moral Philosopher and the Moral Life," in J. Roth, ed., *The Moral Philosophy of William James.* New York, Crowell, 1969.

Jampolsky, G., *Love Is Letting Go of Fear.* Berkeley, Celestial Arts, 1979.

Janis, I., and Mann, L., *Decision-Making.* New York, Free Press, 1977.

Jeffrey, A., trans., *The Koran.* New York, Heritage Press, 1958.

Jensen, J., and Bergin, A., "Mental Health Values of Professional Therapists: a National Interdisciplinary Survey," Brigham Young University (Doctoral Dissertation, 1986).

Johns, R., of the Alcoholism Council, Interview. (Westport, Conn., December 18, 1978).

Johnson, C., ed., *Vedanta.* New York, Harper & Row, 1971.

Johnson, J., *et al.,* "Life Stress, Depression, and Anxiety," *Journal of Psychosomatic Research* (Vol. 22, 1978), pp. 205–8.

Johnson, R., "Changing Patterns of Psychological Distress and Psychotherapeutic Needs Among Medical Students and Law Students," 80th Annual Transpersonal Psychology Conference, 1980.

Johnson, W., *The Inner Eye of Love*. San Francisco, Harper & Row, 1978.

Jonas, H., *The Phenomenon of Life*. New York, Harper & Row, 1966.

Jones, W. H., *et al.*, "The Persistence of Loneliness: Self and Other Determinants," *Journal of Personality* (Vol. 49, No. 1, 1981), pp. 27–47.

Jones, W.T., *et al.*, *Approaches to Ethics*. New York, McGraw-Hill, 1977.

Jorgensen, S., and Gaudy, J., "Self-Disclosure and Satisfaction in Marriage: the Relation Examined," *Family Relations* (Vol. 29, 1980), pp. 281–87.

Jourard, S., *The Transparent Self*. Princeton, N.J., D. Van Nostrand, 1964.

———, *Disclosing Man to Himself*. Princeton, N.J., D. Van Nostrand, 1968.

———, "Healthy Personality and Self-Disclosure," in G. Egan, ed., *Encounter Groups: Basic Readings*. Belmont, Calif., Brooks/Cole, 1971.

Jowett, B., trans., *The Dialogues of Plato*, Vols. 1–4. Oxford, Clarendon Press, 1953.

Jung, C., *Modern Man in Search of a Soul*. New York, Harcourt Brace Jovanovich.

———, *Psychological Reflections*. Princeton, N.J., Princeton University Press, 1953.

———, *Psychology and Alchemy*. Princeton, N.J., Princeton University Press, 1968.

Kafka, F., *Letter to His Father*. New York, Schocken, 1973.

Kahn, E., "Heinz Kohut and Carl Rogers: a Timely Comparison," *American Psychologist* (August 1985), pp. 893–904.

Kanfer, F., "Personal Control, Social Control and Altruism," *American Psychologist* (March 1979), pp. 231–39.

Kanter, J., *Coping Strategies for Relatives of the Mentally Ill*. Washington, D.C., National Alliance for the Mentally Ill, 1984.

———, "Moral Issues and Mental Illness," *Bulletin of the Menninger Clinic* (Vol. 48, No. 6, 1984), pp. 518–39.

———, therapist and author, Interview by telephone. (Alexandria, Virginia, May 20, 1986).

Kasun, J., "Turning Children into Sex Experts," *The Public Interest* (No. 55, 1979), pp. 3–14.

Keen, S., *What to Do When You're Bored and Blue*. New York, Wyden, 1980.

Kenyon, J., "44 Hours to a Better Marriage," *Christian Herald* (February 1978).

Khan, M. Z., *Islam.* New York, Harper & Row, 1962.

Kissen, D., "The Significance of Personality in Lung Cancer in Men," *Annals of the New York Academy of Science* (Vol. 125, 1966), pp. 820–26.

Kizziar, J., and Hagedorn, J., *Search for Acceptance: the Adolescent and Self-Esteem.* Chicago, Nelson-Hall, 1979.

Klerman, G., "The Age of Melancholy?," *Psychology Today* (April 1979), pp. 36–42, 88.

———, et al., *Interpersonal Psychotherapy of Depression.* New York, Basic, 1984.

Koch, G., *Religion of the American Enlightenment.* New York, Crowell, 1968.

Koch, J., and L., "The Urgent Drive to Make Good Marriages Better," *Psychology Today* (September 1976), pp. 33+.

Kopp, S., *If You Meet the Buddha on the Road, Kill Him.* Palo Alto, Calif., Science and Behavior Books, 1972.

Krailsheimer, A.J., trans., [Pascal's] *Pensées.* Baltimore, Penguin, 1966.

Kuhn, R., *The Demon of Noontide.* Princeton, N.J., Princeton University Press, 1976.

Kuppermann, J., *The Foundations of Morality.* Boston, George Allen & Unwin, 1983.

Laing, R. D., *The Politics of Experience.* New York, Pantheon, 1967.

Lamb, R., "Adam Smith's System: Sympathy Not Self-interest," *Journal of the History of Ideas* (XXXV, 1974), pp. 671–82.

Lanier, J., "Mysticism and What about It?", *Spiritual Journeys* (November 1980), pp. 18–19.

Latham, R. E., trans., *Lucretius: On the Nature of the Universe.* New York, Penguin, 1951.

Lauer, J., and Lauer, R., "Marriages Made to Last," *Psychology Today* (June 1985), pp. 22–26.

Lazarus, A., "Learning Theory and the Treatment of Depression," *Behavior Research and Therapy* (Vol. I, 1968), pp. 83–89.

Lefebure, M., *Samuel Taylor Coleridge: a Bondage of Opium.* New York, Stein & Day, 1974.

Levin, D., *The Puritan in the Enlightenment: Franklin and Edwards.* Chicago, Rand McNally, 1963.

Levine, I., *Francis Bacon.* London, Kennikat, 1925.

Levine, S., "Who Should Do Psychotherapy?," *American Journal of Social Psychiatry* (Vol. V, No. 1), pp. 60–65.

Leys, R., "Meyer, Watson, and the Dangers of Behaviorism," *Journal of the History of the Behavioral Sciences* (Vol. 20, 1984), pp. 128+.

Linssen, R., *Living Zen.* New York, Macmillan, 1954.

Lodge, R. C., "Plato and the Moral Standard," *International Journal of Ethics* (Vol. 32, 1922), pp. 21–39.

Lovell-Troy, L., "Anomia Among Employed Wives and Housewives," *Journal of Marriage and the Family* (Vol. 45, No. 2), pp. 301–10.

Mace, D., and V., *Marriage East and West.* Garden City, N.Y., Doubleday, 1960.

Mackenzie, M., *Plato on Punishment.* Los Angeles, U. of California Press, 1981.

Macmillan, M., "Bacon's Moral Teaching," *International Journal of Ethics* (Vol. XVII, 1907), pp. 55-70.

Maeder, T., "Wounded Healers," *The Atlantic Monthly* (January 1989), pp. 37–47.

Maeroff, G., "Values Regain Their Popularity," *N.Y. Times* (April 10, 1984), p. C1.

Manuel, F., *The Religion of Isaac Newton.* Oxford, Clarendon, 1974.

Marshall, G., *Buddha: The Quest for Serenity.* Boston, Beacon, 1978.

Mascaro, J., trans., *The Dhammapada.* Baltimore, Penguin, 1973.

Maslow, A., *Motivation and Personality,* 2nd ed. New York, Harper & Row, 1970.

———, *The Farther Reaches of Human Nature.* New York, Viking, 1971.

Mason, R., "Acceptance and Healing," *Journal of Religion and Health* (Vol. 8, No. 2), pp. 123–42.

May, Robert, *Physicians of the Soul.* New York, Crossroads, 1982.

May, Rollo, *Love and Will.* New York, Norton, 1969.

Mazer, E., "People Who Confide in Others Stay Healthier," *Prevention* (February 1985), p. 6.

McBride, J., "Some Heady Talk about Gut Feeling," *Wall Street Journal* (November 9, 1985).

————, executive-search consultant, Interview by telephone. (Washington, D.C., August 11, 1986).

McCall, M., and Lombardo, M., "What Makes a Top Executive?," *Psychology Today* (February 1983), pp. 26–31.

McDonnell, T. S., *A Thomas Merton Reader.* Garden City, N.Y., Doubleday–Image, 1974.

McNeill, J., *A History of the Cure of Souls.* New York, Harper & Row, 1951.

Meer, J., "Loneliness," *Psychology Today* (July 1985), pp. 28–33.

Melber, J., *The Universality of Maimonides.* New York, Jonathan David, 1968.

Meltzer, M., "Countermanipulation Through Malingering," in A. Biderman and H. Zimmer, eds., *The Manipulation of Human Behavior.* New York, Wiley, 1961.

Menninger, K., *The Crime of Punishment.* New York, Viking, 1966.

Miller, W., "The Addictive Behaviors," in W. Miller, ed., *The Addictive Behaviors.* New York, Pergamon Press, 1980.

————, and Hester, R., "Treating the Problem Drinker," in W. Miller, ed., *The Addictive Behaviors.* New York, Pergamon Press, 1980.

————, "Inpatient Alcoholism Treatment: Who Benefits?", *American Psychologist* (July 1986), pp. 794–805.

Montaigne, *Essays.* New York, Encyclopedia Britannica, 1952.

Mora, G., "Recent American Psychiatric Developments," in *American Handbook of Psychiatry,* Vol. I, chapter 2. New York, Basic, 1959.

————, "Mind-Body Concepts in the Middle Ages," *Journal of the History of the Behavioral Sciences* (Vol. 14, 1978), pp. 344–61.

Moustakas, C., *Loneliness.* Englewood Cliffs, N.J., Prentice-Hall, 1961.

Mowrer, O. H., "Sin, the Lesser of Two Evils," *American Psychologist* (XV, 1960), pp. 301–4.

————, *The Crisis in Psychiatry and Religion.* New York, Van Nostrand Reinhold, 1961.

————, ed., *Morality and Mental Illness*. Chicago, Rand McNally, 1967.

Muggeridge, M., *A Third Testament*. New York, Little, Brown, 1976.

Muller, M., trans., *The Dhammapada* in *Sacred Books of the East*, Vol. XII. New York, Scribner, 1961.

Musto, D., "Lessons of the First Cocaine Epidemic," *Wall Street Journal* (June 17, 1986), p. 30.

Nicholson, R., *The Mystics of Islam*. London, Routledge and Kegan Paul, 1963.

————, ed., *Rumi*. New York, Samuel Weiser, 1974.

Nierenberg, G., *The Art of Negotiating*. New York, Hawthorn, 1968.

Nigro, G., and Galli, I., "On the Relationship Between Machiavellianism and Anxiety Among Italian Undergraduates," *Psychological Reports* (Vol. 56, 1985), pp. 37–38.

Nikhilananda, S., ed., *Vivikananda*. New York, Ramakrishna-Vivikananda Center, 1953.

Novak, M., "The Family Out of Favor," *Harper's* (April 1976), pp. 37–46.

Ogg, S., of National Marriage Encounter, Interview by telephone. (Orlando, Florida, August 5, 1986).

*One Addict's Experience with Acceptance, Faith, and Commitment*. Van Nuys, Calif., N. A. World Service, 1983.

Orlinsky, H. M., *et al.*, trans. and ed., *The Torah*. Philadelphia, Jewish Publication Society of America, 1962.

Ouchi, W., "Trust," *Training and Development Journal* (December 1982), pp. 71–72.

Pacht, A., "Reflections on Perfection," *American Psychologist* (Vol. 39, No. 4, 1984), pp. 386–90.

————, professor and therapist, Interview by telephone. (Madison, Wisconsin, May 21, 1985).

Palmer, E. H., trans., *The Koran*. New York, Collier, 1910.

Paramananda, S., *Plato and Vedic Idealism*. Boston, Vedanta Centre, 1924.

Parker, S., "Eskimo Psychopathology in the Context of Eskimo Personality and Culture," *American Anthropologist* (Vol. 64), pp. 76–96.

Parrinder, G., *The Wisdom of the Early Buddhists.* New York, New Directions, 1977.

Parloff, M., "Can Psychotherapy Research Guide the Policymakers?," *American Psychologist* (April 1979), pp. 296–306.

Pascale, R., "Zen and the Art of Management," in E. Collins, ed., *Executive Success.* New York, Wiley, 1983, pp. 510–23.

Peck, M. S., *The Road Less Traveled.* New York, Simon & Schuster, 1978.

Pennebaker, J., and O'Heeron, R., "Confiding in Others and Illness Rate among Spouses of Suicide and Accidental Death Victims," *Journal of Abnormal Psychology* (Vol. 93, 1984), pp. 473–76.

Pennebaker, J., "Traumatic Experience and Psychosomatic Disease: Exploring the Roles of Behavioral Inhibition, Obsession, and Confiding," *Canadian Psychology* (Vol. 26, 1985), pp. 82–95.

———, and Chew, C., "Behavioral Inhibition and Electrodermal Activity During Deception," *Journal of Personality and Social Psychology* (Vol. 49, No. 5, 1985), pp. 1427–33.

———, and Beall, S., "Confronting a Traumatic Event: Toward an Understanding of Inhibition and Disease," *Journal of Abnormal Psychology,* in press.

———, Hughes, C., and O'Heeron, "The Psychophysiology of Confession: Linking Inhibitory and Psychosomatic Processes," submitted for publication.

Perry, R., *The Thought and Character of William James.* Cambridge, Harvard University Press, 1948.

Peters, T., and Austin, N., *A Passion for Excellence.* New York, Random House, 1985.

Peterson, D., "In Memorium: O. Hobart Mowrer, 1907–1982," *Child and Family Behavior Therapy* (Vol. 4, 1982), pp. 99–101.

Phillips, D., *The Choice Is Always Ours.* New York, Richard R. Smith Pub., 1948.

Phillips, M., *The Seven Laws of Money.* New York, Random House, 1974.

Pickthall, M. M., trans., *The Meaning of the Glorious Koran.* New York, Mentor.

Pieper, J., *Enthusiasm and Divine Madness.* New York, Harcourt, Brace & World, 1962.

Pilkonis, P., and Zimbardo, P., "The Personal and Social Dynamics of Shyness," in C. Izard, ed., *Emotions in Personality and Psychotherapy*. New York, Plenum, 1979.

Polish, J., *The Course of Alcoholism*. New York, Wiley, 1980.

Polivy, J., and Herman, C., "Dieting and Binging," *American Psychologist* (February 1985), pp. 193–201.

Pope, H., and Ferguson, M., "Age and Anomia in Middle and Later Life," *International Journal of Aging and Human Development* (Vol. 15, No. 1), pp. 51–74.

Potok, C., *Wanderings*. New York, Knopf, 1978.

Prabhavananda, S., *The Spiritual Heritage of India*. Hollywood, Calif., Vedanta Press, 1963.

———, *Religion in Practice*. Hollywood, Calif., Vedanta Press, 1968.

———, trans., *The Song of God: the Bhagavad-Gita*. Hollywood, Calif., Vedanta Press, 1975.

———, and Manchester, F., trans., *The Upanishads*. New York, Mentor, 1948.

———, and Isherwood, C., trans., *How to Know God*. Hollywood, Calif., Vedanta Press, 1975.

Price, A., and Wong, M.-L., trans., *Diamond Sutra* and *Sutra of Hui Neng*. Boulder, Colo., Shambhala, 1969.

Prugh, T., "Alcohol, Spirituality, and Recovery," *Alcohol Health and Research World* (Winter 1985/1986), pp. 28–31 and 53.

"Psychiatry on the Couch," *Time* (Vol. 113, No. 14, 1979), pp. 74–82.

Rafford, Rev. R., of Waterbury Hospital, Interview. (Waterbury, Conn., November 12, 1978).

Ram Dass and Gorman, R., *How Can I help?*. New York, Knopf, 1985.

Ramakrishna, *The Gospel of . . . .* New York, Vedanta Society, 1947.

Raxlen, Dr. B., Leuba, M., and Horton, K., Institute for Bio-Behavioral Medicine, Interview. (Bridgeport, Conn., October 18, 1979).

"Reagan's Address to the U.N. General Assembly," *N.Y. Times* (September 25, 1984), p. A-10.

Reilly, R., "America's Destiny Is in Its Beginnings," *Wall Street Journal* (January 2, 1981), p. 6.

"Religion in America: 1982," *Gallup Report* (No. 201 and 202, June–July 1982).

"Religion in America: 50 Years 1935–1985," *Gallup Report* (No. 236, May 1985).

Renou, L., ed., *Hinduism.* New York, George Braziller, 1962.

Rhys Davids, C.A.F., *Buddhist Psychology.* New Delhi, Oriental Reprint, 1974.

Ricklefs, R., "On Many Ethical Issues, Executives Apply Stiffer Standard Than Public," *Wall Street Journal* (November 1, 1983), p. 33.

Rieff, P., "Freudian Ethics and the Idea of Reason," *Ethics* (Vol. LXVII, 1956–1957), pp. 169–83.

Robinson, T.M., *Plato's Psychology.* Buffalo, New York, U. of Toronto Press, 1970.

Rook, K., "Promoting Social Bonding," *American Psychologist* (Vol. 39, No. 12, 1984), pp. 1389–1407.

Rooke, B., ed., *The Collected Works of Samuel Taylor Coleridge*, Vol. I *(The Friend).* Princeton, N.J., Princeton University Press, 1969.

Rosenfeld, A., "Depression: Dispelling Despair," *Psychology Today* (June 1985), pp. 28–34.

Ross, N., *The World of Zen.* New York, Random House, 1960.

Rothman, D., "The State as Parent," in Gaylin, W., *et al.*, eds., *Doing Good: The Limits of Benevolence.* New York, Pantheon, 1978.

Rotter, J., "Trust and Gullibility," *Psychology Today* (October 1980), p. 35+.

————, therapist and author, Interview by telephone. (Storrs, Conn., February 28, 1985).

Rowan, R., "Those Business Hunches Are More Than Blind Faith," *Fortune* (April 23, 1979), pp. 110+.

————, *The Intuitive Manager.* New York, Little, Brown, 1986.

Rubenstein, C., and Shaver, P., "Loneliness in Two Northeastern Cities," in J. Hartog, *et al.*, eds., *The Anatomy of Loneliness.* New York, International Universities Press, 1980.

Rudin, J., *Psychotherapy and Religion.* Notre Dame, Ind., U. of Notre Dame Press, 1968.

Rush, B., "An Inquiry into the Effects of Ardent Spirits on the Human Body and Mind," *Alcohol World* (Summer 1976), pp. 7–9.

Safire, W., and Safir, L., *Good Advice.* New York, Times Books, 1982.

Safran, C., "65,000 Women Reveal How Religion Affects Health, Happiness, Sex and Politics," *Redbook* (April 1977), p. 126+.

Samelson, F., "Organizing for the Kingdom of Behavior: Academic Battles and Organizational Policies in the Twenties," *Journal of the History of the Behavioral Sciences* (January 1985), pp. 33–47.

Sanford, J., *The Kingdom Within.* New York, Lippincott, 1970.

Sarma, D., *The Renaissance of Hinduism.* Benares, Hindu University, 1944.

————, *Renascent Hinduism.* Bombay, Bharatiya Vidya Bhavan, 1966.

Savage, C., and McCabe, O., "Psychedelic Therapy of Drug Addictions," in C. Brown and C. Savage, eds., *The Drug Abuse Controversy.* Baltimore, Friends Medical Science Research Center, 1971.

Savino, M., and Mills, A., "The Rise and Fall of Moral Treatment in California Psychiatry, 1852–1870," *Journal of the History of Behavioral Sciences* (October 1967), pp. 359–69.

*Sayings of Buddha.* New York, Peter Pauper Press, 1957.

Scarf, M., "The More Sorrowful Sex," *Psychology Today* (April 1979), pp. 45–52+.

————, "The Promiscuous Woman," *Psychology Today* (July 1980, pp. 78–87.

————, "The Undiscovered Country of the Depressed," *Psychology Today* (January 1979), pp. 86–89.

Schachtel, E., "On Alienated Concepts of Identity," *American Journal of Psychoanalysis* (Vol. 21, No. 2, 1961), pp. 120–31.

Schmeck, H., "Defective Gene Tied to Form of Manic-Depressive Illness," *N.Y. Times.* (February 26, 1987), pp. A1, B7.

————, "2nd Genetic Defect Linked to Illness," *N.Y. Times.* (March 19, 1987), p. A20.

Seibert, D., and Proctor, W., *The Ethical Executive.* New York, Cornerstone, 1984.

Seidenberg, R., *Marriage Between Equals*. Garden City, N.Y., Doubleday–Anchor, 1973.

Seligson, M., "The Physician of the Future," *New West* (January 1977), pp. 43–49.

Sennett, R., *The Uses of Disorder*. London, Penguin, 1971.

Sermat, V., "Some Situational and Personality Correlates of Loneliness," in J. Hartog, *et al.*, eds., *The Anatomy of Loneliness*. New York, International Universities Press, 1980.

Shafarich, I., "Does Russia Have a Future?," in A. Solzhenitsyn, ed., *From Under the Rubble*. New York, Bantam, 1976, pp. 280–95.

Shah, I., *The Sufis*. Garden City, N.Y., Doubleday–Anchor, 1971.

Shaw, M., "Paradoxical Intention in the Life and Thought of William James," *American Journal of Theology and Philosophy* (Vol. 7, 1986), pp. 5–16.

Shankara, *Crest-Jewel of Discrimination*. Hollywood, Calif., Vedanta Press, 1970.

Sheikh, A., and Panagiotou, N., "The Use of Mental Imagery in Psychotherapy," *Perceptual and Motor Skills* (Vol. 41, 1975), pp. 555–85.

Shostrom, E., *Man, the Manipulator*. New York, Abingdon, 1967.

Sigelman, L., "Is Ignorance Bliss? A Reconsideration of the Folk Wisdom," *Human Relations* (Vol. 34, No. 11), pp. 965–74.

Simmel, G., *Conflict: The Web of Group Affiliation*. New York, Free Press, 1955.

Simon, B., *Mind and Madness in Ancient Greece*. Ithaca, New York, Cornell University Press, 1978.

Singer, J., *The Inner World of Daydreaming*. New York, Harper & Row, 1975.

Smith, V., Coordinator of the Connecticut Self-Help Mutual Support Network, Interview by telephone. (New Haven, Conn., August 13, 1986).

Smith, W., *The Hippocratic Tradition*. Ithaca, New York, Cornell University Press, 1979.

Snyder, M., and Cantor, N., "Thinking about Ourselves and Others," *Journal of Personality and Social Psychology* (Vol. 39, 1979), pp. 222–34.

Snyder, M., and Simpson, J., "Self-Monitoring and Dating Relationships," *Journal of Personality and Social Psychology* (Vol. 47, 1984), pp. 1281–91.

Solar, D., and Bruehl, D., "Machiavellianism and Locus of Control: Two Conceptions of Interpersonal Power," *Psychological Reports* (Vol. 29, 1971), pp. 1079–82.

Solzhenitsyn, A., "As Breathing and Consciousness Return," in A. Solzhenitsyn, ed., *From Under the Rubble.* New York, Bantam, 1976, pp. 1–23.

———, "Repentance and Self-Limitation," in A. Solzhenitsyn, ed., *From Under the Rubble.* New York, Bantam, 1976, pp. 104–42.

Spedding, J., *et al.*, eds., *The Works of Francis Bacon.* New York, Garrett Press, 1980.

Sperling, D., "Best Executives Know Intuition Supplements Logic," *USA Today* (August 22, 1984), p. 2b.

Stall, R., "An Examination of Spontaneous Remission from Problem Drinking in the Bluegrass Region of Kentucky," *Journal of Drug Issues* (Spring 1983), pp. 191+.

Staniforth, M., trans., *The Meditations of Marcus Aurelius.* New York, Penguin, 1964.

Starbuck, E., *The Psychology of Religion.* London, Scribner, 1901.

Steidl, J., of Yale Dana Clinic, Interview. (New Haven, Conn., October 15, 1979).

Steidl, L., psychologist, Interview. (New Haven, Conn., November 16, 1978).

Steinnilber-Oberlin, E., *The Buddhist Sects of Japan.* London, George Allen and Unwin, 1938.

Steinsaltz, A., *The Essential Talmud.* New York, Basic, 1976.

Stewart, K., "Dream Theory in Malaya," in C. Tart, ed., *Altered States of Consciousness.* New York, Wiley, 1969.

Stitskin, L., ed., *Letters of Maimonides.* New York, Yeshiva University Press, 1977.

Streeter, L., *et al.*, "Pitch Changes During Attempted Deception," *Journal of Personality and Social Psychology* (Vol. 35, No. 5, 1977), pp. 345–50.

Stupp, H., *et al.*, *Psychotherapy for Better or Worse: the Problem of Negative Effects.* New York, Jason Aronson, 1977.

Suedfeld, P., "The Benefits of Boredom: Sensory Deprivation Reconsidered," *American Scientist* (Vol. 63, No. 1), pp. 60–67.

Swami, Shri Purohit, trans., *The Geeta.* London, Farber, 1965.

Swidler, A., of Stanford University, Interview. (San Francisco, June 28, 1980).

Tagore, R., trans., *Songs of Kabir.* New York, Samuel Weiser, 1977.

"Talk Is as Good as a Pill," *Time* (May 26, 1986), p. 60.

Tavris, C., *Anger, the Misunderstood Emotion.* New York, Simon & Schuster, 1982.

Thera, N., *The Heart of Buddhist Meditation.* New York, Samuel Weiser, 1965.

Thompson, E. F. ed., *The Wisdom of Omar Khayyam.* New York, Philosophical Library, 1967.

Thoreau, H. D., *A Week on the Concord and Merrimack Rivers.* Princeton, N.J., Princeton University Press, 1980.

Thoresen, C., and Eagleston, J., "Counseling for Health," *The Counseling Psychologist* (Vol. 13, No. 3, 1985), pp. 15–87.

*To the Man Who Wants to Stop Compulsive Overeating, Welcome.* Los Angeles, Overeaters Anonymous, 1980.

Toynbee, A., and Ikeda, D., *The Toynbee-Ikeda Dialogue.* New York, Kodansha, 1976.

Trilling, L., *Sincerity and Authenticity.* Cambridge, Harvard University Press, 1972.

Turner, C., and Willis, R., "The Relationship between Self-reported Religiosity and Drug Use by College Students," *Journal of Drug Education* (Vol. 9, No. 1), pp. 67–78.

Tversky, A., and Kahneman, D., "The Framing of Decisions and the Psychology of Choice," *Science* (Vol. 211, January 30, 1981), pp. 453–58.

Twersky, I., ed., *A Maimonides Reader.* New York, Behrman House, 1972.

"Type A: A Change of Heart and Mind," *Science News* (Vol. 126, No. 7), p. 107.

Unterman, A., *The Wisdom of the Jewish Mystics.* New York, New Directions, 1976.

Vallacher, R., and Solodky, M., "Objectives Self-Awareness, Standards of Evaluation and Moral Behavior," *Journal of Experimental Social Psychology* (Vol. 15, 1979), pp. 254–62.

Van Doren, C., *Benjamin Franklin.* New York, Viking, 1938.

Vaughan, F., *Awakening Intuition.* Garden City, N.Y., Doubleday, 1979.

———, *The Inward Arc.* Boston, Shambhala, 1985.

———, author and therapist, Interview. (Pacific Grove, Calif., June 28, 1980).

———, author and therapist, Interview by telephone. (Mill Valley, Calif., July 17, 1986).

Vesper, K., of Babson College, Interview by telephone. (Babson Park, Mass., February 18, 1981).

Vitz, P., *Psychology as Religion.* Grand Rapids, Eerdmans, 1977.

Vonhoff, H., *People Who Care.* Philadelphia, Fortress, 1960.

Warren, H. C., trans., *Buddhist Writings.* New York, Collier, 1910.

Watson, L., ed., *Light From Many Lamps.* New York, Simon & Schuster, 1951.

Watts, A., *Psychotherapy East and West.* New York, Vintage, 1975.

Weil, A., *The Natural Mind.* New York, Houghton Mifflin, 1972.

Weil, S., *Oppression and Liberty.* Amherst, U. of Massachusetts Press, 1973.

———, *Lectures on Philosophy.* New York, Cambridge University Press, 1978.

Weiss, E., and English, O. S., *Psychosomatic Medicine.* Philadelphia, Saunders, 1957.

Weiss, F., "Self-Alienation: Dynamics and Therapy," *American Journal of Psychoanalysis* (Vol. 21, No. 2), pp. 207+.

Weiss, R., and Butterworth, C., eds., *Ethical Writings of Maimonides.* New York, Dover, 1975.

Wells, T., *Keeping Your Cool Under Fire.* New York, McGraw-Hill, 1980.

———, author and consultant, Interview. (Beverly Hills, Calif., January 18, 1981).

———, author and consultant, Interview by telephone. (May 22, 1986).

White, H., *Peace among the Willows.* The Hague, Martinus Nijhoff, 1968.

White, L. W., Interview. (Monterey, Calif., June 28, 1980).

———, "Recovery from Alcoholism: Transpersonal Dimensions," *The Journal of Transpersonal Psychology* (Vol. II, No. 2, 1979), pp. 117–28.

Wild, J., *Plato's Modern Enemies and the Theory of Natural Law.* Chicago, U. of Chicago Press, 1953.

Winget, C., and Kapp, F., "The Relationship of Manifest Content of Dreams to Duration of Childbirth in Primiparae," *Psychosomatic Medicine* (Vol. 34, 1972), pp. 313+.

Wolpe, J., *Psychotherapy by Reciprocal Inhibition.* Stanford, Calif., Stanford University Press, 1958.

Yonge, C. D., trans., "Epicurus," in B. Rand, ed., *The Classical Moralists.* New York, Houghton Mifflin, 1909.

Zeiss, A., *et al.,* "Nonspecific Improvements in Depression Using Interpersonal Skills Training, Pleasant Activity Schedules, or Cognitive Reinforcement," *Journal of Consulting and Clinical Psychology* (Vol. 47, No. 3, 1976).

Zulueta, T., "Abolishing Mental Hospitals," *World Press* (February 1980), p. 57.

## About the Author

Dr. Lewis M. Andrews is a Connecticut-based writer and consultant. He holds a bachelor's degree in psychology from Princeton University, an M.A. in communications research from Stanford, and a Ph.D. in psychology from the Union Graduate School. In recent years Dr. Andrews has been both a Research Fellow at the Yale Divinity School and a Visiting Scholar at the Columbia Graduate School of Business.

He has authored and co-authored numerous academic and popular books, including the bestseller *Biofeedback*; and his articles have appeared in such diverse publications as *The Saturday Review, Science of Mind* magazine, *The Wall Street Journal, The Nation, Cosmopolitan,* and *New Realities.*

Dr. Andrews currently speaks to business, professional, and community groups around the world on the relationship of spiritual values to emotional health and achievement. Further information about his lectures and workshops can be obtained by writing him directly at P.O. Box 459, Redding Ridge, Connecticut U.S.A. 06876.